Gamebirds of Africa

Guineafowls, Francolins, Spurfowls, Quails, Sandgrouse & Snipes

Rob Little

ACKNOWLEDGEMENTS

My appreciation begins with Dr Mike Mentis who introduced me to grassland francolin research in the KwaZulu-Natal Drakensberg and gave me my first English Pointer during the early 1980s. Thereafter, Prof. Tim Crowe at the FitzPatrick Institute of African Ornithology and the University of Cape Town gave me the opportunity to develop my conservation biology career with gamebird research in the 1990s. Tim also contributed funding for the production and printing of the book.

I thank Tshifhiwa Mandiwana-Neudani, Rauri Bowie and Tim Crowe for their collaboration with recent research into the taxonomy, phylogeny and biogeography of spurfowls and francolins. I am also grateful to David Donsker, Don Turner and Frank Willems for their valuable inputs when considering the taxonomy and biogeography of the recently elevated spurfowl and francolin species.

Special thanks also to my son Bryan Little for compiling the distribution maps, including those for the 15 recently elevated species. Claire Doutrelant and Jérôme Fuchs kindly provided the proposed French names for the 15 recently elevated species, including the proposed French name of Pseudofrancolin for the spurfowls.

A plea to bird photographers across the world resulted in an overwhelmingly generous offer of over 950 photographs from more than 60 accomplished bird photographers for consideration in the book. A difficult and time-consuming task was undertaken to select the most appropriate photographs which splendidly represent the birds. On deciding to publish the revised *Gamebirds of Africa*, various photographers were contacted and many again kindly offered images of the recently elevated species and improved images of other species. The list on page iv reflects the names of the 90 photographers and the number of photographs used from each person in the revised book. Special gratitude goes to André Botha for his photograph of the calling Grey-winged Francolin which illustrates the cover of this book.

The production of this book would not have been possible without the bulk of the funding for the production and printing of this book from the Wild Bird Trust. I thank them for their support and endorsement and Dr Steve Boyes for his thoughtful Foreword.

I am also grateful to Carol Broomhall, Megan Mance and the rest of the team at Jacana Media for taking on the publishing of both editions and who have created a high-quality product which is now a comprehensive handbook on the gamebirds of Africa. I trust it is a worthy addition to the ornithological literature and to the bookshelves of bird enthusiasts, particularly birders, wing-shooters, landowners and anyone with an interest in nature and conservation, throughout Africa and across the rest of the world.

OPPOSITE Calling male Clapperton's Spurfowl (photo by Nik Borrow)

LIST OF PHOTOGRAPHERS

Photographer names and number of photographs used from each photographer.

Abubakar, Mohammed 2
Athanas, Nick 1
Baker, Neil 1
Barelli, Lorenzo 5
Barrett, Nancy 1
Baston, Bill 1
Beaman, Mark 1
Behrens, Ken 2
Bianchi, Sergio 1
Boedts, Bruno 2
Botha, Andre 20
Borrow, Nik 24
Booysen, Maans 27
Braine, Dayne 11
Braine, Sean 3
Chittenden, Hugh 4
Cohen, Callan 4
Daniels, Dick 1
Dereliev, Sergey 2
Drewitt, Allan 1
Doppagne, Stéphane 2
Dorse, Cliff 4
Dowd, Tony 1
Eggert, Ron 1
Francis, Ian 2
Gabremichael, Merid 3
Gaglio, Davide 5
Gedeon, Kai 2
Gibbs, Dalton 1
Ginn, Peter 1

González, Guilierrez 2
Grant, Peter 1
Grosset, Arthur 1
Hansen, Louis 2
Hatfield, Stratton 2
Henry, Dominic 1
Hills, Peter 3
Hoddinott, David 4
Holmen, Florence 1
Holmen, Per 13
Hoodless, Andrew 2
Hyett, Marvin 3
Jasper, Louise 2
Jonker, Marnix 1
Kean, Christopher 1
Keijser, Guido 1
Kennedy, Adam Scott 1
Krishnappa, Yathin 1
Lagerqvist, Markus 3
Lee, Salim 1
Leventis, Tasso 37
Little, Ian 3
Little, Rob 5
Lloyd, Penn 2
Marcel, Ashute Essebi 2
Martins, Antonio 2
Mendelsohn, John 1
Michelini, Victor 1
Mougeot, Francois 3
Odino, Martin 1

Oláh, János 1
Pitteloud, Jacques 14
Poliza, Michael 1
Portier, Bruno 1
Prophet, Matt 1
Pugh, Andy 2
Redman, Nigel 1
Riley, Adam 4
Rovero, Francesco 2
Ryan, Brendan 1
Shapiro, Dubi 2
Shiff, Yael 1
Shirihai, Hadoram 1
Schmidt, Otto 2
Skov, Bjarne 1
Sloan, Margaret 1
Stapelberg, Philip 1
Steyn, Peter 1
Stockenstroom, Eric 2
Suter, Werner 1
Tizard, Robert 4
van Giersbergen, Paul 2
Vasapolli, Dylan 1
Voaden, Nigel 2
Vorster, Eugene 1
Wachira, Washington 2
Walton, Jessie 4
White, Ian 28
Wilby, Derrick 1
Willems, Frank 3

AUTHOR'S NOTE

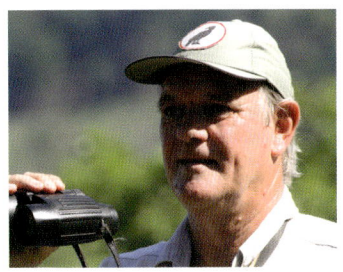
(Photo by Maans Booysen)

Rob Little was born in Durban, KwaZulu-Natal, schooled at King Edward VII High School and his career in conservation began as a forester in 1974. He attained national diplomas in Forestry and Nature Conservation, a BSc degree in Wildlife Resources from the University of Idaho, USA, and a PhD degree on the behavioural ecology, management and utilisation of the Grey-winged Francolin from the University of Cape Town. Between 1974 and 1985, he was a forestry researcher, lecturer in forestry and nature conservation and warden of the Cathedral Peak mountain catchment reserve in the KwaZulu-Natal Drakensberg. Between 1988 and 1997, Rob coordinated the Gamebird Research Programme at the FitzPatrick Institute of African Ornithology, University of Cape Town. Together with Tim Crowe, he published the book *Gamebirds of Southern Africa* (Struik Nature, 2000 & 2011). Rob was Director: Conservation at WWF South Africa from 1997 until 2008. In April 2009 he was appointed Manager of the Centre of Excellence (CoE) at the Fitztitute. He was the Fitztitute's link with the National Research Foundation and the Department of Science & Innovation and managed the research activities which were funded by the CoE using Birds as Keys to Biodiversity Conservation until he retired at the end of 2020. He also recently published the book *Birding in South Africa's National Parks* (Jacana, 2018).

Rob has authored 85 papers in peer-reviewed journals, including book reviews, over 130 popular articles, 5 books and 10 book chapters, including 14 species accounts in *The Atlas of Southern African Birds* (Vol. 1, 1997), 12 species accounts in *Roberts' Birds of Southern Africa* (VIIth Edition, 2005), and 25 species texts in *The Ultimate Companion for Birding in Southern Africa* (Vol. 1, 2014). Rob also guest edited a special issue of *Ostrich* (2015, Vol. 86(1&2)) in memory of esteemed ornithologist Phil Hockey, which attracted 20 papers, 17 with Fitztitute authors and 12 with Phil as co-author. He remained as an associate editor of *Ostrich* from 2015 until 2020.

CONTENTS

FOREWORD	1
INTRODUCTION	3
Africa: Political map	9
GUINEAFOWLS & CONGO PEAFOWL	12
White-breasted Guineafowl	15
Black Guineafowl	18
Helmeted Guineafowl	21
Plumed Guineafowl	26
Crested Guineafowl	29
Vulturine Guineafowl	32
Congo Peafowl	35
FRANCOLINS & PARTRIDGES	40
Crested Francolin	44
Kirk's Francolin	47
Grant's Francolin	51
Coqui Francolin	54
Stuhlmann's Francolin	59
Plain-bellied Francolin	63
Thika Francolin	66
Bar-bellied Francolin	70
Pale-bellied Francolin	73
White-throated Francolin	76
Chestnut-breasted Francolin	79
Schlegel's Francolin	82
Shelley's Francolin	85
Rufous-throated Francolin	88
Ulu Francolin	91
Grey-winged Francolin	94
Orange River Francolin	98
Kunene Francolin	102
Archer's Francolin	105
Red-winged Francolin	108

OPPOSITE An African Snipe that has just probed its bill into the soft sediment (photo by Ian White)

Crawshay's Francolin	111
Finsch's Francolin	114
Moorland Francolin	117
Elgon Francolin	121
Ring-necked Francolin	124
Forest (Latham's) Francolin	127
Barbary Partridge	130
Sand Partridge	133
Udzungwa Forest Partridge	136
Rubeho Forest Partridge	139
Madagascan Partridge	142
Stone Partridge	145
Nahan's Partridge	149

SPURFOWLS ... 154

Red-necked Spurfowl	158
Cranch's Spurfowl	163
Swainson's Spurfowl	167
Yellow-necked Spurfowl	171
Grey-breasted Spurfowl	175
Erckel's Spurfowl	178
Djibouti Spurfowl	181
Chestnut-naped Spurfowl	184
Black-fronted Spurfowl	187
Jackson's Spurfowl	190
Handsome Spurfowl	193
Mount Cameroon Spurfowl	196
Swierstra's Spurfowl	199
Ahanta Spurfowl	202
Scaly Spurfowl	205
Schuett's Spurfowl	208
Grey-striped Spurfowl	213
Double-spurred Spurfowl	216
Heuglin's Spurfowl	219
Clapperton's Spurfowl	222
Hildebrandt's Spurfowl	225
Natal Spurfowl	228

Hartlaub's Spurfowl	232
Harwood's Spurfowl	235
Red-billed Spurfowl	238
Cape Spurfowl	242

QUAILS 248

Common Quail	250
Harlequin Quail	254
Blue Quail	257

SANDGROUSE 262

Pin-tailed Sandgrouse	265
Namaqua Sandgrouse	268
Chestnut-bellied Sandgrouse	271
Spotted Sandgrouse	275
Black-bellied Sandgrouse	278
Yellow-throated Sandgrouse	281
Crowned Sandgrouse	284
Black-faced Sandgrouse	287
Lichtenstein's Sandgrouse	291
Four-banded Sandgrouse	294
Double-banded Sandgrouse	297
Burchell's Sandgrouse	301
Madagascan Sandgrouse	305

SNIPES, GREATER PAINTED-SNIPE & EURASIAN WOODCOCK 310

Greater Painted-snipe	312
Jack Snipe	316
African Snipe	319
Great Snipe	322
Common Snipe	325
Madagascan Snipe	328
Eurasian Woodcock	331

GLOSSARY 334

BIBLIOGRAPHY AND FURTHER READING 336

INDEXES *(Common English, French & scientific names)* 338

FOREWORD

Africa plays host to a rich and diverse gamebird fauna, which are celebrated in this comprehensive and spectacularly illustrated monograph. This book contains a fascinating and authoritative compilation of evolutionary, behavioural and ecological information alongside valuable insights into the lives of these unique and special birds. There is no doubt that this book fills an important gap in our ornithological literature. *Gamebirds of Africa* offers a concise summary of the large but scattered body of accumulated scientific research and field guide literature. This recently updated book is scientifically sound and represents a unique central repository of information on Africa's gamebirds.

The 89 species of upland gamebirds and snipes found in Africa fall into seven groups: guineafowls and Congo Peafowl (7 species); francolins and partridges (33 species); spurfowls (26 species); quails (3 species); sandgrouse (13 species); and snipes and Eurasian Woodcock (7 species). The book is informative and readable, carefully collating detailed information on gamebird identification, distribution, habitat use, habits, foraging, nesting ecology, breeding biology and conservation status for each species. Added to this, spectacular photographs illustrate the overall appearance, diagnostic features, behavioural activities and, in some cases, preferred habitats of each species. This book will be a worthy addition to the ornithological literature and to the bookshelves of bird enthusiasts.

The author, Rob Little, has had a long career in gamebird research and conservation biology. Rob coordinated the Gamebird Research Programme at the FitzPatrick Institute of African Ornithology at the University of Cape Town in the 1990s. Together with Tim Crowe, he published the book *Gamebirds of Southern Africa*. Rob was then appointed as the Director of Conservation at WWF South Africa from 1997 until 2008. In 2009, he became the manager of the Centre of Excellence at the Fitztitute, coordinating the research and education activities using birds as keys to conservation. He has a passion for this fascinating group of birds and provides unique and thought-provoking insights into their life histories in this superbly written book.

The Wild Bird Trust committed to fund the production and printing of this handbook to support the Trust's primary aim of keeping birds safe in the wild using a combination of applied research and conservation action. The Trust encourages the use of flagship bird species, like many gamebirds, as 'ecosystem ambassadors' in their natural habitats. The Trust works hard to advance the research in, education about, and conservation of all bird species in the wild. Endorsement of this book speaks to the Trust's current focus on the conservation of African bird species.

OPPOSITE A male Burchell's Sandgrouse takes off from a watering hole (photo by Ian White)

The Trust congratulates the author and Jacana Media for the publication of this book, which will no doubt stimulate a deeper appreciation for and interest in Africa's gamebirds. We encourage ornithologists, birders, wing-shooters, landowners and anyone with an interest in nature or conservation, throughout Africa and across the world, to add this book to their library collection. Very importantly, the resultant awareness of the threats that face each species will support their future conservation and help us all recognise the role they play in the ecosystems they depend on.

Dr Rutledge 'Steve' Boyes
Wild Bird Trust
28 July 2020

INTRODUCTION

Gamebirds of Africa summarises and presents useful and pertinent facts in an informative and readable fashion. Numerous photographs accompany the descriptive text and, where possible, reflect the appearance, characteristics and sexual dimorphism features and special behavioural activities or favoured habitat features to assist with the identification of the species. Recent research into the taxonomy, phylogeny and biogeography of the francolins and spurfowls is presented (see the Bibliography) and the book covers the 89 species of upland gamebirds and snipes found in Africa. These 89 species comprise six groups: guineafowls and Congo Peafowl (7 species) francolins and partridges (33 species), spurfowls (26 species), quails (3 species), sandgrouse (13 species) and snipes and Eurasian Woodcock (7 species). Three endemic Madagascan species (a partridge, a sandgrouse and a snipe) and four African species (introduced Helmeted Guineafowl, Harlequin Quail, Common Quail and Greater Painted-snipe) which are also found in Madagascar, are included for regional completeness.

Gamebirds have been utilised by humans for food and sport for centuries because they are believed to withstand 'sustainable harvesting' and have also been domesticated for food production and for ornamental aviculture. They are a familiar, yet often under-appreciated, group of birds, members of which can be seen along roadsides, open farmlands, in urban fringes and even within cities, towns and gardens. It is therefore not surprising that the Helmeted Guineafowl *Numida meleagris* appears more regularly as African curios on mantelpieces in living rooms and on printed African textiles than any other bird.

Helmeted Guineafowls are the best known African gamebird and are icons of the African landscape (photo by Andre Botha).

All gamebirds can be divided broadly by habitat into two artificial groups – landfowl and waterfowl – which today have representatives on all continents except Antarctica. Landfowl and waterfowl together occupy the second oldest branch of the avian evolutionary tree, after ostrich-like birds. The landfowl, including pheasants, quails, grouse, partridges, francolins, spurfowls, guineafowls and turkeys, occupy virtually all terrestrial habitats ranging from lowland deserts and tropical rainforests to Siberian tundras and the snowy slopes of the highest mountains of the Himalayas. Modern waterfowl, such as ducks, geese and snipes, are largely dependent on aquatic habitats.

In the strict sense of the word, most landfowl are chicken-like species in the avian taxonomic order Galliformes. Traditionally, the Galliformes are divided into nine major groups: megapodes, cracids (guans, chachalacas and curassows), guineafowls, grouse, turkeys, pheasants, partridges (including francolins and spurfowls), Old World quails and New World quails. Megapodes and cracids are the most ancient galliforms and are confined respectively to the tropical and subtropical regions of Australasia and South America. Megapodes have, as their name implies, large feet and differ from all other birds in that their eggs are incubated artificially, such as by heat from rotting vegetation piled in a compost-heap-like nest or from sand heated by volcanic activity. Cracids differ from the other galliforms in that they spend relatively little time scratching on the ground for food, preferring rather to pluck fruits and flowers from the branches of trees or to pick up fallen items from the ground.

Investigation of the genetics and anatomy of living species and fossils, as well as plumage, calls and behaviour, suggests that the major evolutionary break in the galliform evolutionary tree is the African guineafowls. Thus, the primary breakup of the mega-continent Gondwana into Australasia, South America and Africa more than 90 million years ago led to the creation of the three most ancient groups of galliforms on now well-separated continents. The next major event probably dates back to about 55 million years ago when partridge/francolin-like galliforms dispersed fairly simultaneously from Africa to North America and Asia respectively, giving rise to the rest of Earth's gamebirds: quails, partridges, peafowls, junglefowls, pheasants, turkeys and grouse. The American quail descendants are relictually represented in Africa by the evolutionarily enigmatic Stone Partridge *Ptilopachus petrosus* from the African savannas north of the tropics and Nahan's Partridge *P. nahani* from the forests of the Democratic Republic of the Congo and Uganda. The Eurasian landfowl are descended from the Udzungwa Forest Partridge *Xenoperdix udzungwensis* discovered during the early 1990s from forests confined to the tops of the Udzungwa Mountains in Tanzania.

Evidence shows that pheasants, partridges, quails and francolins as understood throughout the 20th century are not natural evolutionary groups but rather mosaics of evolutionarily unrelated species. Even the best-known gamebird, the Junglefowl *Gallus gallus* (which is the wild ancestor of the domestic chicken), has shifted its 'perch' on the gamebird evolutionary tree from that of the pheasants to one including a mix of 'francolins' and 'partridges'. To make matters more confusing, 'the' Partridge *Perdix*

perdix links with the true pheasants (for example, *Phasianus* species with which it shares more than 14 tail feathers), which, in turn, do not include the peafowls *Pavo* species, the peacock pheasants *Polyplectron* species and the argus 'pheasants' (*Rheinartia* and *Argus* species), which are in fact related to one another. Furthermore, the most evolutionary artificial groups of all are the partridges and 'francolins', whose members appear to link variously with the New World quails, the Old World quails and the peacock pheasants.

Natal Spurfowl chicks showing their broad head-stripes (photo by Ian White).

The distinction between the partridge-like francolins ('true' francolins related to Asiatic *Francolinus* species) and the pheasant-like francolins (spurfowls) is apparent in the plumage of their downy chicks. They differ in facial markings and the markings on their backs and crowns. Francolins have quail-like back feathers with strong barring and a streak along the quill shaft. The back feathers of spurfowls have no shaft streak and are, at best, extremely irregularly barred. The crowns of francolin chicks are multi-striped as opposed to the few broad stripes of spurfowl chicks.

From a conservation perspective, research on gamebirds is essential because, time and again, the one biological 'bond' that unites gamebirds (their ability to be 'harvested' sustainably) has been broken. In particular, information on gamebird behavioural ecology and demographics can highlight the roles of changes to the natural environment by humans that can, on the one hand, produce some of the most spectacular wing-shooting in the world, but can also destroy it and harm biodiversity across the board. The bottom-line is that relatively easy-to-apply management of the landscape can be a 'win-win' conservation success, whereas mismanagement can result in disaster. Unfortunately, it is safe to say that much of Africa has been subjected to extensive habitat transformation and degradation, mostly through conversion to croplands, extensive frequent burning, as well as to urban areas and rural settlement. I trust that the information provided on the human threats to gamebirds will stimulate effective implementation of practical conservation guidelines and best practice that restore and maintain gamebird habitats and populations.

The aim of this book

This book collates and summarises the large, but scattered, body of literature on the biology of African gamebirds. Much of the information contained is gleaned from the *Handbook of the Birds of the World* (Del Hoyo *et al.* 1994, 2013), *The Birds of Africa Volume II* (Urban *et al.* 1986), *Birds of Africa south of the Sahara* (Sinclair & Ryan 2010) and *Gamebirds of Southern Africa* (Little & Crowe 2011). The species texts present information on the classification, description, distribution and habitat, habits, food and feeding, breeding, status and conservation of each species in a readable format. By doing this, I hope to encourage birders, conservationists, landowners and wing-shooters to appreciate this special group of birds and to manage gamebirds as 'umbrella' species, whose conservation promotes that of biodiversity conservation in general.

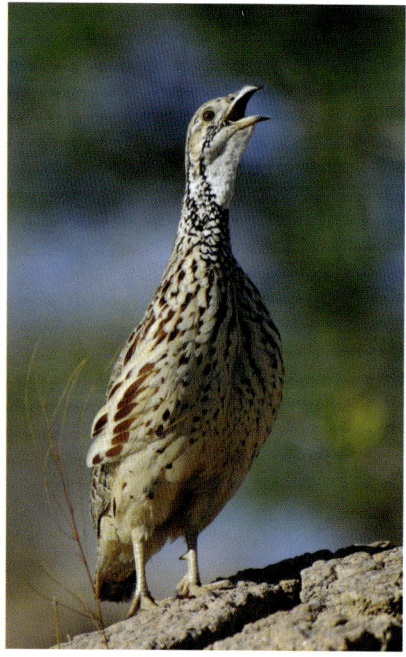

This Kunene Francolin is calling from a conspicuous perch to advertise his presence in his territory (photo by Dayne Braine).

How to use and interpret this book

The main content of the book is contained within six sections, which represent the overall groups covered by the book. Each group section has an introduction that briefly highlights the diagnostic features of that group, and the natural history and evolutionary relationships between the members of the group.

Each species account opens with the currently accepted English and French common names, followed by the current scientific name of the bird. The third line of the opening text refers to the original scientific name and details of its discovery, including the surname of the scientist who was the first to describe the species, the year in which this was done, and the place of the first record. The naming of the gamebirds and snipes of Africa largely follows the International Ornithological Congress (IOC) World Bird List (version 5.3, Gill & Donsker 2015). English and French common names have been proposed for the two 'new' spurfowls and the 13 'new' francolin species including the use of Pseudofrancolin as the French common name for the spurfowls.

The distribution map for each species reflects the current distribution of the species within the continent. Due to the scale of the maps, only relatively vague interpretations of distribution can be ascertained at a local scale. The distribution maps for the recently elevated francolin species, particularly the coqui-type *Campocolinus* species, are not totally resolved and need further verification.

Classification

This section gives the most current information on the species' evolutionary status and affinities. The most closely related species are given where appropriate. Where the species varies significantly geographically, distinctive forms are recognised as subspecies, which are listed, along with their general geographical distribution. This information largely follows the IOC World Bird List (version 5.3, Gill & Donsker 2015), Tim Crowe's overview of gamebird evolution (The Conversation, 24 February 2016) and two recently published papers by Mandiwana-Neudani *et al.* (2019, *Ostrich* 90: 2 & 3).

Description

This section will help the reader to identify the species in the field and to distinguish adults, juveniles and chicks, using, where available, information on overall form and plumage. Some comments are also given to differentiate from similar species. Identification can also be assisted by referring to the photographs which, where possible, reflect the general appearance, characteristic and sexual dimorphism features of each species.

Distribution and habitat

Here I reflect the species' geographical range and their habitat preferences. Information should be interpreted in conjunction with the distribution map of each species.

Habits

This summarises what is known about the species' behavioural ecology, any movement patterns, and their displays and calls, both day by day and throughout the year.

Food and feeding

This section describes any specific foraging behaviour and identifies food types taken on a seasonal basis.

A male Crested Guineafowl offering a courtship food item to a hen while she dust-baths (photo by Maans Booysen)

Breeding

This section gives information on the species' mating system (for example, if it is monogamous), breeding (egg-laying) and factors (such as rainfall) that may influence its timing. The architecture of its nest, clutch size, egg colour and size, incubation period and the growth and development of chicks and juveniles is also presented where known.

Status and conservation

This indicates the status of the species' populations evaluated on a geographical basis, emphasising any potential threats of local populations and where and if (and when) it may be utilised sustainably by wing-shooters.

The glossary

Because the species accounts contain biological information, terms may be used with which some readers are not familiar. These are explained or defined in the glossary.

Bibliography and suggested reading

The bibliography at the end of the book presents a brief list of key references on which I relied for information. While the bibliography is not fully comprehensive, it is sufficiently detailed to allow any reader to source the key studies of the 89 species represented in the book. Further reference material can be found in the reference sections of the *Handbook of the Birds of the World* (Del Hoyo *et al.* 1994, 2013), *The Birds of Africa Volume II* (Urban *et al.* 1986), *Birds of Africa south of the Sahara* (Sinclair & Ryan 2010) and *Gamebirds of Southern Africa* (Little & Crowe 2011).

Africa: Politcal Map

PART 1

Guineafowls & Congo Peafowl

GUINEAFOWLS AND CONGO PEAFOWL

Classification

Guineafowls make up the Afrotropical endemic family Numididae, with six species in four genera:

Agelastes Bonaparte, 1850, containing two species:

- White-breasted Guineafowl *A. meleagrides* of West Africa
- Black Guineafowl *A. niger* of Central Africa

Numida Linnaeus, 1764, containing one species:

- Helmeted Guineafowl *N. meleagris* are characteristic of virtually all open-country habitats outside deserts and alpine systems throughout sub-Saharan Africa.

Guttera Wagler, 1832, containing two species:

- Plumed Guineafowl *G. plumifera* are confined largely to the primary rainforests of central equatorial Africa.
- Crested Guineafowl *G. pucherani* of western, central and southern Africa, which inhabit forest edges, gallery forest along rivers, and secondary forest regrowth.

Acryllium Gray, GR, 1840, containing one species:

- Vulturine Guineafowl *A. vulturinum* extends the realm of the guineafowl into the semi-deserts of eastern Kenya, southern Ethiopia and Somalia.

Recent research suggests that the Kenya Crested Guineafowl *G. edouardi* of East Africa may be recognised as a full species in the future. Although the Congo Peafowl *Afropavo congensis* is more closely related to Asian peafowls, *Pavo* species, and the pheasants in the family Phasianidae than to the guineafowls, they are placed with the guineafowls here because they may have more of a field affiliation with them in Africa.

Description

- Guineafowl species differ from one another primarily in the colour of the naked skin on their head and eye surrounds, in the colour of other facial structures and adornments, and in the pitch of their advertisement cackles. These anatomical and behavioural characteristics are functional components within the individual species' mating systems, allowing them to instinctively distinguish potential sexual partners of their own species from members of the other guineafowl species. There is sometimes striking, effectively qualitative, geographical variation in head colour

PREVIOUS PAGE Crested Guineafowl subspecies *Guttera pucherani pucherani* (photo by Lorenzo Barelli) and adornments among various subspecies (or geographical races). However, none of this variation has any demonstrable adaptive value, plays any role in mate recognition or inhibits interbreeding between members of the various subspecies. For example, when domesticated Helmeted Guineafowl, previously derived from the West African subspecies, is bred in captivity with members of other subspecies from as far afield as Somalia and East Africa, or is released into populations of wild Helmeted Guineafowl in southern Africa, it interbreeds freely without any apparent loss of fertility. Indeed, within the zones of natural geographical contact between subspecies of the Helmeted Guineafowl, in particular, there is apparently free interbreeding, producing anatomically intermediate forms of all persuasions.

- The other prominent feature that distinguishes one guineafowl 'type' from another is the pitch of the advertisement calls, which seems to be an adaptation that allows effective communication in different habitats. For example, the Black Guineafowl, which lives in dense primary rainforest, has a low-pitched, almost musical call designed to penetrate thick vegetation. The calls of the Crested Guineafowl, which lives in less dense, secondary forest and riverine bush, are somewhat higher pitched. The call of the Helmeted Guineafowl, which lives in open savanna habitat, is higher pitched still. Finally, the Vulturine Guineafowl *Acryllium vulturinum*, which inhabits more open, semi-arid scrubby grassland, has the highest-pitched call of all.

Natural history

Guineafowls occur in virtually all African habitats from dense rain forest to semi-desert, only excluded from extreme deserts and extensive wetland landscapes. They are generally gregarious, forming flocks during the non-breeding season and flocks can even converge in areas of optimal foraging. They are icons of the African landscape and are depicted on more African curios than any other bird on the continent.

They tend to have large clutches and chicks, commonly known as keets, that remain with the parents into the non-breeding season to form flocks. Guineafowl are favoured for food by many rural communities and as such are captured or even domesticated, particularly the Helmeted Guineafowl, to breed for the table.

Evolutionary placement

- The evolution of guineafowls, like that of the Australasian megapodes (Megapodiidae) and the largely South American cracids (Cracidae), was influenced by the break-up of Gondwana (the southern mega-continent comprising Australia, India, Africa and South America) more than 100 million years ago.
- Guineafowls bridge the evolutionary gap between the relatively advanced, pheasant-like birds and the anatomically relatively primitive megapodes and cracids.
- Therefore, Africa is the likely origin of a guineafowl-like gamebird that was the ancestor of modern galliform gamebirds.

- Evolution has produced, in some instances, new species and genera of guineafowl reproductively isolated from one another and, in others, merely geographical variants that interbreed freely.
- The Congo Peafowl is endemic to the Congo Basin, and is one of three extant species of peafowl, the other two being the Indian Peafowl *Pavo cristatus* originally from India and Sri Lanka, and the Green Peafowl *P. muticus* native to Burma and Indochina.
- The Congo Peafowl was only described as a species in 1936 by Dr James Chapin who noticed that local Congolese headdresses contained long reddish-brown feathers that were not consistent with any known central African bird. He later found two specimens in the Royal Museum of Central Africa with similar feathers labelled as the 'Indian Peacock' which he discovered to be the Congo Peafowl, a completely different species. In 1955 he located seven live specimens of the species.
- The Congo Peafowl has physical characteristics of both peafowls and guineafowls which may indicate that the Congo Peafowl is a link between the two families.

Conservation

Five of the six guineafowl species are relatively secure with only the White-breasted Guineafowl being severely threatened, and thus listed as Vulnerable (The IUCN Red List of Threatened Species, version 2015-4). While all six species are impacted by hunting pressure, including shooting and snaring, at various levels across their range, the forest species are most impacted by habitat fragmentation and loss due to deforestation and the more open habitat species are influenced by agriculture, including pesticides and the injudicious use of fire.

White-breasted Guineafowl
Pintade à poitrine blanche

Agelastes meleagrides

Agelastes meleagrides ('Temm.' Bonaparte, 1850), the type locality is probably Ghana

White-breasted Guineafowls photographed in Tai Forest, Ivory Coast
(both photos by Ian Francis)

Classification

The White-breasted Guineafowl is most closely related to the Black Guineafowl *A. niger*. They are monotypic with no recognised subspecies.

Description

- They are easily identified by their completely bare pink or red head and neck, conspicuous white neck collar and breast, and otherwise black body.
- Their bill is greenish brown and their legs are greyish black.
- Juveniles have no white collar, the head and upper neck are covered with brownish-black downy feathers, with two tawny crown stripes, and their belly is white.
- Downy keets are greyish brown with pale ochre stripes on a dark sepia head and neck.

Distribution and habitat

- They are uncommon to rare from south-eastern Sierra Leone, Liberia, Ivory Coast to western Ghana.
- See status and conservation for indications of their local extinction.
- They inhabit primary West African lowland rainforests, which have an open or sparse undergrowth, or older regrowth adjacent to primary forest.

Habits

They occur in loose groups of up to 20 birds, and are shy and difficult to approach. Although they rarely leave the protective forest cover, they do not favour dense undergrowth. They roost in bushy trees in the understory. They utter a metallic twitter when foraging, a loud, even-pitched whistle to muster the flock, and a descending, flute-like whistle by isolated individuals.

Food and feeding

They forage on the ground below fruiting trees, scratching among soil and leaf litter with their feet like domestic chickens. Their diet consists mainly of berries and fallen seeds of forest trees, and insects including termites, ants, crickets, beetle larvae, as well as millipedes, spiders and small molluscs.

Breeding

Not much is known about their breeding biology. Breeding is during October to May, peaking from November to January. They nest on the ground in dense undergrowth. The clutch of up to 12 eggs are reddish buff with white pores and measure 45.0 x 35.0 mm.

Status and conservation

They are severely threatened by hunting pressure and habitat destruction and may disappear except from a few protected areas if efforts are not made to secure more representative portions of their populations. Populations in Ghana, Sierra Leone and Guinea may be largely extinct, and they are rare in Liberia and Ivory Coast. Although shy and secretive, they are easily trapped and hunters also lure them by imitating the call and killing them with a slingshot. A recent census conducted in the Tai Forest, Ivory Coast, suggests that they are still fairly numerous, despite the poaching and habitat-related issues, along with civil unrest. But their status in Ivory Coast and Liberia remains precarious in the long term. Their conservation status is therefore listed as Vulnerable (The IUCN Red List of Threatened Species v 2015-4).

White-breasted Guineafowls in typical dense forest habitat (photo by Allan Drewitt)

Black Guineafowl
Pintade noire
Agelastes niger

Phasidus niger (Cassin, 1857), Cape Lopez, Gabon

Black Guineafowl photographed in Gabon (photo by Tasso Leventis)

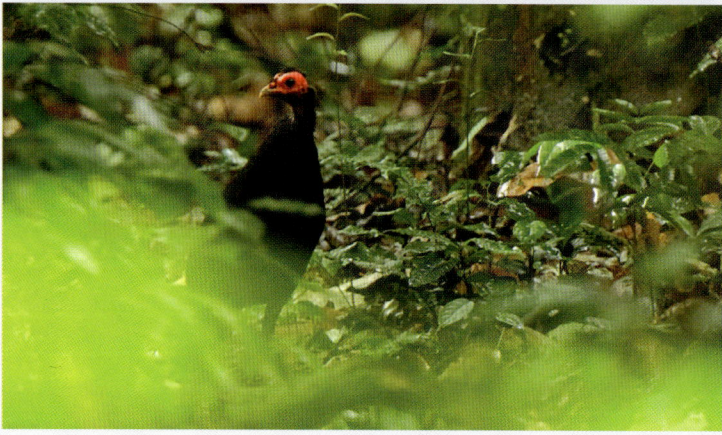

Black Guineafowl photographed in Gabon (photo by David Hoddinott)

Classification

The Black Guineafowl was previously placed in the monotypic genus *Phasidus*, but they are most closely related to the White-breasted Guineafowl *A. meleagrides*. There are no subspecies recognised.

Description

- They are a relatively small (average 700 g), entirely plain, black guineafowl with a bare dull red head and throat and a short black downy crown and hind-neck crest.
- The rest of the plumage is unmarked black, and the wings and tail are unmarked.
- The bill is greenish grey and the legs are greyish brown.
- Their lack of plumes on a pinkish head and unspotted plumage distinguish them from the larger Plumed Guineafowl *Guttera plumifera*, which has a similar distribution.
- The sexes are similar in appearance with the male being slightly larger.
- Juveniles are dull black, have a feathered neck, dull brown head and a greyish white belly.
- Downy keets are mainly dark rufous and black above.

Distribution and habitat

- They are endemic to Central Africa from Cameroon, Equatorial Guinea, Gabon and far-northern Angola, through the central Democratic Republic of the Congo to the western edge of the Rift Valley.
- They are scarce to locally common, but seldom seen.
- They are found chiefly in dense primary lowland rain forest mostly with rank undergrowth, also in forest edges and on old, overgrown fields.

Habits

They are usually encountered as elusive pairs or small groups of less than 10 individuals, which frequent the forest floor and rapidly run within dense primary forest thickets for cover. They are presumed to roost in trees or bushes. They have a resonant rising, rather melodious '*huwhee-huwhee-huwhee-huwhe- wheet-wheet-wheet* …' whistling call, and a '*keet keet*' contact call.

Food and feeding

They forage as a flock on the forest floor, scratching with their feet. Their diet consists of hard seeds, green leaves, fruits, beetles, ants, termites, millipedes and small frogs.

Breeding

They are probably monogamous. In north-eastern Democratic Republic of the Congo, they breed in almost any month, but mainly during the drier months of December to February. The nest, clutch size and incubation period are undescribed. The deeply pitted eggs are pale, reddish brown, sometimes washed with yellow or violet and measure 42.0 x 34.0 mm.

Status and conservation

They are probably less threatened by habitat loss than White-breasted Guineafowl because their range is much more extensive, but are nonetheless vulnerable to forest destruction and hunting. The viability of protected areas within their range is probably vital to their long-term conservation.

Helmeted Guineafowl
Pintade sauvage

Numida meleagris

Phasianus meleagris (Linnaeus, 1758),
Upper Nile, Nubia, Sudan

Helmeted Guineafowl subspecies *N. m. coronata* keets in the Kruger National Park, South Africa (photo by Jessie Walton)

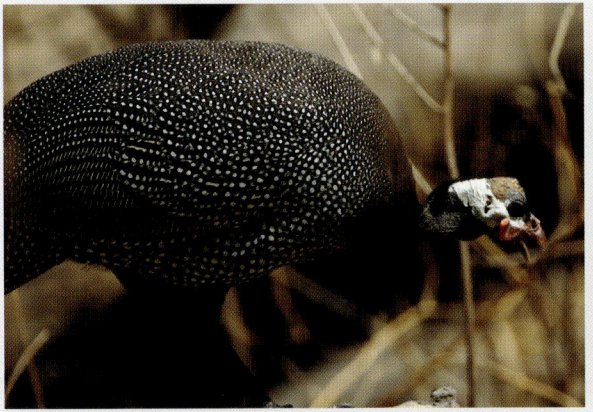

Helmeted Guineafowl subspecies *N. m. galeatus* from Nigeria (photo by Tasso Leventis)

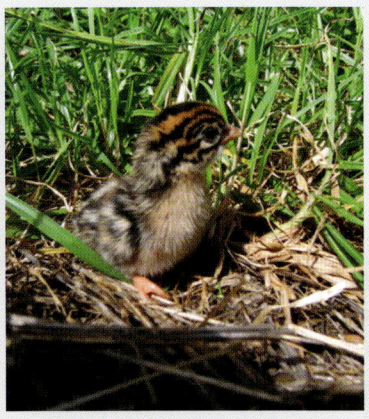

A one-day-old Helmeted Guineafowl chick (photo by Rob Little)

GAMEBIRDS

Helmeted Guineafowl subspecies *N. m. reichenowi* from Tanzania (photo by Tasso Leventis)

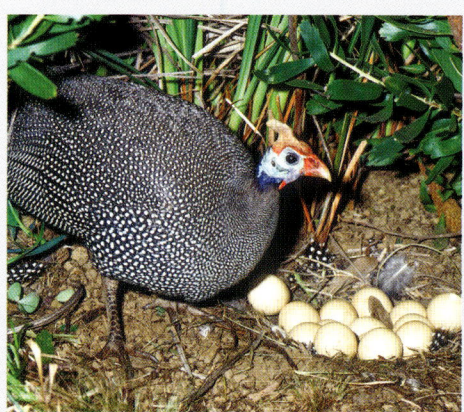

A typical Helmeted Guineafowl nest and clutch (photo by Peter Steyn)

Helmeted Guineafowl in flight (photo by Davide Gaglio)

Helmeted Guineafowl subspecies *N. m. coronata* at a water hole in South Africa (photo by Andre Botha)

Classification

Nine subspecies are recognised:

N. m. sabyi Hartert, 1919, between the Oum er Rbia and Sebou rivers in north-western Morocco

N. m. galeatus Pallas, 1767, in West Africa, east to southern Chad, and south to central Democratic Republic of the Congo and northern Angola, has a distinctive white face and rounded, red wattles

N. m. meleagris (Linnaeus, 1758) in eastern Chad, east to Ethiopia and south to northern DRC, Uganda and northern Kenya, has a small helmet, a blue face, rounded blue wattles and a short, cartilaginous, bristly 'moustache'

N. m. somaliensis Neumann, 1899, in north-eastern Ethiopia and Somalia, has a very long moustache and triangular wattles, which are blue at the base and red at the tips

N. m. reichenowi Ogilvie-Grant, 1894, in Kenya and central Tanzania has a huge, sabre-shaped helmet and rounded, red wattles

N. m. mitratus (Pallas, 1764) in Tanzania, eastern Mozambique, Zambia, Zimbabwe and northern Botswana

N. m. marungensis Schalow, 1884, in the southern Congo Basin, south to western Angola and east to the Zambezi Basin, and in the Luangwa Valley in Zambia, has a long helmet and pennant-shaped, blue wattles with red tips

N. m. papillosus Reichenow, 1894 [including *N. m. damarensis* (Roberts, 1917)] in the drier parts of western Botswana and Namibia

N. m. coronata Gurney, 1868, in South Africa

If pressed to apply an extreme phylogenetic concept, based on albeit limited molecular and morphological phylogenetically informative evidence, it is possible to argue for five species taxa within *Numida*: *galeatus* + *sabyi*, *meleagris* sensu lato (including *major* and *somaliensis*), *reichenowi*, *marungensis*, *cornonata* sensu lato (including *damarensis/papilosus*, *cornonata* and *mitratus*) (Tim Crowe pers. com.).

Description

- They have a bony casque or 'helmet' and bare fleshy wattles.
- Sexes are similar, however, males exhibit the hump-backed display, walking erect and on their toes with wings raised and held close to his body.
- Females tend to walk flat-footed and appear slouched in posture.
- Juveniles have a tawny-buff head with two blackish lateral crown stripes and no casque.

GAMEBIRDS

- Their plumage is drab grey-brown, barred with reddish-brown and speckled with black.
- The head retains the feathers of the downy keet almost until full grown.
- The helmet appears at about 40 days.
- Keets have light brown and buff facial stripes with a dark brown crown stripe.
- The back plumage is mottled brown and grey, with two longitudinal buffy stripes bordered with black, straddling a central broad brown stripe.

Distribution and habitat

- They are widespread in most open-country terrain, from near-desert to the edges of forests, especially in savannas mixed with cultivation.
- They are absent from some arid areas, which lack drinking water and elevated roosts.
- They have expanded their range where humans have added these missing habitat features, with even telephone poles can serve as nightly roosts.
- Humans have further promoted this range expansion by translocating wild birds into new areas, including to Madagascar.
- This has also promoted the release of domesticated Helmeted Guineafowl into the wild.
- Evidence of domestication is white feathers on the wings or body, whitish instead of blue facial skin and orange not brown-black legs.

Habits

During the non-breeding season, flocks of 15–40 birds are formed, with larger aggregations being multiple flocks converging on a super-abundant resource. Flocks descend from their roost at dawn, move to a drinking site, then socialise and dust-bath. Thereafter, they move into foraging areas or mixed bush-grassland shade cover until late afternoon. A couple of hours before sunset, they may move to a watering site to socialise and drink. Just before sunset they return to their roost. They rarely fly, only if pressed or to mount their roost. They have a cackling, staccato '*kek, kek, kek, kek, kaaaaaa, ka, ka, ka, ka, kaaaaaa, ka, ka*' alarm call. Females have a two-note 'buckwheat' contact call used during the breeding season. Flock members keep in contact by emitting a single-noted '*cheenk*' call.

Food and feeding

Their diet consists of bulbs, primarily *Cyperus* species, the stems of plants and spillage from harvested grain, but will readily shift to grass and forb seeds. While breeding, they eat invertebrates, including agricultural pests, especially grasshoppers and termites. They do not normally take growing maize plants or maize from cobs still attached to healthy plants.

Breeding

Breeding is triggered by rainfall. The female selects the nest site in tall grass at the base of a tussock or under a bush. The nest is a well-concealed scrape in the earth, lined with feathers and grass stems. The clutch of 6–20 (and sometimes more), broad, slightly pointed oval eggs are white to pale brown with fine speckling. They are hard and thick-shelled and measure 52.6 x 40.2 mm. Incubation by the female lasts 24–27 days. Both parents aggressively defend their precocial keets, which can join their parents on the roost when 2–3 weeks old.

Status and conservation

Threats include disease, predation by natural and feral carnivores, and snaring and poisoning by humans. However, the primary causes of population declines are habitat fragmentation and destruction associated with extensive crop farming. These involve large-scale planting and the elimination of weeds and insects by the use of herbicides and insecticides, which destroy nesting cover and food resources.

Female Helmeted Guineafowl incubating her clutch (photo by Rob Little)

Plumed Guineafowl
Pintade plumifère

Guttera plumifera

Numida plumifera (Cassin, 1857), Cape Lopez, Gabon

Perched Plumed Guineafowl in Central African Republic (photo by Christopher Kean)

Plumed Guineafowls among dense forest undergrowth in Gabon (photo by Nik Borrow)

Classification

The Plumed Guineafowl is most closely related to the Crested Guineafowl *G. pucherani*. There are two subspecies recognised:

G. p. plumifera Cassin, 1857 in southern Cameroon down to northern Angola

G. p. schubotzi Reichenow, 1912 in northern and eastern Democratic Republic of the Congo

Description

- They are slightly smaller than Crested Guineafowl, but differ in appearance by having a long erect crest of stiff black plumes from the forehead to the rear of the crown, which is not curly.
- They have a dark grey, not a blue-grey, face and neck, but also have light blue spots on a black body.
- Adults have longish black facial wattles, not red, and no red on the throat.
- *G. p. schubotzi* has patches of orange skin in front of the ear and on the hind neck.
- Juveniles lack spots and have faintly scaled underparts.
- Downy keets are buffy with dark longitudinal stripes.

Distribution and habitat

- They are locally common to uncommon, but rarely seen, endemic to Central Africa.
- Their distribution is from southern Cameroon, Equatorial Guinea, coastal Gabon and Congo, across northern Congo and the Democratic Republic of the Congo, through the Congo basin eastwards to the western edge of the Rift Valley.
- Their distribution is similar to that of Black Guineafowl *Agelastes niger* but probably more patchy.
- They inhabit primary lowland rainforest and sometimes mature secondary growth.
- They do not venture into cultivated clearings.

Habits

They are shy, and non-breeding birds gather in flocks of up to 50 birds. When disturbed, they scatter and run rather than fly, but if flushed will fly into the thick foliage of tall trees and remain motionless until the threat has passed. They roost together in tall trees. They have a far-carrying '*kow kow khep, kow kow khep* …' trumpeting alarm call and a sharp '*tchik tchik*' contact call.

Food and feeding

They forage together on the forest floor, scratching up large areas of leaf litter with their feet in search of food. Their diet consists of roots, seeds, fruits, leaves and invertebrates, including snails, slugs, millipedes, spiders, roaches, grasshoppers, crickets, hemipterans, beetles, termites and ants.

Breeding

They are monogamous and breed during the wetter months. The nest is a simple scrape in the ground among dry leaves, with which it is lined. The average clutch is 10 eggs, which are pale buff, with numerous darkened pits, and measure 49.0 x 38.0 mm. Incubation lasts for 23 days.

Status and conservation

They are not threatened, but their range may be decreasing and becoming fragmented because of forest and thicket habitat destruction, combined with hunting pressure.

Crested Guineafowl
Pintade de Purcheran

Guttera pucherani
Numida pucherani (Hartlaub, 1861), Zanzibar

ABOVE Crested Guineafowl subspecies *G. p. verreauxi* in Nigeria (photo by Tasso Leventis)

LEFT Crested Guineafowl subspecies *G. p. edouardi* in southern Africa (photo by Maans Booysen)

BELOW Crested Guineafowl subspecies *G. p. pucherani* in East Africa (photo by Lorenzo Barelli)

Classification

Five subspecies are recognised, although this may be reviewed in the future:

G. p. pucherani Hartlaub, 1861 in south-western Somalia to central Tanzania, Zanzibar and Tumbatu Island has red bare skin around the eye and genetic differences, which may warrant full species status in the future.

G. p. verreauxi Elliot, DG, 1870; includes *G. p. kathleenae* and *G. p. schoutedeni*) in Guinea Bissau, east to north-western Cameroon and through the DRC to western Kenya, and south to Angola and western Zambia

G. p. sclateri Reichenow, 1898 in the Sanaga River region of western Cameroon

G. p. barbata Ghigi, 1905 in south-eastern Tanzania, southwards to northern Mozambique and Malawi

G. p. edouardi Hartlaub, 1867 in eastern Zambia through southern Mozambique to north-eastern South Africa has grey skin on the nape (this is blue in the other subspecies).

The localised *G. p. symonsi* in the Karkloof Forest of KwaZulu-Natal, South Africa is not considered a valid subspecies.

Description

They have a thick crest of soft curly black feathers, crimson eyes (brown in *G. p. verreauxi*) and a pale grey 'hood' of skin on the back of their head.

- Their lower-neck and upper-breast feathers are black, giving a dark overall appearance.
- Their body and wing feathers have a bluish tinge and pale bluish-white spots, with pale whitish-brown outer secondary flight feathers, visible at rest and as a pale band in the mid-wing in flight.
- Juveniles are duller, with heavily scaled plumage.
- Keets have a dark brown forehead and crown with a lighter rufous-buff cap.
- The sides of the head are brown, with irregular, multiple buff streaking.
- The back has a broad, central, dark brown stripe flanked by two stripes on either side, the inner stripe being buff, the outer dark brown.
- The underparts are rufous-buff, lighter on the throat.

Distribution and habitat

- They are widespread but fragmented from southern West Africa across Central and East Africa to southern Africa.
- Their preferred habitats are forest edge, secondary and gallery forest, and they spend much of their time skulking in thick bush.

- Although associated with forest and woodland habitats, they are found in both moist and semi-arid sites.
- They are a species of wild habitats, seldom venturing into cultivated farmlands.

Habits

They are relatively secretive and wary, although can be fairly tame in the vicinity of bush camps. They are sedentary and roost at night in trees. They are gregarious during the non-breeding season, with flocks averaging fewer than 20 birds. During the early morning, the flock will move into forest glades to preen and socialise in the sun. Before sunrise and after sunset, they will venture onto bush tracks where they are vulnerable to collisions with motor vehicles. When disturbed they cock their tail and scurry around in a seemingly confused manner. The alarm call is a staccato '*chuk-chuk-chukchukerr*', which has a low pitch. They are noisy, often heard before they are seen and sometimes call well into the night and during the pre-dawn hours. Members of the flock keep in contact by emitting a low-pitched '*chuk*' call.

Food and feeding

They forage mainly on the ground, scratching in leaf litter with their feet, but will also fly into trees to pick fruit and berries. They feed on the seeds, fruits and berries of Rubiacceae, Amaranthaccae, Compositae, Malvaceae and Fabaceae. They also eat soft shoots, stems, green leaves, bulbs and roots, but are not attracted to maize scattered on the ground. Animal food includes spiders, beetles, grasshoppers, termites and millipedes. They often scavenge scraps of fruit and seed-bearing faeces dropped by monkeys from the trees above, where both benefit by reacting to each other's predator-alarm calls.

Breeding

They are monogamous and the male courtship-feeds his mate. Peak breeding activity is largely linked to rainfall. The nest is a shallow scrape in the ground in thick cover, often situated near a log, perhaps to shield it from the view of terrestrial predators. The clutch of four to eight deep buff to pinkish eggs measure 52.4 x 41.3 mm, and are less pointed than those of Helmeted Guineafowl *Numida meleagris*. Incubation by the female lasts 23 days. Keets can fly at 14 days and moult into juvenile plumage at about a month.

Status and conservation

There is no evidence of substantial expansion or contraction in their range. Although nowhere severely threatened, local range decreases might be due to destruction of forest and thicket habitats. They are not a favoured wing-shooting species and do not appear to be significantly affected by hunting pressure.

Vulturine Guineafowl
Pintade vulturine

Acryllium vulturinum

Numida vulturina (Hardwicke, 1834), Tsavo, Kenya

A group of Vulturine Guineafowls from Ethiopia (photo by Tasso Leventis)

Perched Vulturine Guineafowls in Kenya (photo by Peter W. Hills)

GUINEAFOWLS & CONGO PEAFOWL

Classification

The Vulturine Guineafowl is monotypic, being the only species in the genus *Acryllium* Gray, GR, 1840. There are no subspecies recognised.

Description

- They are a distinctive and attractive tall slender guineafowl with long legs, a long thin neck and a long pointed tail.
- The bare head and neck are bluish grey with a patch of short dense chestnut down on the nape.
- The breast and back are bright cobalt-blue, overlaid with black-and-white lanceolate feathers.
- The secondaries are edged with lilac.
- The rest of the wings and the remainder of the body are black, with white spots.
- Their bill is light grey and their legs are black.
- Juveniles are duller greyish-brown, with black, brown and rufous bars and spots.
- Downy keets are yellowish buff, mottled with dark brown, with the centre of the crown dark brown, a dark curving streak below the eye and two curved cheek stripes.

Distribution and habitat

- They are locally common from southern Ethiopia, north-western and southern Somalia, and semi-arid eastern Kenya to far north-eastern Tanzania.
- They prefer arid, open scrub and dry savanna, but will also inhabit montane forest patches and tall riverine woodlands.

Habits

They occur in flocks of 20–30 individuals outside of the breeding season. They roost in tall trees and retire to thick bush in the heat of the day. When disturbed the flock will cluster in a group and walk or run to nearby cover. If flushed, they will fly 50–100 m and then run, seldom landing in a tree. The characteristic call is a high-pitched, metallic '*chink-chink-chink-cheenk-cheenk krrrrrrrr*' rattle, which is faster and higher pitched than that of Helmeted Guineafowl *Numida meleagris*.

Food and feeding

They forage mostly on the ground scratching with their feet, but will climb into bushes to feed on berries and fruits. Their diet consists of roots, bulbs, seeds and leaves of grasses and herbs, berries and fruit (*Commiphora* spp. and *Ficus* spp.), green buds and shoots. They also eat insects, scorpions, spiders and small molluscs. They are apparently independent of fresh water, and do not drink even where water is readily available in the dry season.

Breeding

The timing of breeding is triggered by rainfall, peaking in June and December/January. The nest is a simple scrape in the ground in thick grass or bush cover, sparsely lined with grass. The clutch of 4–8 creamy white or pale brown, smooth and slightly pitted, broad oval and slightly pointed eggs measure 50.0 x 36.0 mm. Incubation is for 23–25 days. In general, information on their breeding biology in the wild is lacking.

Status and conservation

They are generally not threatened, except by local hunting pressure.

Congo Peafowl
Paon du Congo

Afropavo congensis

Afropavo congensis (Chapin, 1936), Sankuru District, central Democratic Republic of the Congo

ABOVE A male Congo Peafowl photographed in the Bronx Zoo, New York, USA (photo by Marvin Hyett)

LEFT A roosting female Congo Peafowl from the Lomako Forest, the Democratic Republic of Congo (photo by Mark Beaman)

Classification

The Congo Peafowl is more closely related to the Asian peafowls, *Pavo* species, and the pheasants in the family Phasianidae than to the guineafowls in the family Numididae. They are monotypic with no subspecies recognised.

Description

- They are larger (ca 1 400 g) and much more brightly coloured than the Black Guineafowl *Agelastes niger* and the Crested Guineafowl *Guttera puncherani*.
- Males are deep iridescent violet-green, with a red throat, blue breast and bristled black-and-white crown tuft.
- Females are duller than the males, with a greenish back, a rufous head tuft and underparts, and green-barred rufous wings.
- Juveniles have duller upperparts with a brown-tinged back and dull black underparts.
- Downy chicks have a black crown, nape and hind neck, tawny yellow sides of the head with a narrow black line along the eyelid and above the eye, and a small black patch just behind the eye and on the ear covert.

Distribution and habitat

- They are endemic to the equatorial forests of central and eastern Democratic Republic of the Congo and their overall biology is poorly known.
- They may be locally common in remote areas, favouring undisturbed primary rainforest below 1 200 m above sea level with extensive undergrowth on well-drained soils.
- They are known to occur in the Maiko, Salonga and Ituri Forest National Parks.
- They avoid seasonally flooded areas.

Habits

They occur in pairs or small groups and are very secretive within the dense understory. They are mostly crepuscular, retreating to hide in undergrowth during most of the day. They can also be active well into the night, particularly when the moon is full. They roost high in trees at night. When disturbed they will cock and spread their tail and erect their crest. The call is a repeated duet '*goway-gowaa*' with the male calling first, and is higher-pitched than the female.

Food and feeding

They forage on the forest floor among the dense undergrowth. Their preferred diet includes the seeds and fruits of trees and forest understory plants, including *Celtis adolfi-friedericii*, *C. ituriensis*, *Sapium ellipticum*, *Ficus* spp., *Strombosia grandifolia*, *Xymalos monospora* and *Caesalpinia decapetala*, as well as ants, termites and their larvae, and other terrestrial and aquatic invertebrates.

Breeding

They are monogamous, aggressive and males display standing erect with their tail and wings spread, similar to other peafowls *Pavo* spp. and turkeys *Meleagris* spp. They also display sideways like other phasianids. The eggs are laid in a flat spot in a branched fork of a tree. The clutch of 2–4 eggs are plain rufous-brown or cream and measure 60.0 x 45.0 mm. Incubation by the female lasts for 25–28 days. The chicks are brooded by the female in the nest for two days, whereafter they descend to the ground.

Status and conservation

Their populations may be impacted by hunting and they are susceptible to disease and parasites. As they are also restricted to secluded forest areas, forest destruction will be a major limiting factor. Their conservation status is therefore listed as Vulnerable (The IUCN Red List of Threatened Species v 2015-4).

A male Congo Peafowl photographed in the Bronx Zoo, New York, USA (photo by Marvin Hyett)

PART 2
Francolins & Partridges

FRANCOLINS & PARTRIDGES

Classification

- Recent research has recommended the changes of the francolin genera *Dendroperdix* for the Striated Group to *Ortygornis* (Reichebach, 1853) and *Peliperdix* for the Red-tailed Group to *Campocolinus* (Crowe et al. 2020 *Ostrich* 91(2): 134–136).
- That research also elevated 13 francolin subspecies to species status and lumped other subspecies into more inclusive entities with only 14 subspecies in contrast to 52 previously (Mandiwana-Neudani et al., 2019 *Ostrich* 90(3): 191–221).
- Twenty-five of the 26 African francolin species of the genera *Ortygornis*, *Campocolinus* and *Scleroptila*, within the family Phasianidae, are grouped into three sub-groups according to diagnostic plumage features: striated, red-tailed and red-winged (see Table 1).
- The Forest (Latham's) Francolin retains the genus *Peliperdix* and represents its own evolutionary trajectory and is not included in the francolin groups.
- The seven 'partridge' species are members of the genera *Alectoris*, *Ammoperdix*, *Xenoperdix*, *Margaroperdix* and *Ptilopachus*.
- The enigmatic Nahan's Francolin *Ptilopachus nahani* is rather a sister species to the Stone Partridge *P. petrosus*, both of which are relatives of the New World Quails (Odontophoridae) and thus are placed in their own subfamily, Ptilopachinae.

The recent francolin taxonomy and phylogeny research employed a Consilience Species Concept that assessed evidence to find several congruent sources of evidence with regards to morphology, behaviour, calls, genetics and ecology. That approach tends to recognise more species than Mayr's Biological Species Concept (BSC) that places heavy evidence on inter-taxon reproductive compatibility and fewer species than Cracraft's Phylogenetic Species Concept (PSC) that merely seeks 'diagnosable' entities, placing heavy evidence on 'differences' between populations.

PREVIOUS PAGE Male Plain-bellied Francolin in the Lake Nakuru National Park, Kenya (photo by Martin Odino)

FRANCOLINS & PARTRIDGES

Table 1: Recognised francolin species groups (*Ortygornis*, *Campocolinus* & *Scleroptila* spp.)

Striated	Red-tailed	Red-winged
Crested	Coqui	Shelley's
Ortygornis sephaena	*Campocolinus coqui*	*Scleroptila shelleyi*
Grant's	Stuhlmann's	Rufous-throated
O. grantii	*C. stuhlmanni*	*S. whytei*
Kirk's	Plain-bellied	Ulu
O. rovuma	*C. hubbardi*	*S. uluensis*
	Thika	Grey-winged
	C. thikae	*S. afra*
	Bar-bellied	Orange River
	C. maharao	*S. levalliantoides*
	Pale-bellied	Kunene
	C. spinetorum	*S. jugularis*
	White-throated	Archer's
	C. albogularis	*S. gutturalis*
	Chestnut-breasted	Red-winged
	C. dewittei	*S. levaillantii*
	Schlegel's	Crawshay's
	C. schlegelii	*S. crawshayi*
		Finsch's
		S. finschi
		Moorland
		S. psilolaema
		Elgon
		S. elgonensis
		Ring-necked
		S. streptophora

Description

- Francolins are relatively small, 'Old World', partridge/quail-like terrestrial gamebirds weighing 220–550 g.
- They have quail-like back feathers (chestnut, barred with black and white, and with a white shaft streak).
- Their legs are generally yellow and males have only one short, relatively blunt spur situated about half-way down the lower leg.

Natural history

Francolins tend to be sedentary and occur in grassland habitats, grading towards those with scattered bush, to a few inhabiting extensive patches of thicket. They sit tight on the ground when disturbed and at night, eventually flushing as a group with a whir of wings, dropping back to the ground after the flush-flight. Their calls tend to be musical and whistling, and they react strongly to calls played back to them. The incubating hen sits very tight, particularly late in the incubation period. Their chicks have a narrow, dark crown patch on their heads, bordered by several black and white stripes above and around the eye. Chicks are precocial, leaving the nest after about two hours after hatching, and are cared for by both parents. If a predator approaches, the parent closest to the chicks will attempt to distract the predator by limping away, feigning injury.

The distribution maps for the recently elevated species, particularly the coqui-type *Campocolinus* species, are not totally resolved and need further verification.

Evolutionary placement

- Traditionally, francolins (and spurfowls) have been classified with partridges in the tribe Perdicini within the family Phasianidae, although the only anatomical feature that supports this grouping unambiguously is that they both have 14 tail feathers.
- Until recently, all 41 species of francolins and spurfowls (36 African and 5 Asiatic) were lumped into a single genus, *Francolinus*, but divided among 7 groups, at least one member of which may be found in all habitats throughout sub-Saharan Africa outside of true desert.
- Many birders, farmers and wing-shooters divide these groups into two assemblages:
  - partridges (which make up the striated, red-tailed and red-winged francolin groups); and
  - francolins (of the bare-throated, montane, scaly and vermiculated groups).
- Anatomical and genetic research suggests that 'francolins' and 'spurfowls' are indeed natural but distantly related evolutionary groupings.
- Gross and histological anatomical similarities within, and differences between, francolin and spurfowl syrinxes support their division into 'true' francolins and spurfowls.
- Francolins are on a 'perch' of the gamebird evolutionary tree, distant from spurfowls, and are more closely related to the Asiatic francolins, the Junglefowl *Gallus gallus* and the Bamboo Partridge *Bambusicola thoracica*.
- Spurfowls, on the other hand, group with quails and a range of 'partridges' (for example, the Chukar Partridge *Alectoris chukar*) from the Northern Hemisphere.
- Since African francolins link with Asiatic francolins, including the Black Francolin *Francolinus francolinus*, the type species of the genus (the first francolin described to science), they have retained the common name 'francolin'.

- The five 'Old World' African partridges are members of the family Phasianidae and of four genera:
    - *Alectoris* Kaup, 1829;
    - *Ammoperdix* Gould, 1851;
    - *Xenoperdix* Dinesen, Lehmberg, Svendsen, Hansen and Fjeldså, 1994; and
    - *Margaroperdix* Reichenbach, 1853.
- Although the Stone Partridge *Ptilopachus petrosus* and Nahan's Partridge *P. nahani* (previously francolin/spurfowl) are most closely related to the New World Quails (Odontophoridae), they are placed in this section to be with the other partridges.

Conservation

Francolins are generally less opportunistic in their use of altered and transformed habitats than spurfowls and are wilder, preferring natural habitats over the extensive use of agricultural lands. They are also less abundant and are only in some cases available at levels that can sustain wing-shooting, such as the Grey-winged Francolin *Scleroptila afra*. General threats which impact on the stability of francolin populations are the injudicious use of fire, overgrazing by livestock and expanding rural settlements.

Six of the 33 species threatened: Udzungwa Forest Partridge *Xenoperdix udzungwensis* and Rubeho Forest Partridge *X. obscuratus* are listed as Endangered, Nahan's Partridge *Ptilopachus nahani* is listed as Vulnerable and Ring-necked Francolin *Scleroptila streptophora*, Moorland Francolin *S. psilolaema* and Elgon Francolin *S. elgonensis* are listed as Near Threatened (The IUCN Red List of Threatened Species v 2016-3), although this last listing may still be conservative. Ten other francolin species are listed as of Least Concern, although there needs to be further assessment for the recently elevated species.

Crested Francolin
Francolin huppé

Ortygornis sephaena

Perdix sephaena (Smith, A, 1836), Marico River, Limpopo Province, South Africa

Female Crested Francolin from Botswana (photo by Ian White)

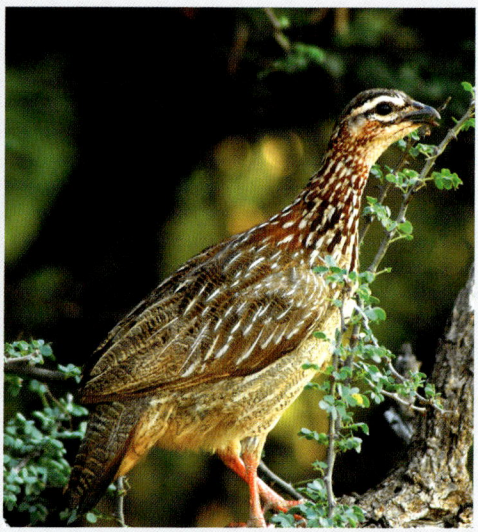

Female Crested Francolin from South Africa (photo by Dominic Henry)

Male Crested Francolin from Namibia (photo by Dayne Braine)

Crested Francolin from east of Hwange National Park, Zimbabwe (photo by Maans Booysen)

Classification

Crested Francolin are related to Grey Francolin *Francolinus pondicerianus* and Swamp Francolin *F. gularis* of Asia, although their closest relatives in Africa are Grant's Francolin *O. grantii* and Kirk's Francolin *O. rovuma*.

Recent research suggests that all three African striated francolin group species should be reassigned to the genus *Ortygornis* Reichenbach, 1853; Mandiwana-Neudani *et al.*, 2019, *Ostrich* 90(3): 191–221.

Crested Francolin are monotypic with no subspecies recognised:

The putative subspecies *O. s. zambesiae* Mackworth-Praed, 1920 in west-central Mozambique to north-western Namibia and southern Angola is synonymised with Crested Francolin.

Two previous subspecies of Crested Francolin have been elevated to full species status: Grant's Francolin *O. grantii* and Kirk's Francolin *O. rovuma*, including the subspecies *O. r. spilogaster*.

Description

- They have a bantam-like build and characteristic white striped-and-streaked head, extending down the centre of the back and breast feathers.
- Their neck, upper breast and back are rich reddish-brown with broad white shaft-streaks, contrasting with narrow greyish barring on the lower breast and the paler unpatterned belly.
- The rump is yellowish-brown and the vent pinkish, while the tail feathers are black, and are conspicuous when the tail is fanned in flight.
- They have a black bill and purplish-red legs and feet.
- Males have a dark brown cap with a grey outer edge that contrasts with the broad white eyebrow stripe.
- Males have long, curved leg spurs.
- Females are similar in appearance to males but less boldly marked.
- The back plumage is barred in females and speckled in males.
- Juveniles resemble adult females but are paler above and the white streaking on the feather shafts is broader and more clearly defined.
- Downy chicks are rufous-brown above, with darker streaking on the crown and back.
- The side of the head, above and below the eye, has multiple fine black-and-white stripes.
- The underparts are buffy-white, darker on the breast.

Distribution and habitat

- They are distributed from southern Mozambique, southern Zambia, Zimbabwe to southern Angola, northern Botswana and Namibia to north-eastern South Africa and Swaziland.
- Their preferred habitats are thickets and woodlands, particularly thornveld, often with sparse ground cover, as well as bush-encroached savanna.

Habits

They are territorial and secretive, coveys of 2–5 birds being seen along roadsides and in openings in woodlands. During the heat of the day, they retire to dense undergrowth, where the sound of their scratching in leaf litter discloses their presence. When disturbed, they prefer to run rather than to flush, scampering into dense vegetation. When flushed, they fly low and fast, weaving between trees. Unlike other grassland francolins, they will perch in trees to avoid ground predators. They also often roost overnight on a horizontal branch within the crown of a tree. The advertisement call, uttered mostly in the early morning and less so at sunset, is a closely synchronised, repeated '*kee, kik, kerrik*' antiphonal duet.

Food and feeding

They feed on corms and bulbs, green shoots, leaves, fruits and berries of *Grewia occidentalis*, *Rhus lancea*, mistletoe seeds (Loranthaceae) and *Ziziphus mucronates*, and insects during the breeding season. They are also known to feed on tree resin (*Senegalia mellifera* and *S. caffra*), which they glean from the bark while perching in trees. They will ingest seeds and invertebrates from the droppings of large herbivores, such as African Elephant *Loxodonta africana*, Buffalo *Syncerus caffer* and rhinoceros (Rhinocerotidae).

Breeding

They are monogamous, breeding during October to May in South Africa, December to March in Zimbabwe and October to March (mainly December–January) in Zambia. The nest is a scrape in the ground under dense, low bush, lined with grass and leaves. The clutch of 4–9, usually 6 rounded eggs are unmarked cream or pinkish-buff and measure 39.7 x 30.4 mm. Incubation by the female lasts 19–20 days. Males guard the nest area, warning the incubating female of impending danger by uttering a soft '*koo woo koo woo kirr kirr kirr kirr*' call.

Status and conservation

Although their densities can vary between sites, they are not threatened, being neither rare nor vulnerable. The only potential threat is the clearing of bush for domestic fuel, agriculture and grazing.

Kirk's Francolin
Francolin de Kirk

Ortygornis rovuma

Perdix sephaena (Smith, A, 1836), Marico River, Limpopo Province, South Africa

Dendroperdix. s. rovuma (Gray, GR, 1867), Zanzibar, Tanzania

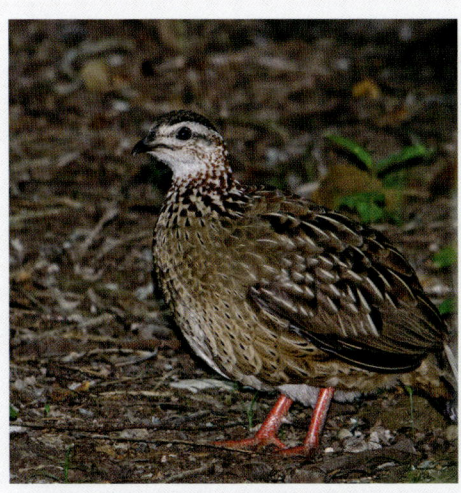

Male Kirk's Francolin subspecies *O. r. rovuma* at M'phingwe Camp, Catapu forestry concession, Caia District, central Mozambique (photo by Dylan Vasapolli)

Female Kirk's Francolin subspecies *O. r. rovuma* in the Coutadas wildlife utilisation areas of central Mozambique (photo by Per Holmen)

Male Kirk's Francolin subspecies *O. r. spilogaster* from Somaliland (photo by Nik Borrow)

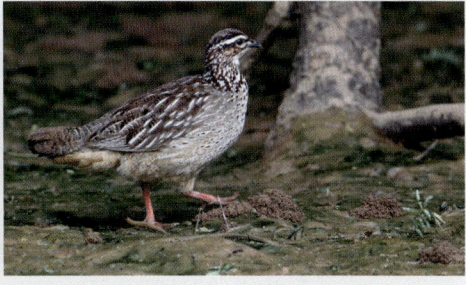

Female Kirk's Francolin subspecies *O. r. spilogaster* at Sof Omar, Bali Province, Ethiopia (photo by Paul van Giersbergen)

Classification

- Recent research suggests that the Striated Francolins should be reassigned to the genus *Ortygornis* (Reichenbach, 1853) and that Kirk's Francolin be elevated from Crested Francolin *O. sephaena rovuma* Mandiwana-Neudani *et al.*, 2019, *Ostrich* 90(3): 191–221.

Kirk's Francolin are most closely related to their sister species Grant's Francolin *O. grantii*.

Thereafter, they are related to Crested Francolin *O. sephaena*, and the Grey Francolin *Francolinus pondicerianus* and Swamp Francolin *F. gularis* of Asia.

Two subspecies are recognised:

O. r. rovuma Gray, GR, 1867, from Kenya to central Mozambique is streaked onto the belly and flanks.

O. r. spilogaster Salvadori, 1888 in eastern Ethiopia, Somalia and north-eastern Kenya.

Description

- They have a bantam-like build and characteristic white striped and streaked head, extending down the centre of the back and breast feathers.
- They have a collar with chestnut triangular marks, barely extending onto the breast, drop-shaped chestnut streaks on the belly, and lack barring on the belly.
- The Ethiopian subspecies *spilogaster* is barred and streaked on the breast, with extensive barring that is similar to the markings of Crested Francolin.
- The Somalian population '*somaliensis*' is synonymised with *O. s. spilogaster*, although the streaking is not as extensive.
- They have a black bill and purplish-red legs and feet.
- Males have long curved leg spurs.
- Females are similar but less boldly marked.
- The back plumage is barred in females and speckled in males.
- Juveniles resemble adult females but are paler above and the white streaking on the feather shafts is broader and more clearly defined.
- Downy chicks are rufous-brown above, with darker streaking on the crown and back.
- The side of the head, above and below the eye, has multiple fine black-and-white stripes.
- The underparts are buffy-white, darker on the breast.

FRANCOLINS & PARTRIDGES

Distribution and habitat

- They are distributed from north-western Somalia, eastern Ethiopia, north-eastern Kenya, southern Somalia (*O. r. spilogaster*), to coastal Kenya and Tanzania, southern Malawi down to central Mozambique (*O. r. rovuma*).
- Where *rovuma* meets *spilogaster* in Somalia is not entirely clear.
- In Ethiopia, *spilogaster* and *grantii* are difficult to separate and in some areas occur on the same ground although generally *grantii* is west of the Rift Valley, and *spilogaster* to the east. Birds as far west as Moyale on the border with Kenya are *spilogaster,* while birds in Awash National Park, east of Addis Ababa, are *grantii*.
- Similarly, in south-eastern Kenya, the coastal *rovuma* appears to merge with *grantii* in the Tsavo region, while inland limits of *rovuma* in the eastern Tanzania lowlands, especially the Selous Game Reserve, are unknown.
- Their preferred habitats are scattered thickets and relatively sparse ground cover in lowland woodlands and coastal forests.
- In Somalia, *spilogaster* occur in tamarisk scrub in dry riverbeds and thickets of *Salvadora persica* and *Euphorbia* spp. Along rivers and edges of pans.

Habits

They are largely sedentary and shy, coveys of 2–5 birds being seen along roadsides and in woodland glades. Where the habitat is short of shade they retire to dense undergrowth during the heat of the day. When disturbed, they prefer to run rather than to flush, scampering into dense vegetation. When flushed, they fly low and fast, weaving between trees. The territorial advertisement call, uttered mostly in the early morning and less so at sunset, is a rhythmic repeated '*kerrik ke keeek*' antiphonal duet.

Food and feeding

They feed on sedge corms, seeds, green shoots, leaves, fruits and berries with invertebrates including termites and their larvae also added to their diet during the breeding season. They are reported to feed on the outskirts of towns and villages in Somalia, but generally forage in or near cover, mainly in the early morning and evening.

Breeding

They breed mostly during January–June in Ethiopia, May–August in Somalia and June and July in Mozambique. The nest is a well concealed scrape in the ground under dense, low bush, lined with grass and leaves. The clutch is 5–6 rounded cream or pinkish buff eggs, sometimes marked with pale brown speckles. The eggs measure 37.0 x 29.0 mm in Mozambique and 41.0 x 30.5 mm in Somalia. Incubation by the female lasts 19–20 days. The pair both care for the young birds.

Status and conservation

Populations of Mozambique and Tanzania are thought to be relatively stable. However, they are considered to have declined in the coastal strip of Kenya. Potential threats are extensive timber logging and hunting, particularly in lowland woodlands and forests outside of protected areas.

Grant's Francolin
Francolin de Grant

Ortygornis grantii

Perdix sephaena (Smith, A, 1836), Marico River, Limpopo Province, South Africa

Dendroperdix s. grantii (Hartlaub, 1866), southern Sudan and western Ethiopia to north-central Tanzania

LEFT Male Grant's Francolin on the south-eastern shore of Lake Langano, Ethiopia (photo by Merid N Gabremichael)

TOP-RIGHT An allopreening pair of Grant's Francolins in the Tsavo East National Park, Kenya (photo by Washington Wachira)

RIGHT Grant's Francolin in the Kilimanjaro Golf and Wildlife Estate, Tanzania (photo by Per Holmen)

Classification

Recent research suggests that the Striated Francolins should be reassigned to the genus *Ortygornis* (Reichenbach, 1853) and that Grant's Francolin be elevated from Crested Francolin *O. sephaena grantii* Mandiwana-Neudani *et al.*, 2019, *Ostrich* 90(3): 191–221.

Grant's Francolin are most closely related to their sister species Kirk's Francolin *O. rovuma*.

Thereafter, they are related to Crested Francolin *O. sephaena*, and the Grey Francolin *Francolinus pondicerianus* and Swamp Francolin *F. gularis* of Asia.

Grant's Francolin are monotypic with no subspecies recognised.

Description

- They have a bantam-like build and characteristic white striped and streaked head, extending down the centre of the back and breast feathers.
- They resemble the Crested Francolin but have a reduced band of chestnut triangle marks on the breast, narrow whitish grey somewhat U-shaped streaks on the breast and an unpatterned belly.
- Where they are sympatric with Ring-necked Francolin *Scleroptila streptophora*, the latter has yellow not red legs and the chestnut upper breast feathers extend continuously around the nape and neck.
- They have a black bill and purplish-red legs and feet.
- Males have a dark brown cap with a grey outer edge that contrasts with the broad white eyebrow stripe.
- Males have long, curved leg spurs.
- Females are similar but less boldly marked.
- The back plumage is barred in females and speckled in males.
- Juveniles resemble adult females but are paler above and the white streaking on the feather shafts is broader and more clearly defined.
- Downy chicks are rufous-brown above, with darker streaking on the crown and back.
- The side of the head, above and below the eye, has multiple fine black-and-white stripes.
- The underparts are buffy-white, darker on the breast.

Distribution and habitat

- They are distributed from south-eastern Sudan, central Ethiopia and north-western Somalia, south through Kenya, Uganda and northern Tanzania.
- In south-eastern Kenya, *O. grantii* appears to merge with the coastal *O. rovuma* in the Tsavo region, with birds in Tsavo East National Park still being *O. grantii*.
- In Ethiopia, birds in Awash National Park, east of Addis Ababa, are Grant's Francolin.
- Their preferred habitats are patchy thickets and open woodlands, dense riparian bush, forest edges, bush-encroached grasslands and overgrown cultivation.

Habits

Coveys of 3–5 up to 10 individuals can be seen along roadsides, on lawns and in openings in woodlands. During the heat of the day, they retire to the shade of a bush where they can be particularly secretive to avoid disturbance. They are shy and when disturbed they prefer to run rather than to flush, scampering into dense vegetation. When flushed, they fly low and fast, weaving between trees. Unlike other grassland francolins, they will perch in trees to avoid ground predators and will also often roost within the crown of a tree. The advertisement call, uttered at dawn and particularly at dusk, is a closely synchronised repeated '*kee, kik, kerrik*' antiphonal duet.

Food and feeding

They feed on corms and sedge bulbs, green shoots, leaves, seeds, fruits and berries. They will also eat termites, other invertebrates and their larvae particularly during the breeding season.

Breeding

They are monogamous and territorial, with breeding mostly during May and June in Ethiopia, April–June in Kenya, and December–April in Tanzania. The nest is a small depression with a few dry grass stems as a lining often at the foot of a small bush. The clutch of 5–9 rounded eggs are cream or pinkish-buff, sometimes with pale brown speckles measure 39.7 x 30.4 mm. Incubation by the female lasts 19–20 days. Males guard the nest area during incubation and assist the hen with the care of the fledglings.

Status and conservation

Although their densities can vary between sites, they are not threatened, being neither rare nor vulnerable. They are probably the most widespread and plentiful gamebird in Kenya. The only potential threat is the clearing of bush for domestic fuel, agriculture and livestock grazing.

Coqui Francolin
Francolin coqui

Campocolinus coqui

Perdix coqui (Smith, A, 1836), near Kurrichane, Zeerust, North West Province, South Africa

Calling male Coqui Francolin subspecies *C. c. coqui* in the Kruger National Park, north-eastern South Africa (photo by Hugh Chittenden)

Female Coqui Francolin subspecies *C. c. coqui* at Madikwe Game Reserve in the North West Province, South Africa (photo by Maans Booysen)

Male Coqui Francolin subspecies *C. c. coqui* from Pilanesberg National Park, North West Province, South Africa (photo by Per Holmen)

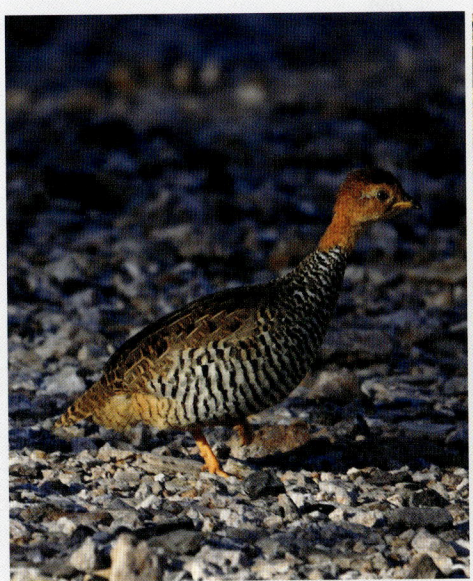
Male Coqui Francolin subspecies *C. c. kasaicus* from Luita, Katanga in the DR Congo (photo by Nigel Voaden)

Female Coqui Francolin subspecies *C. c. kasaicus* from Luita, Katanga in the DR Congo (photo by Nigel Voaden)

Classification

Recent research suggests that the red-tailed francolins group should be reassigned to the genus *Campocolinus* Crowe *et al.* 2020, *Ostrich* 91(2): 134–136.

Coqui Francolin are most closely related to Plain-bellied Francolin *C. hubbardi* and Stuhlmann's Francolin *C. stuhlmanni* within their sister clade and to Schlegel's Francolin *C. schegelii* and White-throated Francolin *C. albogularis* beyond the sister clade.

The recent francolin taxonomy research employed a Consilience Species Concept that assessed evidence to find several congruent sources of evidence with regards to morphology, behaviour/calls, genetics and ecology.

The taxonomic and ecological separation of these two taxa requires further testing by analysing specimens along a transect across their inferred 'ranges' to test levels of difference with regards to morphology, behaviour and genetics.

Four subspecies are recognised:

C. c. coqui Smith, A, 1836 in Angola, south-central Zambia, far south-western Zimbabwe south to South Africa;

C. c. ruahdae Van Someren, 1926 in southern Uganda and north-western Tanzania;

C. c. vernayi Roberts, 1932 in east-central Namibia, western Zambia and central Botswana;

C. c. kasaicus White CMN, 1945 in the Congo, DRC and north-western Zambia.

The putative subspecies '*hoeschianus*' and '*angolensis*' are clinal variants of *C. c. vernayi*, while '*campbelli*', '*lynesi*', '*kasaicus*' and '*ruandae*' are synonymised with *C. coqui*.

Five previous subspecies of Coqui Francolin have been elevated to full species status: Pale-bellied Francolin *C. spinetorum*, Bar-bellied Francolin *C. maharao*, Plain-bellied Francolin *C. hubbardi*, Thika Francolin *C. thikae* and Stuhlmann's Francolin *C. stuhlmanni*.

Description

- Coqui Francolin are sexually dimorphic. Males have a plain mustard-yellow head with a darker chestnut crown, and a black-and-white barred breast and shoulders. Black barring on varying shades of buff belly in C. c. coqui.
- *C. c. kasaicus* from the DRC and north-eastern Angola have a dark brown malar stripe, grey wings and barring on a white breast and belly.
- *C. c. ruahdae* have broad, black widely spaced barring on the underparts.

- *C. c. vernayi* is paler overall than nominate *coqui*, has more reddish on the head and has a reddish pinkish wash on the wings.
- The orange-buff tail of both sexes is conspicuous in flight.
- The legs and feet are rich yellow.
- Males have sharp leg spurs, longer than other members of the Red-tailed Group.
- Females have a characteristic black and white face pattern which resembles Shelley's Francolin *S. shelleyi* but have a broad white stripe above the eye and onto the neck.
- Juveniles resemble adult females, but are paler above, with rufous-buff mottling.
- Their underparts are buffy, with faint black barring.
- Downy chicks are rufous-brown above, with dark streaking on the crown and back.
- The sides of the head above and below the eye have black and white striping.
- The underparts are buffy-white.

Distribution and habitat

- They are distributed from Uganda and north-western Tanzania to the DRC, Angola, Namibia, Botswana, west-central Zambia and southern Zimbabwe to South Africa and southern Mozambique.
- Subspecies *C. c ruahdae* has a disjunct population in northwest Tanzania and southern Uganda ranging from Ngara, Biharamulo, Kagera and Bukoba districts north to the Ankole and Toro grasslands including Lake Mburo and Queen Elizabeth National Parks.
- The distribution boundary between this species and that of Stuhlmann's Francolin particularly in Zambia is unclear and needs verification. Coqui Francolin occurs through west-central Zambia with Stuhlmann's Fracolin occurring along the eastern side of the country.
- There are suggestions that *C. c. vernayi* extends into the Kalahari sands of western Zambia.
- They inhabit tall grasslands (50–100 cm grass height), savanna or well-grassed miombo (*Brachystegia*) and less so mopane (*Colophospermum mopane*) woodlands, and in drier country on sand dunes with good bush cover.
- They do not regularly venture far into agricultural lands.

Habits

They occur in pairs or small coveys of up to 12 individuals. Coveys are territorial and are difficult to see, reluctant to flush, choosing to run low through grass cover to avoid detection. In bushy habitat, they will flush from the far side of a bush. Once flushed, they fly relatively far, dodging between trees, and seldom flush a second time. When approached by a vehicle, they crouch, relying on their cryptic camouflage, resulting in many road-kills. They have two characteristic calls: a repetitive, two-syllable '*co-qui*', or a loud, tinny trumpet-like '*ter, ink, ink, terra, terra, terra, terra, terra*', with the second or third of the eight notes being loudest and the last notes fading away. Calling birds often perch on a termite mound, tree stump or boulder.

Food and feeding

Their diet consists of fewer underground corms and bulbs than other grassland francolins, with more seeds and small fruits consumed. They forage by using a sideways motion of the bill. Their breeding season diet includes beetles, grasshoppers, mantises and winged ants. They are known to drink dew or raindrops from grass blades and are probably not dependent on standing water.

Breeding

Breeding can occur during most months of the year but is mostly during the rainy season, October to April (peak November to February) in South Africa, late August to March in DRC, October to November and May in Uganda. The nest is a shallow hollow in dense cover lined with grass and leaves. The clutch of 4–05 oval, plain, cream or pinkish-buff eggs measure 32.5 x 27.3 mm. Incubation is by the hen, but the incubation period is not known. Chicks can fly at 7–10 days.

Status and conservation

There is no evidence that the distribution of this species has changed significantly in recent times, although the population in Uganda *C. c. ruahdae* is suspected to have declined significantly. Potential threats are changes in grass cover as a result of too frequent fires and continuous grazing by livestock, cultivation for crops and motor vehicle road-kills.

Stuhlmann's Francolin
Francolin de Stuhlmann
Campocolinus stuhlmanni

Perdix coqui (Smith, A, 1836), Near Kurrichane, Zeerust, North West Province, South Africa

Francolinus stuhlmanni (Reichenow, 1889), Bagamoyo, Usegua north of Dar-es-Salaam, Tanzania

A pair of Stuhlmann's Francolins near the northern limit of their range in the Shimba Hills National Reserve, south-west of Mombasa, Kenya (photo by Nancy Barrett)

Male Stuhlmann's Francolin in southern Tanzania (photo by Neil Baker)

Male Stuhlmann's Francolin on the Ngamo Plain, Hwange National Park, Zimbabwe (photo by Brendan Ryan)

Male Stuhlmann's Francolin at Panda, central Mozambique (photo by Per Holman)

Classification

Recent research suggests that the red-tailed francolins should be reassigned to the genus *Campocolinus* Crowe *et al.* 2020, Ostrich 91(2): 134–136.

Recently elevated from Coqui Francolin – *C. coqui stuhlmanni* Mandiwana-Neudani *et al.* 2019, Ostrich 90(3): 191–221.

That recent francolin taxonomy research employed a Consilience Species Concept that assessed evidence to find several congruent sources of evidence with regards to morphology, behaviour/calls, genetics and ecology.

They are most closely related to the subspecies *C. c. kasiacus* of the Coqui Francolin sister clade.

The taxonomic and ecological separation of these two taxa requires further testing by analysing specimens along a transect across their inferred 'ranges' to test levels of difference with regards to morphology, behaviour and genetics.

Stuhlmann's Francolin are monotypic with no subspecies recognised.

Description

- Stuhlmann's Francolin are sexually dimorphic, males have a plain mustard-yellow head with a darker chestnut crown, and a black-and-white barred breast and shoulders.
- They resemble Coqui Francolin C. *coqui* except that the extent of barring on the white belly and flanks is reduced and more broadly spaced, but not virtually absent as in Plain-bellied Francolin C. *hubbardi*.
- The orange-buff tail of both sexes is conspicuous in flight.
- The legs and feet are yellow, and males have sharp leg spurs.
- Females resemble Shelley's Francolin *Scleroptila shelleyi* but have a broad white stripe above the eye and onto the neck.
- Juveniles resemble adult females, but are paler above, with rufous-buff mottling.
- Their underparts are buffy, with faint black barring.
- Downy chicks are rufous-brown above, with dark streaking on the crown and back.
- The sides of the head above and below the eye have multiple black-and-white striping.
- The underparts are buffy-white.

Distribution and habitat

- They occur from coastal Kenya, through Tanzania, Malawi, eastern Zambia, north-western Zimbabwe to central Mozambique.
- In East Africa, their distribution is coastal from eastern Tanzania to the central Kenyan coast. Over much of southern and eastern Tanzania, up the coastal lowlands north to Kilifi and the Arabuko-Sokoke-Dakatcha woodlands near Malindi in Kenya.
- The distribution map for this species and for the other elevated coqui-type *Campocolinus* species are not totally resolved and need further verification.
- The distribution boundary between this species and that of Coqui Francolin, particularly in Zambia, is unclear and needs verification. Stuhlmann's Francolin occurs along the eastern side of Zambia with Coqui Francolin occurring through west-central Zambia.
- They inhabit grasslands and savanna or well-grassed miombo (*Brachystegia*) often in more mesic woodland habitats than Coqui Francolins.
- They do not regularly venture far into agricultural lands.

Habits

They occur in pairs or small coveys of up to 10 individuals. Coveys are territorial and are difficult to see, reluctant to flush, choosing to run low through grass cover to avoid detection. In bushy habitat, they will flush from the far side of a bush. Once flushed, they fly relatively far, dodging between trees, and seldom flush a second time. When approached by a vehicle, they crouch relying on their cryptic camouflage, when many road-kills result. They have two characteristic calls; a repetitive, two-syllable '*co-qui*', or a loud, tinny trumpet-like '*ter, ink, ink, terra, terra, terra, terra, terra*', with the second or third notes being loudest and the last notes fading away. The first call is lower in tone and more grating and the second call much slower and more deliberate than those of Coqui Francolin. Calling birds often perch on a termite mound, tree stump or boulder.

Food and feeding

Their diet consists of fewer underground corms and bulbs than other grassland francolins, with more seeds and small fruits consumed. They forage by using a sideways motion of the bill. Their breeding season diet includes beetles, grasshoppers, mantises and winged ants. They are known to drink dew or raindrops from grass blades and are probably not dependent on standing water.

Breeding

Breeding can occur during most months of the year but has a peak during November–February in Zambia, September–April in Malawi and April–June in Tanzania. The nest is a shallow hollow in dense cover lined with grass and leaves. The clutch of 4–5 oval plain cream or pinkish-buff eggs measure 32.5 x 27.3 mm. Incubation is by the hen, but the incubation period is not known. Chicks can fly at 7–10 days.

Status and conservation

They are common in eastern Zambia and Tanzania, but largely confined to protected areas in Malawi (e.g. Vwaza Marsh Wildlife Reserve, Kasungu National Park, Nkhotaota Wildlife Reserve and Dzalanyama Forest Reserve). Potential threats are changes in grass cover as a result of too frequent fires and continuous grazing by livestock, cultivation for crops and motor vehicle road-kills.

Plain-bellied Francolin
Francolin à ventre uni
Campocolinus hubbardi

Perdix coqui (Smith, A, 1836), Near Kurrichane, Zeerust, North West Province, South Africa

Peliperdix c. hubbardi (Ogilvie-Grant, 1895), Lake Victoria basin

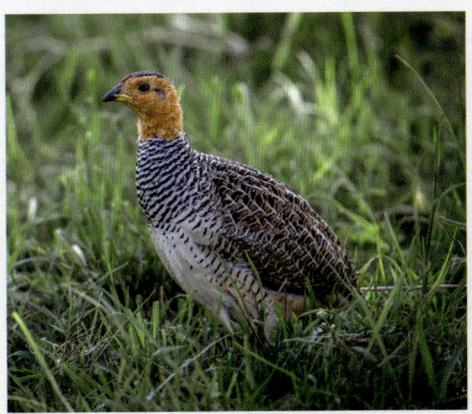

Male Plain-bellied Francolin in Kenya (photo by Jacques Pitteloud)

Male Plain-bellied Francolin in the Serengeti National Park, Tanzania (photo by Tasso Leventis)

LEFT Female Plain-bellied Francolin in the Lake Nakuru National Park, Kenya (photo by Philip Stapelberg)

RIGHT Female Plain-bellied Francolin in the Maasai Mara, Kenya (photo by Marnix Jonker)

Classification

Recent research suggests that the red-tailed francolins should be reassigned to the genus *Campocolinus* Crowe *et al.* 2020, *Ostrich* 91(2): 134–136.

Recently elevated from Coqui Francolin *C. coqui hubbardi* Mandiwana-Neudani *et al.* 2019, *Ostrich* 90(3): 191–221.

That recent francolin taxonomy research employed a Consilience Species Concept that assessed evidence to find several congruent sources of evidence with regards to morphology, behaviour/calls, genetics and ecology.

They are most closely related to their sister species Thika Francolin *C. thikae*.

The taxonomic and ecological separation of these two species requires further testing by analysing specimens along a transect across their inferred 'ranges' to test levels of difference with regards to morphology, behaviour and genetics.

Plain-bellied Francolin are monotypic with no subspecies recognised.

Description

- Plain-bellied Francolin are sexually dimorphic, males have a plain mustard-yellow head with a greyish mottled crown, and a black and white barred breast and shoulders.
- They resemble Coqui Francolin except that the extent of barring on the abdomen is extremely reduced, narrow and confined to the flanks, with an unbarred buff belly.
- Females, like the other coqui-type francolin females, resemble Shelley's Francolin *Scleroptila shelleyi*, but they have a blackish crown rather than the dull chestnut crown of female Coqui Francolin.
- The orange-buff tail of both sexes is conspicuous in flight.
- The legs and feet are rich yellow, and males have sharp leg spurs.
- Juveniles resemble adult females, but are paler above, with rufous-buff mottling.
- Their underparts are buffy, with faint black barring.
- Downy chicks are rufous-brown above, with dark streaking on the crown and back.
- The sides of the head above and below the eye have multiple black and white striping.
- The underparts are buffy-white.

Distribution and habitat

- They are localised in East Africa, occurring in western and southern Kenya, and northern Tanzania, from the central Rift Valley and Mt Eburru south to Narok District, the Loita Plains and the Masai Mara in Kenya to the Serengeti-Maswa grasslands, and north Tabora District in Tanzania. Also, in the Lake Victoria basin

from the former South Nyanza to the Mara in Kenya down to the Mwanza and Simiyu regions of northern Tanzania, including the Lake Manyara National Park.
- Reports of an intergrade zone with *C. c. ruahdae* around Tabora requires further clarification.
- The distribution map for this species and for the other elevated coqui-type *Campocolinus* species are not totally resolved and need further verification.
- They are mostly found in open grassland savanna and arid woodlands.
- They do not regularly venture far into agricultural lands.

Habits

They occur in pairs or small coveys of 4–6 individuals. Coveys are territorial and are reluctant to flush, usually running in a crouched posture to the nearest cover. Once flushed and carefully marked where they land are even more difficult to locate and flush again. They will seldom land in a tree when flushed and only when hard pushed, for example by dogs. Their shrill call is heard in the early morning and again in the evening, but it is difficult to locate in the open country in which the birds are generally found. They have two characteristic calls; a repetitive, two-syllable '*co-qui*' call, which is more evenly spaced and deliberate than that of Coqui Francolin, or a loud, tinny trumpet-like '*ter, ink, ink, terra, terra, terra, terra, terra*' call, with the second or third notes being loudest and the last notes fading away. Calling birds often perch on a termite mound, tree stump or boulder. Calling is most frequent during the onset of the breeding season and then mostly quiet when the hen is incubating. They roost on the ground usually as a covey group together.

Food and feeding

Their diet consists mostly of seeds and small fruits. They forage by using a sideways motion of the bill. Their breeding season diet includes ants, beetles and insect larvae. They are known to drink dew or raindrops from grass blades and are probably not dependent on standing water.

Breeding

Breeding occurs mostly during the rainy season. The nest is a shallow hollow in dense cover lined with grass and leaves. The clutch of 4–5 oval plain cream or pinkish-buff eggs measure 42.0 x 31.0 mm. Incubation is by the hen, but the incubation period is not known. Chicks can fly at 7–10 days.

Status and conservation

There is no evidence that the distribution of this species has changed significantly in recent times. Threats are changes in grass cover as a result of too frequent fires and continuous grazing by livestock, cultivation for crops and motor vehicle road-kills.

Thika Francolin
Francolin de Thika
Campocolinus thikae

Perdix coqui (Smith, A, 1836), near Kurrichane, Zeerust, North West Province, South Africa

P. c. thikae (Grant & Mackworth-Praed, 1934) in southern Kenya

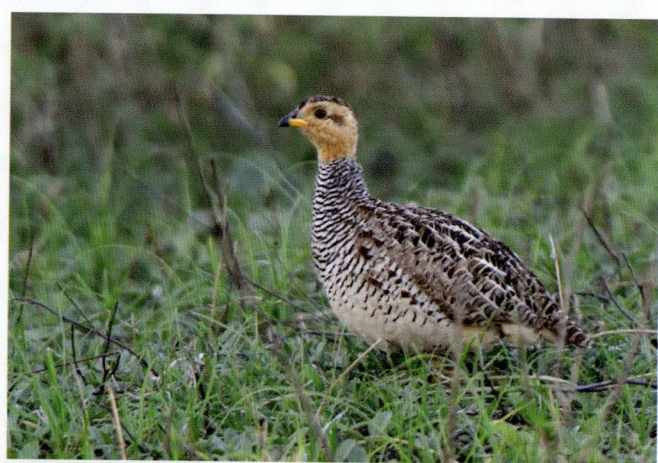

Male Thika Francolin near Nanja, Tanzania (photo by Per Holmen)

Female Thika Francolin in Tarangire National Park, Tanzania (photo by Per Holmen)

Classification

Recent research suggests that the red-tailed francolins should be reassigned to the genus *Campocolinus* Crowe *et al.* 2020, *Ostrich* 91(2): 134–136.

Recently elevated from Coqui Francolin *C. coqui thikae* Mandiwana-Neudani *et al.* 2019, *Ostrich* 90(3): 191–221.

That recent francolin taxonomy research employed a Consilience Species Concept that assessed evidence to find several congruent sources of evidence with regards to morphology, behaviour/calls, genetics and ecology.

They are most closely related to their sister species Plain-bellied Francolin *C. hubbardi*.

The taxonomic and ecological separation of these two species requires further testing by analysing specimens along a transect across their inferred 'ranges' to test levels of difference with regards to morphology, behaviour and genetics.

Thika Francolin are monotypic with no subspecies recognised.

Description

- Thika Francolin are sexually dimorphic, males have a plain mustard-yellow head with a darker chestnut crown, and a black-and-white barred breast and shoulders.
- They resemble Plain-bellied Francolin *C. hubbardi* except that they have rufous wings.
- Barring on the abdomen is, like in *hubbardi*, extremely reduced, confined to the flanks and the female has light pinkish-washed barring on the breast.
- The orange-buff tail of both sexes is conspicuous in flight.
- The legs and feet are yellow, and males have sharp leg spurs.
- Females have a characteristic black-and-white marked head similar to that of Shelley's Francolin *Scleroptila shelleyi* but have a broad white stripe above the eye and onto the neck.
- Juveniles resemble adult females, but are paler above, with rufous-buff mottling.
- Their underparts are buffy, with faint black barring.
- Downy chicks are rufous-brown above, with dark streaking on the crown and back.
- The sides of the head above and below the eye have multiple black and white striping.
- The underparts are buffy-white.

Distribution and habitat

- They occur in south-central Kenya and north-eastern Tanzania.
- They are generally uncommon and scattered east of the Rift Valley in the eastern plateau country from the Embu District and the Ithanga Hills east of the town of Thika, south-eastwards through the Kitui, Machakos and Kajiado districts to the Tsavo National Park complex, while in northern Tanzania from the Longido and Arusha districts down to the Tarangire National Park.
- The distribution map for this species and for the other elevated coqui-type *Campocolinus* species are not totally resolved and need further verification.
- They inhabit tall grasslands, savanna or well-grassed woodlands, and do not regularly venture far into agricultural lands.

Habits

They occur in pairs or small coveys of up to 8 individuals. Coveys are territorial and largely remain in the cover of dense grass. They are reluctant to flush, running low through grass cover to avoid detection. In bushy or rocky habitat, they will often flush from the far side of a bush or rock. When flushed, they fly relatively far and seldom flush a second time. When approached by a vehicle, they crouch relying on their cryptic camouflage, when many road-kills result. They have two characteristic calls; a repetitive, two-syllable '*co-qui*', or a loud, tinny trumpet-like '*ter, ink, ink, terra, terra, terra, terra, terra*', with the second or third notes being loudest and the last notes fading away. Calling birds often perch on a termite mound, tree stump or boulder.

Food and feeding

Their diet consists of grass seeds, green leaves and small fruits. They forage by using a sideways motion of the bill. Their breeding season diet includes beetles, grasshoppers, mantises and winged ants. They are known to drink dew or raindrops from grass blades and are probably not dependent on standing water.

Breeding

Breeding can occur during most months of the year but is mostly during the rainy season. The nest is a shallow hollow in dense cover lined with grass and leaves. The clutch of 4–5 oval plain cream or pinkish-buff eggs measure 32.5 x 27.3 mm. Incubation is by the hen, but the incubation period is not known. Chicks can fly at 7–10 days.

Status and conservation

Although considered to be a species of Least Concern by the IUCN, Stone Partridges, including their eggs are used at significant levels for food, in magical rituals and for traditional medicine by local human communities in West Africa, particularly in Benin. A loss of their habitat and hunting have caused them to be locally threatened.

Currently, the Stone Partridge has no protected status and is sourced primarily from wild populations for human use. Furthermore, ornithological studies that inform their population and ecological requirements are lacking in West Africa, and there is a need for further fieldwork to inform conservation action.

Bar-bellied Francolin
Francolin à ventre rayé
Campocolinus maharao

Perdix coqui (Smith, A, 1836), near Kurrichane, Zeerust, North West Province, South Africa

Peliperdix c. maharao (Sclater, WL, 1927), Abyssinia, southern Ethiopia

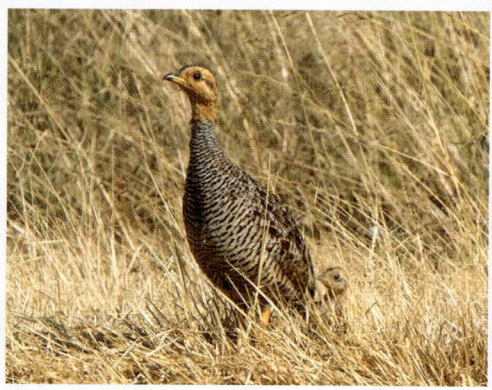

Male Bar-bellied Francolin with a chick near Bogol Manyo, Genale Valley, Ethiopia (photo by Arthur Grosset)

Male Bar-bellied Francolin near Yabelo, southern Ethiopia (photo by Ken Behrens)

Female Bar-bellied Francolin near Ngele, southern Ethiopia (photo by Ken Behrens)

Female Bar-bellied Francolin near Ngele, southern Ethiopia (photo by Nick Athanas)

Classification

Recent research suggests that the red-tailed francolins should be reassigned to the genus *Campocolinus* Crowe *et al.* 2020, Ostrich 91(2): 134–136.

Recently elevated from Coqui Francolin *C. coqui maharao* Mandiwana-Neudani *et al.* 2019, Ostrich 90(3): 191–221.

They are most closely related to Plain-bellied Francolin *C. hubbardi*.

Bar-bellied Francolin are monotypic with no subspecies recognised.

Description

- Bar-bellied Francolin are small and sexually dimorphic.
- They resemble Coqui Francolins *C. coqui* except that they have rufous wings, narrower barring on the uderparts and a faint wash of pinkish grey over the barring on the breast of the female.
- Males have a plain mustard-yellow head with a darker chestnut crown, and a black-and-white barred breast and shoulders.
- Unlike Plain-bellied Francolin, its close sister-clade relative, it has widespread but narrow abdominal barrings.
- The orange-buff tail of both sexes is conspicuous in flight.
- The legs and feet are rich yellow.
- Males have sharp leg spurs.
- Females, like the other coqui-type francolin females, resemble Shelley's Francolin *Scleroptila shelleyi*.
- Juveniles resemble adult females, but are paler above, with rufous-buff mottling.
- Their underparts are buffy, with faint black barring.
- Downy chicks are rufous-brown above, with dark streaking on the crown and back.
- The sides of the head above and below the eye have multiple black-and-white striping.
- The underparts are buffy-white.

Distribution and habitat

- They have a localised distribution in southern Ethiopia and northern Kenya.
- In Ethiopia, they occur from south of Addis Ababa extending southwards straddling Negele and Yabelo to the Kenyan border.
- Birds in the Huri Hills, west of Turbi Forest in northern Kenya, represent the

- southern limit of this otherwise Ethiopian species.
- The distribution map for this species and for the other elevated coqui-type *Campocolinus* species are not totally resolved and need further verification.
- They inhabit grassy areas in dry thorn savanna or sandy plains in considerably drier landscapes than occupied by their *Campocolinus* sister species in East Africa.
- They mostly avoid hilly and stony ground and do not regularly venture far into agricultural lands.

Habits

They occur in pairs or small coveys of seldom more than 4–6 individuals. Coveys are territorial and reluctant to flush, choosing to run low through grass cover to avoid detection. In bushy habitat, they will flush from the far side of a bush. Once flushed, they fly relatively far and seldom flush a second time. They also seldom if ever land in a tree after being flushed. They have two characteristic calls; a repetitive, two-syllable '*co-qui*', or a loud, tinny trumpet-like '*ter, ink, ink, terra, terra, terra, terra, terra*', with the second or third notes being loudest and the last notes fading away. Calling birds often perch on a prominent site or call from within grass cover. Calling is most frequent approaching the breeding season and generally ceases when the hen is incubating. They roost on the ground often the whole covey grouped together. Flushed individuals utter shrill squeaks.

Food and feeding

Their diet consisting of grass seeds, leaves and small fruits. Their breeding season diet includes beetles, grasshoppers, winged ants and insect larvae. They are probably not dependent on standing water.

Breeding

Breeding can occur during most months of the year but peaks during May and June in Ethiopia. The nest is a shallow hollow in dense cover lined with grass and leaves. The clutch of 4–5 oval plain cream or pinkish-buff eggs measure 32.5 x 27.3 mm. Incubation is by the hen, but the incubation period is not known. Chicks can fly at 7–10 days.

Status and conservation

They are uncommon to locally common in Ethiopia. Potential threats are degradation of grass cover as a result of too frequent fires and continuous grazing by livestock, and cultivation for crops.

Pale-bellied Francolin
Francolin à ventre pâle
Campocolinus spinetorum

Perdix coqui (Smith, A, 1836), near Kurrichane, Zeerust, North West Province, South Africa

Francolinus coqui spinetorum (Bates, 1928), eastern Burkina Faso, 45 km southwest of Say Niger

Only available images of Male Pale-bellied Francolins in the Fika Local Government Area, north-eastern Nigeria (photos by Haruna Mohammed Abubakar)

Classification

Recent research suggests that the red-tailed francolins should be reassigned to the genus *Campocolinus* Crowe *et al.* 2020, *Ostrich* 91(2): 134–136.

Recently elevated from Coqui Francolin *C. coqui spinetorum* Mandiwana-Neudani *et al.* 2019, *Ostrich* 90(3): 191–221.

They are most closely related to their sister Coqui Francolin clade, particularly *C. c. vernayi*.

Pale-bellied Francolin is monotypic with no subspecies recognised.

Description

- Pale-bellied Francolin are sexually dimorphic.
- They resemble the Coqui Francolin C. *coqui* except that they have a rufous crown and primaries, paler upperparts and an unbarred buff belly.
- Males have a broadly barred breast, which is unbarred and washed with pinkish grey in the female.
- The orange-buff tail of both sexes is conspicuous in flight.
- The legs and feet are yellow, and males have sharp leg spurs.
- Females, like the other coqui-type francolin females, resemble Shelley's Francolin *Scleroptila shelleyi*.
- Juveniles resemble adult females, but are paler above, with rufous-buff mottling.
- Their underparts are buffy, with faint black barring.
- Downy chicks are rufous-brown above, with dark streaking on the crown and back.
- The sides of the head above and below the eye have multiple black-and-white striping.
- The underparts are buffy-white.

Distribution and habitat

- They are widespread but with patchy isolated populations in West Africa, from Mauritania, Mali, Burkina Faso, to Niger and Nigeria.
- The distribution map for this species and for the other elevated coqui-type *Campocolinus* species are not totally resolved and need further verification.
- They inhabit tall grassland savanna or woodlands, and in drier country on sandy areas with bush cover.
- They do not regularly venture far into agricultural lands.

Habits

They occur in pairs or small coveys of up to 8 individuals. Coveys are territorial and mostly remain secretive within grass cover. They are reluctant to flush, choosing to run low through grass cover to avoid detection. In bushy habitat, they will flush from the far side of a bush. Once flushed, they fly relatively far, dodging between trees, and seldom flush a second time. When approached by a vehicle, they crouch, relying on their cryptic camouflage, when road-kills may result. There characteristic calls; a repetitive, two-syllable '*kwee…kree*', or a loud, tinny trumpet-like '*ter, ink, ink, terra, terra, terra, terra, terra*' which is rapid and the tempo is more truncated than that of the other coqui-type francolins. Calling birds are often hidden in the grass or may perch on a mound, tree stump or boulder.

Food and feeding

Their diet consists of grass seeds, grains, leaves and small fruits, with beetles, grasshoppers, ants and insect larvae consumed during the breeding season. They are probably not dependent on standing water.

Breeding

Breeding occurs mostly during the rainy season with a peak in July in Nigeria. The nest is a shallow hollow in dense cover lined with grass and leaves. The clutch of 4–5 oval plain cream or pinkish-buff eggs measure 34.0 x 27.3 mm. Incubation is by the hen, but the incubation period is not known. Chicks can fly at 7–10 days.

Status and conservation

There is no evidence that the distribution of this species has changed significantly in recent times. However, the population in Mali may have declined and in north-eastern Nigeria they are regarded as rare. While populations in the W National Park or W Regional Park in Niger, Benin and Burkina Faso and in the Tamou Faunal Reserve in Niger are relatively secure. Potential threats are changes in grass cover as a result of too frequent fires and continuous grazing by livestock, and cultivation for crops.

White-throated Francolin
Francolin à gorge blanche
Campocolinus albogularis

Francolinus albogularis (Hartlaub, 1854), Gambia

White-throated Francolin subspecies *P. c. buckleyi* from the Benoue National Park, Adamawa Province, Cameroon (photo by Nik Borrow)

White-throated Francolin subspecies *P. c. buckleyi* from the Mole National Park, Ghana (photo by Adam Riley)

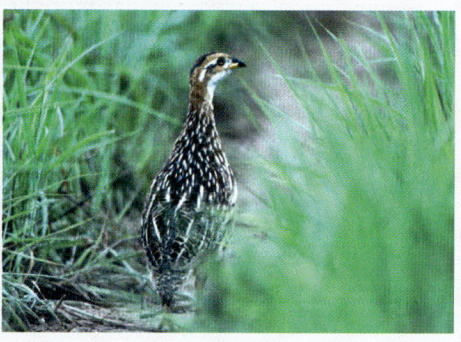

White-throated Francolin subspecies *P. c. buckleyi* from Nigeria (photo by Tasso Leventis)

Classification

Recent research suggests that the red-tailed francolins group should be reassigned to the genus *Campocolinus* Crowe *et al.* 2020, *Ostrich* 91(2): 134–136.

They are most closely related to Chestnut-breasted Francolin *C. dewittei* and Schlegel's Francolin *C. schlegelii*.

There are two subspecies recognised:

C. a. albogularis Hartlaub, 1854 in Senegal and Gambia to Guinea;

C. a. buckleyi Ogilvie-Grant, 1892 from eastern Ivory Coast to northern Cameroon.

The putative subspecies '*gambagae*' is synonymised with *C. a. buckleyi*.

One previous White-throated Francolin subspecies has been elevated to full species status: Chestnut-breasted Francolin *C. dewittei* Mandiwana-Neudani *et al.* 2019, *Ostrich* 90(3): 191–221.

Description

- The White-throated Francolin is similar in appearance to the Chestnut-breasted Francolin and the Coqui Francolin *C. coqui*, but has a distinct white throat contrasting with orange-red cheeks and no black barring on the hindneck and underparts of the male.
- They are best identified by their small size and buffy head, with grey crown and ear coverts, white supercilium, and plain buff unbarred underparts.
- The male underparts of *albogularis* are quite distinct from any other forms of red-tailed francolins, being chestnut on the breast with orange-red shaft streaks, richer on the abdomen, lacking any dark barring.
- The subspecies *buckleyi* including the genetically and morphologically highly similar synonymised '*gambagae*' has more heavily barred underparts and an unpatterned abdomen.
- Females are duller, with less well-defined quail-type patterning, and narrow fine, dark bars on their breast and flanks which has a faint pinkish or rufous wash.
- Females also have a poorly defined black facial pattern and necklace.
- The chestnut wings and tail of both sexes are conspicuous in flight.
- Juveniles have more barred underparts.
- Downy chicks are buff brown above and paler below.

Distribution and habitat

- They have a disjunct distribution across West Africa in Senegambia and Guinea (*C. a. albogularis*) and the eastern population from Ivory Coast, south-western Mali to central Nigeria and northern Cameroon (*C. a. buckleyi*).
- They prefer grassy plains and open savannas, often in recently burnt areas, and will also venture into disturbed areas and the edges of cultivated lands.
- In Nigeria, they have a preference for habitats with ironstone substrata.
- The nominate subspecies in Senegambia is restricted to Guinean savanna.

Habits

They occur in pairs or small coveys. They are shy and sit tight or reluctantly scurry off through the grass sward if disturbed. If flushed, they fly fast and low with their neck extended. Their calls are a far-carrying, high-pitched trumpet-like '*ter-ink-inkity-ink*' or a repeated '*co-qui*', both somewhat similar sounding to that of the Coqui Francolin, but the former is shorter and faster and slightly higher but stable pitched, with six notes.

Food and feeding

Their diet consists mostly of grass seeds and green plant material as well as grasshoppers, termites, beetles, ants and other insects.

Breeding

They are monogamous and breed during September and October in Senegambia and during June in Nigeria. Their nest is a scrape lined with grass and leaves. The clutch of 4–7, usually 6, rounded, buff to pale brown, slightly glossy and finely pitted and brown-speckled eggs measure 32.4 x 26.4 mm.

Status and conservation

They are uncommon to rare across most of their range but are widespread and tolerant of disturbed habitats.

Chestnut-breasted Francolin
Francolin à poitrine marron
Campocolinus dewittei

Francolinus albogularis (Hartlaub, 1854), Gambia

C. a. dewittei (Chapin, 1937) in south-eastern Democratic Republic of Congo, north-western Zambia and eastern Angola.

LEFT Male Chestnut-breasted Francolin 50km east of Luacano in northern Moxico Province, Angola (photo by John Mendelsohn)

TOP-RIGHT Chestnut-breasted Francolin on the Minyanya Plain in north-western Zambia (photo by Frank Willems)

RIGHT Flushed Chestnut-breasted Francolin showing the chestnut flight feathers at the Kembo River crossing in Cuando Cubango Province, south-eastern Angola (photo by Maans Booysen)

Classification

Recent research suggests that the red-tailed francolins should be reassigned to the genus *Campocolinus* Crowe *et al.* 2020, *Ostrich* 91(2): 134–136.

Chestnut-breasted Francolin has been recently elevated from White-throated Francolin – *Peliperdix (Campocolinus) albogularis dewittei* Mandiwana-Neudani *et al.* 2019, *Ostrich* 90(3): 191–221.

They are most closely related to White-throated Francolin *C. albogularis* and Schlegel's Francolin *C. schlegelii*.

The clinal variant subspecies *meinertzhageni* is synonymised with *C. dewittei.*

They are monotypic with no subspecies recognised.

Description

- The Chestnut-breasted Francolin is similar to the White-throated Francolin and Coqui Francolin *C. coqui* but are more richly coloured and have a distinct white throat and no black barring on the hindneck and underparts of the male, which also has a chestnut breast band.
- They are best identified by their small size and buffy head, with grey crown and ear coverts, white supercilium and plain buff unbarred underparts.
- Males have one stout spur on each leg.
- Females are duller, with fine, dark bars on their breast and flanks which is heavier but not as extensive as that of the White-throated Francolin.
- The chestnut wings and tail of both sexes are conspicuous in flight.
- Juveniles have more barred underparts.
- Downy chicks are buff brown above and paler below.

Distribution and habitat

- They are distributed south of the Democratic Republic of the Congo (DRC) forests in moist montane grasslands and dambo floodplains in eastern Angola and marginally into north-western Zambia.
- They prefer grassy plains and open savannas, often in recently burnt areas, and will venture into disturbed areas and the edges of cultivated lands.
- The eastern Angolan and north-western Zambia '*meinertzhageni*' is found in montane grasslands and is restricted to the upper Zambezi flood plains.
- Fairly common in the source lakes area of the Okavango system in central Angola and in the drier sections of the relatively flat Minyanya Plain in Zambia.

- They are also relatively common on the Marungu Plateau in the Kataga Province of the DRC, to the west of the southern half of Lake Tanganyika.

Habits

They occur in pairs or small coveys. They are shy and sit tight or reluctantly scurry off through the grass sward if disturbed. If flushed, they fly fast and low with their neck extended. Their calls are a far-carrying, high-pitched trumpet-like '*ter-ink-inkity-ink*' or a repeated '*co-qui*', both similar to that of Coqui Francolin, but faster and slightly higher pitched, with up to 10 notes, rather than 4–6.

Food and feeding

Their diet consists mostly of grass seeds and green plant material, as well as grasshoppers, termites, beetles, ants and other insects.

Breeding

They breed during the early rains of October–December in the Democratic Republic of the Congo. Their nest is a scrape lined with grass and leaves. The clutch of 4–7, usually 6, rounded buff to pale brown, slightly glossy and finely pitted and brown-speckled eggs measure 32.4 x 26.4 mm.

Status and conservation

Although they are considered common in some parts where the grassland habitats are still in a healthy state, they are otherwise scattered and relatively scarce, although they can be tolerant of patches of disturbed habitats.

Schlegel's Francolin
Francolin de Schlegel
Campocolinus schlegelii

Francolinus schlegelii (Heuglin, 1863), Bongo River (Bussere River), Bahr el Ghazal, Sudan

LEFT Female Schlegel's Francolin with black-blotched breast bars (photo by Nik Borrow)

BELOW Male Schlegel's Francolin with finely barred breast (photo by Nik Borrow)

FRANCOLINS & PARTRIDGES

Classification

Recent research suggests that the red-tailed francolins group should be reassigned to the genus *Campocolinus* Crowe *et al.* 2020, *Ostrich* 91(2): 134–136.

They are most closely related to White-throated Francolin *C. albogularis* and Coqui Francolin *C. coqui*, particularly *C. c. kasiacus*.

Previously recognised as both a subspecies of *Peliperdix* (*Campocolinus*) *coqui* (Peters 1934, Sibley and Munroe 1990) and a full species (Hall 1963, Mackworth-Praed 1970).

They are monotypic with no subspecies recognised.

Description

- Schelgel's Francolin is the Central African counterpart of the White-throated Francolin, but both sexes have an orange rather than a white throat and with their rusty-orange or rufous-yellow head look more like the male Coqui Francolin.
- However, they differ from Coqui Francolin by having a grey-brown crown and eye-stripe line from the lores to the ear coverts.
- Their back is more similar in appearance to that of *C. albogularis* than to *C. coqui*, although the quail-type patterning is much reduced, and the sexual dimorphism is pronounced.
- The underparts are distinctly barred black on buff-white.
- Their bill is black with a yellow base and their legs are yellow.
- Females have browner upperparts that are less richly coloured than males, which have broad buff shaft streaks, and the female belly is less heavily barred.
- Juveniles are similar in appearance to adult females, but have rufous-buff barring on the mantle and scapulars.
- The downy chick is undescribed.

Distribution and habitat

- They are scarce, occurring from west-central Cameroon (Adamawa Plateau), through northern Central African Republic and southern Chad to western South Sudan (Bahr el Ghazal).
- They are localised and uncommon, inhabiting rank grasslands in well-wooded savanna, particularly where the tree *Isoberinia doka* is common.
- They avoid human settlements, but will forage in the edges of cultivated lands.

Habits

They occur in pairs or small coveys. When flushed, their flight is slow, short and silent. They roost overnight on the ground, huddled together with their heads facing outwards. Their repeated trumpet-like '*ter, ink, terrra*' call is similar to that of the Coqui and White-throated Francolins, but is longer and faster with seven more clearly defined elements and is slightly lower pitched.

Food and feeding

Their diet consists of grass seeds, leaves, agricultural grain and caterpillars.

Breeding

They are monogamous and breed during September–November, at least in South Sudan. Their nest is a shallow hollow in the ground lined with grass and leaves. The clutch of 2–5 smooth cream-coloured eggs measure 35.5 x 26.0 mm. Their incubation period is unknown.

Status and conservation

Although they are known to be generally localised and uncommon to rare, their population status and threats are largely unknown.

Shelley's Francolin
Francolin de Shelley
Scleroptila shelleyi

Francolinus shelleyi (Ogilvie-Grant, 1890), Hartley Hills, Umfuli River, Mashonaland, Zimbabwe

ABOVE Calling Shelley's Francolin (photo by Andre Botha)

TOP RIGHT Shelley's Francolin near Utrecht, KwaZulu-Natal, South Africa (photo by Maans Booysen)

RIGHT Ruffled Shelley's Francolin (photo by Andre Botha)

Classification

Shelley's Francolin are most closely related to Orange River Francolin *S. levalliantoides* and Kunene Francolin *S. jugularis*.

They are monotypic with no subspecies recognised.

Two previous Shelley's Francolin subspecies have been elevated to full species status: Ulu Francolin *S. uluensis* and Rufous-throated Francolin *S. whytei* (Mandiwana-Neudani *et al.* 2019, *Ostrich* 90(3): 191–221).

Description

- They are difficult to distinguish from Orange River Francolin, Archer's Francolin *S. gutturalis* and Red-winged Francolin *S. levaillantii*, having similar markings and the same pale buff to white throat.
- However, the black speckled necklace is distinct and thinner than that of Red-winged Francolin and broader than that of Orange River Francolin and Archer's Francolin.
- The white lower breast feathers are boldly blotched and mottled with two or more broad black bands on the belly (these feathers are buff to rufous in the other three species).
- The legs and feet are yellow.
- Males have leg spurs.
- Juveniles resemble adults, but the black-and-white breast barring is irregular and the outer margins of the primary flight feathers are marked with buff.
- Downy chicks are rufous-brown above, with strong, darker stripes on the crown and back, and buffy below.
- They have characteristic multiple, alternating black and buff stripes above and around the eye.

Distribution and habitat

- Their distribution through south-eastern Africa is from southern Tanzania through southern Zambia, Mozambique to South Africa.
- In Zambia, Shelley's Francolin occur east of the Luangwa Valley up the northern boundary of the Eastern Province and south of 14°S across the drier half of the country, with Rufous-throated Francolin in the northern wetter half of the country.
- They inhabit moist, rocky hillsides, open grasslands, wooded savanna, thornveld and open areas in miombo (*Brachystegia*), mopane (*Colophospermum mopane*) and other woodlands, often on stony terrain or amongst rocky outcrops below 2 000 m above sea level.

- They prefer taller sweetveld in the east, whereas Red-winged Francolin inhabit shorter sourveld dominated by red grass *Themeda triandra*.
- Shelley's Francolins are separated from Orange River Francolin, which occur in drier, tall, sparse grasslands of western southern Africa.

Habits

Usually in sedentary pairs or small coveys of 6–8 birds, they sit tight when approached, but will run through grasslands to avoid being flushed. Where the home range includes moist sites, they will often use marshes and sponges to roost overnight. They generally fly to their roosting site, thus avoiding being tracked by predators. They often use the edges of cultivated lands, but do not spend much time within agricultural lands. Their musical call consists of two low notes followed by two higher notes, '*I'll drink YER BEER*', repeated three or four times, usually from a vantage point such as a termite mound or rock. This call is not as high pitched and is more deliberate than that of the Orange River Francolin, being uttered at a much slower pace. They also have a shrill flush call.

Food and feeding

They forage by digging for corms and bulbs of plants with their bills. Their diet also includes seeds and grains, and is supplemented with invertebrates during the breeding season.

Breeding

They are monogamous, solitary nesters. In southern Africa, peak nesting occurs from October–January. The nest is a relatively deep scrape in dense grassland or under a bush, well lined with grass and roots. The clutch of 4–5 (occasionally six or seven) sometimes pitted oval eggs are buff or whitish and measure 38.0 x 31.1 mm. Incubation by the female lasts for 20–22 days. Chicks can flutter-fly at 12 days and can fly strongly at five weeks.

Status and conservation

Although they are not threatened, there is some evidence of a reduction in their range due to grassland deterioration resulting from continuous grazing by domestic livestock and frequent burning. Fires in these grasslands destroy both nests and chicks, and expose nesting sites to severe hailstorms.

Rufous-throated Francolin
Francolin à gorge rousse
Scleroptila whytei

Francolinus shelleyi (Ogilvie-Grant, 1890), Hartley Hills, Umfuli River, Mashonaland, Zimbabwe

F. s. whytei (Neumann, 1908), Nyika Plateau

Rufous-throated Francolin in Kasanka National Park, Zambia (photo by Frank Willems)

TOP Rufous-throated Francolin in Mutinondo Wilderness, north-eastern Zambia (photo by Frank Willems)

BOTTOM Rufous-throated Francolin on the Nyika Plateau, Malawi (photo by Maans Booysen)

Classification

Recently elevated from Shelley's Francolin *S. shelleyi whytei* Mandiwana-Neudani *et al.* 2019, *Ostrich* 90(3): 191–221.

They are most closely related to Finsch's Francolin *S. finschi*.

Also known as Whyte's Francolin, Francolin de Whyte.

Rufous-throated Francolin are monotypic with no subspecies recognised.

Description

- They are different to Shelley's *S. shelleyi* and Ulu *S. uluensis* Francolins, having a plain grey-brown crown, rufous-buff supercilium, face and throat with no white markings, an indistinct necklace immediately below the throat and reduced black and white barring on the upper breast.
- They also have a moderately developed throat patch blotched with reddish chestnut which distinguishes them from other red-winged francolin group species.
- The belly is buffy white with regular broad black bars on a background of rufous buff, shading to dull blackish-grey lower belly and undertail coverts.
- The legs and feet are yellow.
- Males have leg spurs.
- Juveniles like those of Shelley's Francolin resemble adults, but the black and white breast bars are spaced irregularly and the outer margins of the primary flight feathers are marked with buff.
- Downy chicks are rufous-brown above, with strong, darker stripes on the crown and back, and buffy below.
- They have characteristic multiple, alternating black-and-buff stripes above and around the eye.

Distribution and habitat

- Their distribution is across south-eastern Democratic Republic of the Congo, northern Zambia and far northern Malawi, north of Mzimba.
- In Zambia, Rufous-throated Francolin occur in the northern wetter half of the country down to 14°S and across to the Luangwa Valley, with Shelley's Francolin in the drier south.
- They prefer montane and hilly grasslands and open miombo (*Brachystegia*) and mopane (*Colophospermum mopane*) woodland.
- They frequently occupy rocky areas.

Habits

Usually in pairs or small coveys of 6–8 birds, they sit tight when approached, but will run through grasslands to avoid being flushed. When flushed, they fly a short distance dropping back into the grassland where they then sit tight. Their call, mostly uttered at dawn and dusk, consists of two low notes followed by two higher notes, repeated three or four times, very similar to that of Shelley's Francolin.

Food and feeding

Their diet consists largely of roots, corms and bulbs of savanna plants, supplemented with invertebrates including grasshoppers, beetles, termites and small molluscs during the breeding season.

Breeding

They are monogamous, solitary nesters. In Zambia, nesting occurs during most months from February to December, while in Malawi they nest during May to November. Peak laying is in September in Zambia and August–November in Malawi. The nest is a shallow scrape concealed in dense grassland or under a bush, lined with grass and roots. The clutch of 4–6 sometimes pitted oval eggs are creamy buff or pinkish white. Incubation is by the female and last for 22 days.

Status and conservation

Although they are not threatened, reportedly being common to locally rare, they are considered sparse in Zambia and northern Malawi. They are affected by grassland deterioration resulting from continuous grazing by domestic livestock and frequent burning.

Ulu Francolin
Francolin d'Ulu
Scleroptila uluensis

Francolinus shelleyi (Ogilvie-Grant, 1890), Hartley Hills, Umfuli River, Mashonaland, Zimbabwe

S. shelleyi uluensis (Ogilvie-Grant, 1892), Ulu Hills south of Nairobi, Kenya

LEFT Ulu Francolin in Nairobi National Park, Kenya (photo by Bruno Boedts)

RIGHT Ulu Francolin in Kenya (photo by Jacques Pittteloud)

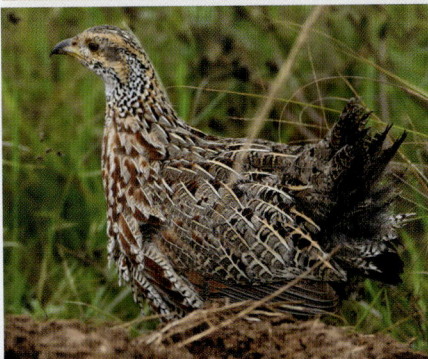

Ruffled Ulu Francolin in Nairobi National Park, Kenya (photo by Bruno Boedts)

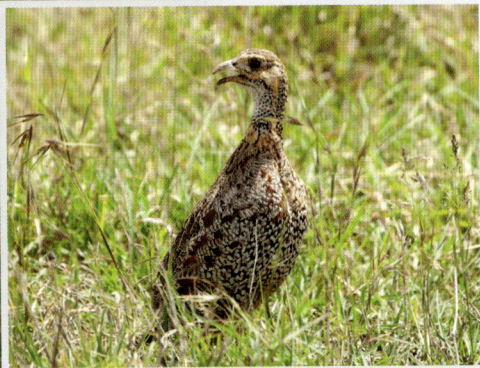

Ulu Francolin in Ol Pejeta Conservancy, Laikipia, Kenya (photo by Adam Scott Kennedy)

Classification

Recently elevated from Shelley's Francolin *S. shelleyi uluensis* Mandiwana-Neudani *et al.* 2019, *Ostrich* 90(3): 191–221.

Ulu Francolin are most closely related to Archer's Francolin *S. gutturalis*.

Ulu Francolin are monotypic with no subspecies recognised.

Description

- They are similar in appearance to Shelley's Francolin, but have a line of black-tipped white feathers behind the ear coverts, the necklace is somewhat less distinct, and the throat patch is variable sometimes with speckling.
- The bill is markedly shorter than that of Shelley's Francolin and is blackish brown.
- The legs and feet are dull yellow.
- Males have leg spurs.
- Juveniles resemble adults, but they have irregular black-and-white breast barring and the outer margins of the primary flight feathers are marked with buff.
- Downy chicks are rufous-brown above, with strong, darker stripes on the crown and back, and buffy below.
- They have characteristic multiple, alternating black and buff stripes above and around the eye.

Distribution and habitat

- Their distribution is from central and southern Kenya into western Tanzania, from the Laikipia District, Ol Pejeta Conservancy, Lewa Downs and around the base of Mt Kenya south to Hell's Gate National Park, Naivasha, Ngong Hills, Nairobi, Machakos and Kajiado districts, also from Tsavo West National Park to Lake Jipe, Mkomazi, Arusha and Tarangire National Parks, the Crater Highlands and at 1 500m above sea level at Mbulu (south-west of Lake Manyara).
- There is a dark montane form '*macarthuri*' in the high grasslands of the Chyulu Hills, and birds recorded at 3 000m above sea level on Mt Kilimanjaro may also belong to this form.
- Their distribution also extends westwards marginally into south-western Uganda, Rwanda and Burundi.
- They prefer thick, open grasslands and lightly wooded savanna, often on rocky areas.

Habits

Locally common, they are usually in pairs or small coveys of 4–6 birds which sit tight when approached but will run through grass cover when approached and to avoid being flushed. When flushed the birds scatter in all directions with a loud scream. They are shy and probably often overlooked. The call uttered mostly at dawn and dusk is a repeated short and deliberate '*tirich-ch-che'e*' which rises and then falls. They roost on the ground in covey groups.

Food and feeding

They forage by digging for roots, corms and bulbs of plants with their bill. Their diet also includes seeds and agricultural grains and is supplemented with invertebrates, including grasshoppers, termites and beetles, particularly during the breeding season.

Breeding

They are monogamous, solitary nesters. They breed mostly during the dry season from March–July. The nest is a relatively deep scrape well concealed in dense grassland or under a bush and lined with grass and roots. The clutch of 4–5 pitted oval eggs are buff or creamy white and measure 40.0 x 33.0 mm. Incubation by the female lasts for 20–22 days. Chicks can flutter-fly at 12 days and can fly strongly at 5 weeks.

Status and conservation

Although they are not threatened, there is some evidence of a reduction in their range and numbers due to grassland deterioration resulting from continuous grazing by domestic livestock and frequent burning.

Grey-winged Francolin
Francolin à ailes grises

Scleroptila afra

Francolinus africanus (Latham, 1790), Cape Province, South Africa

ABOVE Grey-winged francolins at Langebaan, West Coast, South Africa (photo by Jessie Walton)

RIGHT Calling male Grey-winged Francolin (photo by Andre Botha)

FRANCOLINS & PARTRIDGES

ABOVE Grey-winged Francolin nest and clutch (photo by Rob Little)

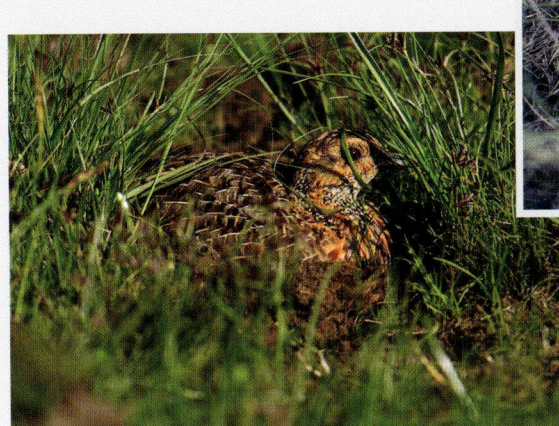

Incubating female Grey-winged Francolin (photo by Andre Botha)

One-day-old Grey-winged Francolin chick showing typical fine head stripes of francolin chicks (photos by Rob Little)

Grey-winged francolins near Uitenhage, Eastern Cape Province, South Africa (photo by Maans Booysen)

Classification

Grey-winged Francolin have previously been considered conspecific with Moorland Francolin *S. psilolaema* of East Africa. But they are geographically separated and differ markedly in appearance and genetically, thus rather being considered endemic to their respective ranges.

However, they remain most closely related to Moorland Francolin.

They are monotypic with no subspecies recognised.

A previously suggested subspecies *S. a. proximus* (Clancey, 1957) of the Drakensberg system in north-eastern South Africa is genetically identical and is not supported.

Description

- Grey-winged Francolin is one of the montane red-winged francolin group.
- They are a medium-sized francolin, and the sexes are not distinguishable other than that the adult male has short, robust leg spurs.
- They differ from the other francolins in the Red-winged Group by having very little red on their wings, and they have a distinctive grey-freckled throat, not white or buff.
- Juveniles resemble adults but have duller plumage and white on the throat.
- Downy chicks are rufous-brown above, with darker streaking on the crown and back.
- The sides of the head, above and below the eye, have multiple fine black and white stripes.
- The underparts are buffy-white, washed with rufous on the breast.

Distribution and habitat

- They are endemic to South Africa and Lesotho.
- They thrive in the highland grasslands of the Drakensberg, from Mpumalanga along the KwaZulu-Natal escarpment and the Lesotho Maluti range to the Eastern Cape.
- They prefer patches of sparse, short grass on shallow, igneous soils on ridge tops and shelves, where grasslands are lightly grazed by wild herbivores and burnt less frequently than every two years.
- Their distribution is more patchy and their numbers are lower in the Western Cape, where they occur in karoo scrub and coastal renosterbos down to sea level.
- They are more tolerant of heavy grazing than the Red-winged Francolin *S. levaillantii*.

Habits

They are sedentary and territorial, with non-breeding coveys consisting of 4–20 individuals. Coveys usually sit tight if disturbed, but will run if the cover is too sparse. They seldom fly except when flushed, or when flying to their overnight roost site in the late afternoon. The covey roosts overnight on open ground, huddling together. They have a high-pitched, whistling advertisement call '*pip-pip-pip-pip pi-pip wi-pleeu*' which is most often heard at sunrise, and also a flush call '*pre-pre-pre-pre-preeu-preeu-preeu-preeu*' when a covey is disturbed. The '*wi-pleeu*' phrase of the advertisement call is repeated in series and is often punctuated antiphonally by another bird giving a '*pipeeu*' call.

Food and feeding

Their diet consists of underground corms, rhizomes and bulbs of the sedge and iris families (*Cyperus*, *Mariscus* and *Moraea* species) during the non-breeding season (February–September), and of invertebrates during the chick-rearing period (October–January). Seeds are also an important part of the autumn diet.

Breeding

Although breeding peaks during August and September, the breeding season is prolonged (from August–March) in the summer-rainfall grasslands and contracted (July–December) in the winter-rainfall region of the Western Cape. The nest is a scrape under a grass tuft, lined with grass and occasionally feathers. The average clutch of 5–6 yellowish-brown eggs, sometimes lightly speckled with brown and slate, measure 39.9 x 30.1 mm. Incubation by the female is for 21–22 days.

Status and conservation

Nest predation by Yellow Mongoose *Cynictis penicillata*, crows *Corvus* species and Common Egg-eater *Dasypeltis scabra* snakes is a concern, particularly in heavily grazed grasslands. Other causes of nest failure are fires and trampling by livestock. Although a fine-scale fire mosaic favours grassland francolins, burning should cease before the end of August. A sustainable Grey-winged Francolin wing-shooting industry is a viable commercial agricultural by-product in the Eastern Cape, South Africa, and provides an incentive for conservation of these grasslands.

Orange River Francolin
Francolin de L'Orange
Scleroptila levalliantoides

Perdix levalliantoides (Smith, A, 1836), Upper Reaches of Orange River, South Africa

LEFT Orange River Francolin subspecies *S. l. levalliantoides* near Secunda, Mpumalanga Province, South Africa (photo by Maans Booysen)

RIGHT Male Orange River Francolin subspecies *S. l. levalliantoides* (photo by Andre Botha)

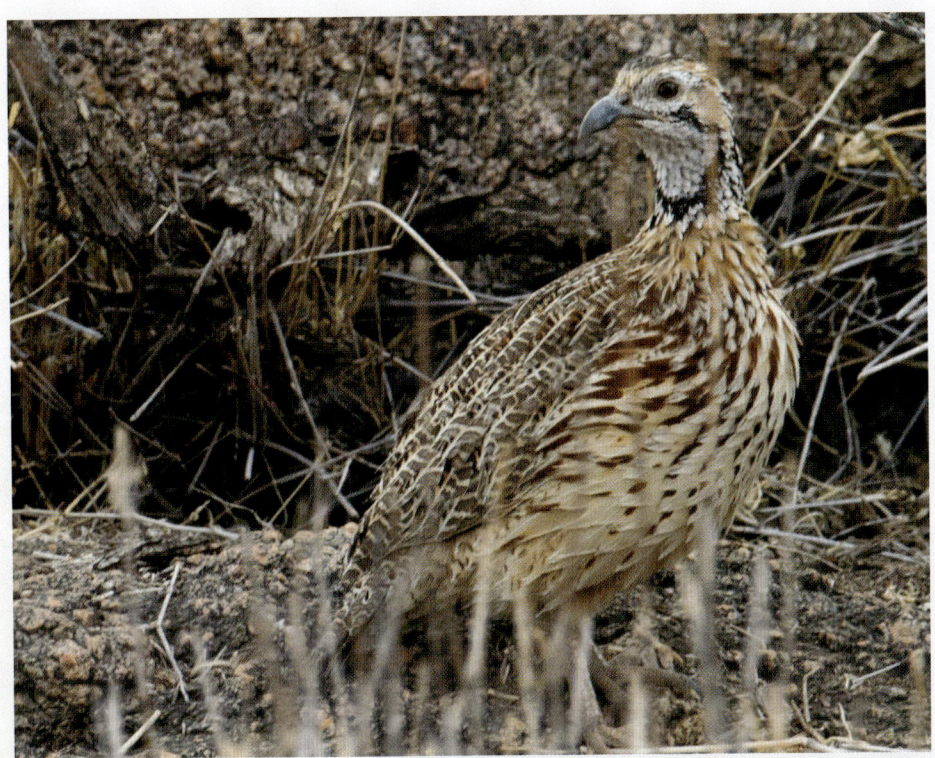
Male Orange River Francolin subspecies *S. l. pallidior* at Namibgrens, south-west of Windhoek, Namibia (photo by Dayne Braine)

Male Orange River Francolin subspecies *S. l. pallidior* (photo by Ian White)

Classification

Their closest relative is the Kunene Francolin *S. jugularis* thereafter the Archer's Francolin *S. gutturalis* of East Africa.

Two subspecies are recognised:

S. l. levalliantoides (Smith, A, 1836) in southern Botswana, north-western and central South Africa;

S. l. pallidior (Neumann, 1908) in east-central Namibia and west-central Botswana.

The putative subspecies *'kalaharica'* is a paler clinal variant of *S. l. pallidior*.

One previous subspecies of Orange River Francolin has been elevated to full species status: Kunene Francolin *S. jugularis* Mandiwana-Neudani *et al.* 2019, *Ostrich* 90(3): 191–221.

Description

- They have a blackish-brown crown and nape, with the feathers edged with buff; a yellow-brown supercilium, grading into white, yellowish-brown sides of the head and hind neck flecked with black and a moderately developed buff throat patch with the breast blotched with buff and reddish brown.
- The throat is white with a characteristic black necklace, with a narrow black-and-white band behind the eye, which runs down either side of the neck, broadening, but does not meet on the throat.
- The upper breast and flanks are buff with red-brown blotches, while the belly is plain buff.
- The flight feathers are distinctly red in flight.
- The legs are dull yellow, and males have leg spurs.
- Juveniles are similar in appearance to adult females, but the black-and-white banding on the head and neck is less well defined and the underparts are barred irregularly with black and buff.
- Downy chicks have reddish-brown underparts, with dark brown streaks on the crown and mid-back, with the ones on the back being flanked by buffy streaks.
- The sides of the head are buffy, and the brown eye has several black-and-white stripes above and below it.

Distribution and habitat

- They are distributed through east-central Namibia, much of south-central Botswana into west-central South Africa, now a southern African endemic species.

- They inhabit mostly flat landscapes, often on sandy soils, except in central Namibia, where they occupy hilly terrain.
- Typical habitats are semi-arid open, sandy grasslands of the dry savannas and the central Kalahari in the east and wooded, busy grasslands in the west.
- Although typically a grassland species, they prefer patches of moderately dense cover and often frequent the edges of cultivated lands.

Habits

They are usually seen in pairs or coveys of 3–5 birds. When approached, they sit tight and then run into thicker cover. Flushed birds will gain height before peeling off over trees. They dust-bath and roost in flat, open patches. Their repeated advertisement call '*kibitele, kibitele*' is similar to that of the Shelley's Francolin *S. shelleyi*, but is more rapid and higher pitched, with the accent on the third note. Calling birds often perch on a conspicuous object such as a rock. Most calling is in the early morning and evening, particularly during the early breeding season. Other subdued, grating calls are used to communicate between individuals in a covey at close quarters or to indicate alarm at the approach of a predator or other threat.

Food and feeding

Their diet comprises corms, bulbs, seeds and some green shoots, supplemented with leaf bugs, beetles, ants, termites and grasshoppers during the breeding season.

Breeding

They are monogamous, solitary nesters. Although breeding can be at any time of the year, peak breeding is during June and July in northern Botswana, during March and April in south-eastern Botswana and in east-central Namibia, and during August to October in South Africa. The nest is a scrape, usually in dense grass cover and lined with dry grass. The clutch of 5–8 pale coffee-coloured or yellowish oval eggs, sometimes lightly speckled with brown, measure 36–5 x 28.7 mm. Incubation by the female lasts for 20–21 days. Chicks can flutter-fly at 12–14 days and accomplished flight is at 5–6 weeks.

Status and conservation

Like some other grassland francolins, they are susceptible to habitat manipulation, particularly where poorly managed grazing has resulted in degraded grasslands. A few consecutive years of overgrazing, even on otherwise well-managed nature reserves, can cause local extinctions.

Kunene Francolin
Francolin de Kunene

Scleroptila jugularis

Perdix levaillantoides (Smith, A, 1836), upper reaches of Orange River

S. l. jugularis (Büttikofer, 1889) in south-western Angola

Male Kunene Francolin at Hobatere Lodge, north-western Namibia (photo by Dayne Braine)

Female Kunene Francolin near Ruacana, north-western Namibia (photo by Cliff Dorse)

Male Kunene Francolin portrait (photo by Dayne Braine)

FRANCOLINS & PARTRIDGES

Classification

Recently elevated from Orange River Francolin *S. lavalliantoides jugularis* Mandiwana-Neudani *et al.* 2019, *Ostrich* 90(3): 191–221.

Their closest relative is its sister species Orange River Francolin *S. lavalliantoides*.

Kunene Francolin is monotypic with no subspecies recognised.

Description

- They are generally paler than Orange River Francolin, with a broadly mottled black-and-white head and neck, and the chestnut spotting on the underparts is much reduced.
- They have a white throat and characteristic black necklace which extends onto the breast.
- The upper abdomen and flanks are spotted with black.
- The flight feathers are distinctly red in flight.
- Their legs are dull yellow and males have leg spurs.
- Juveniles are similar in appearance to adult females, but the black-and-white banding on the head and neck is less well defined and the underparts are barred irregularly with black and buff.
- Downy chicks have reddish-brown underparts, with dark brown streaks on the crown and mid-back, with the ones on the back being flanked by buffy streaks.
- The sides of the head are buffy, and the brown eye has several black and white stripes above and below it.

Distribution and habitat

- They are confined to western Damaraland of north-western Namibia, extending marginally into south-western Angola.
- They inhabit mostly hilly terrain and flat dry landscapes, often on sandy soils.
- Typical habitats are open sandy grasslands of the dry savannas and wooded busy grasslands.
- Although typically a grassland species, they favour patches of moderately dense cover and often frequent the edges of cultivated lands.

Habits

They are usually seen in pairs or coveys of 3–5 birds which are territorial, particularly before the breeding season. When approached, they sit tight and then run into thicker cover. Flushed birds will gain height before peeling off over trees. They dust-bath and roost in flat, open patches. Their repeated advertisement call, often given from a raised surface such as a dune, is similar to that of Orange River Francolin but is followed by a low whistle. Most calling is in the early morning and evening, particularly during the early breeding season.

Food and feeding

Their diet comprises corms, bulbs, seeds and some green shoots, supplemented with leaf bugs, beetles, ants, termites and grasshoppers during the breeding season.

Breeding

They are monogamous, solitary nesters. Although breeding can be at any time of the year, peak breeding is during June and July in northern Namibia and during August in south-western Angola. The nest is a scrape, usually in dense grass cover and lined with dry grass. The clutch of 5–8 pale coffee or yellowish cream-coloured oval eggs, sometimes lightly speckled with brown, measure 36.5 x 28.7 mm. Incubation by the female lasts for 20–21 days. Chicks can flutter-fly at 12–14 days and accomplished flight is at 5–6 weeks.

Status and conservation

Although they occur in relatively sparse open arid grasslands, they are susceptible to habitat manipulation, particularly where poorly managed goat grazing has resulted in degraded grasslands.

Archer's Francolin
Francolin d'Archer

Scleroptila gutturalis

Scleroptila gutturalis (Rüppell, 1835), north-eastern Africa

LEFT Archer's Francolin (photo by János Oláh)

BELOW Archer's Francolin (photo by Callan Cohen)

Classification

This species' closest relative is its sister species the Ulu Francolin *S. uluensis*.

The two previous micro-geographically variable and clinally variant subspecies of Archer's Francolin, *S. g. lorti* Sharpe, 1897 and *S. g. archeri* Sclater, WL, 1927, of Ethiopia, South Sudan, Somalia and northern Uganda are synonymised with *S. gutturalis* to form one monotypic species.

Description

- The Archer's Francolin was previously considered a race of the Orange River Francolin *S. levalliantoides*.
- Their buff, not white, throat patch and line behind the eye, weakly defined necklace and paler greyish to buff underparts which are lightly streaked black without barring distinguish them from the Ulu Francolin.
- They are darker than the Moorland Francolin *S. psilolaema*, lacking streaking on their buff throat, and they have paler, less rufous underparts.
- Juveniles are similar in appearance to adult females but are duller with less defined facial striping and gorget pattern.
- Downy chicks are not described.

Distribution and habitat

- They are a locally common endemic to north-eastern Africa, in Ethiopia, Eritrea, southern South Sudan, northern Somalia and northern Uganda.
- They are scarce in Kidepo and Mount Moroto in northern Uganda and in the Huri Hills and Mount Kulal in norther Kenya.
- Their preferred habitats are arid savanna steppes with open and slightly wooded grasslands and boulder-strewn scrub-covered hill slopes.

Habits

They usually occur in territorial pairs or small coveys which are shy and elusive. Their presence is usually only detected by their call, mostly in the early morning and late afternoon. When approached they will freeze within grassy cover and flush with vigorous wing beats and alarm squeals. Similar to the behaviour of the other Red-winged Group of francolins, they roost overnight as a covey on the ground. Their repeated '*ki-keet ki-kit*' call is similar to that of the Ulu Francolin, but is faster, shorter and more abrupt. They also have a high-pitched, squealing flight call when flushed.

Food and feeding

Their diet consists mostly of bulbs and corms (*Moraea* spp.), seeds, berries and fallen grain, as well as bugs, termites, beetles and grasshoppers particularly during the breeding season.

Breeding

They are monogamous, nesting in a well-concealed scrape under a grass tuft. Laying dates are recorded as February to April and August for Ethiopia. The clutch of 5–8 pale pink to yellowish-brown eggs, sometimes with brown speckling, measure 41.2 x 31.2 mm. Their incubation behaviour is unknown.

Status and conservation

They are generally not threatened, but although they are locally common their population status is uncertain. Common threats to their occurrence are the degradation of their grassland and savanna habits by excessive grazing by domestic livestock and annual burning.

Red-winged Francolin
Francolin de Levaillant
Scleroptila levaillantii

Perdix levaillantii (Valenciennes, 1825), Swellendam, Western Cape Province, South Africa

TOP RIGHT Red-winged Francolin in Rietvlei Nature Reserve, Gauteng Province, South Africa (photo by Maans Booysen)

TOP LEFT Red-winged Francolin with a flying termite (photo by Andre Botha)

LEFT Incubating female Red-winged Francolin (photo by Ian Little)

Classification

Red-winged Francolin is closely related to Crawshay's Francolin *S. crawshayi*.

They are monotypic with no subspecies recognised.

S. levaillantii Valenciennes, 1825 in eastern South Africa and Swaziland

Two previous subspecies of Red-winged Francolin have been elevated to full species status: Crawshay's Francolin *S. crawshayi*, including the subspecies *S. c. crawshayi* and *S. c. kikuyuensis* Mandiwana-Neudani *et al.* 2019, *Ostrich* 90(3): 191–221.

Description

- They are the largest of the Red-winged Group, with prominent rufous markings on the side and hind neck and a broad black-and-white collar but lack a black border to the white throat.
- The white stripe below the eye and down to the collar is less distinct than that of Crawshay's Francolin.
- They have a large, robust bill, which allows for digging out relatively large bulbs.
- Males have relatively small leg spurs.
- Juveniles resemble adults, but are duller, and the black-and-white barring on the lower neck and upper breast is less distinct.
- Downy chicks are rufous-brown above, with dark brown streaks on the crown and mid-back, the latter flanked by buffy streaks.
- The sides of their head are buffy, with multiple black-and-white stripes above and below the eye.
- The underparts are buffy, but somewhat darker on the breast.

Distribution and habitat

- They are endemic to South Africa and Swaziland.
- In South Africa, they occur in the southern Mpumalanga highlands, the highlands and Midlands of KwaZulu-Natal, the eastern Free State and the Eastern Cape, with remnant populations along the southern coast of the Eastern and Western Cape.
- In the eastern parts of South Africa, they inhabit montane sour grasslands, dominated by red grass *Themeda triandra*.
- They thrive in rank vigorous habitats, usually over deep soils.
- They are more sensitive to burning or grazing of grasslands than other members of the Red-winged Group.
- In heavily grazed and frequently burnt grasslands, they are restricted to wetland fringes and rocky outcrops.

Habits

They occur in relatively small coveys of 4–8 birds. They are rarely flushed, but are commonly heard calling from hill tops early in the morning and sometimes at dusk. When flushed, they explode out of the grass with a flurry of wings. The escape flight usually ends in a long glide before dropping into dense grass or sedge cover, seldom to be flushed again. The distinctive, high-pitched whistle call is rendered as '*chee-chee-chee-chee kla-CHEE-choo*', accelerating into repeated '*klik-a-chee-choo, klik-a-chee-choo*' phrases.

Food and feeding

They feed primarily on bulbs or corms, scraping with the heavy bill around rocky outcrops and wetland fringes where favoured food plants, such as *Hypoxis*, *Rhodohypoxis*, *Hesperantha*, *Oxalis*, *Gladiolus* and *Moraea* species, abound. Their diet is supplemented with insects during the breeding season.

Breeding

Peak breeding largely follows the early rains, August to February in KwaZulu-Natal and later during March to July in the Eastern Cape. The nest-site is often in close proximity to wetland edges within two- to three-year-old grass. The nest is a shallow scrape between grass tufts lined with live and dead grass. The clutch of 5–8 creamy yellow eggs, usually faintly spotted with dull brown, measure 40.1 x 32.3 mm. Incubation by the female lasts 22 days. Chicks are precocial and are cared for by both parents.

Status and conservation

There are numerous examples of local declines in their numbers and areas of confirmed absence in apparently suitable habitat in southern Africa. They are sensitive to annual burning and overgrazing, as well as to unburnt moribund grassland. Biennial burning and light grazing by wild herbivores provides important sanctuaries for this species. Other major threats are expanding commercial forestry and the damming and draining of wetlands.

Crawshay's Francolin
Francolin de Crawshay
Scleroptila crawshayi

Perdix levaillantii (Valenciennes, 1825), Swellendam, Western Cape Province, South Africa

S. l. crawshayi (Ogilvie-Grant 1896) in northern Malawi

Crawshay's Francolin subspecies *S. c. crawshayi* in the Nyika National Park, Malawi (photo by Maans Booysen)

Crawshay's Francolin subspecies *S. c. crawshayi* in regenerating bracken grassland in the Nyika National Park, Malawi (photo by Maans Booysen)

Crawshay's Francolin subspecies *S. c. kikuyuensis* in the Mara Triangle, south-western Kenya (photo by Stratton Hatfield)

Classification

Recently elevated from Red-winged Francolin *S. levaillantii crawshayi* Mandiwana-Neudani *et al.* 2019, *Ostrich* 90(3): 191–221.

Their closest relative is Red-winged Francolin *S. levaillantii*.

Two subspecies are recognised:

S. c. kikuyuensis Ogilvie-Grant, 1897 has two populations in Angola, north-western Zambia, and south-eastern Democratic Republic of the Congo (DRC), as well as in Uganda, Rwanda, Burundi, north-western Tanzania and western Kenya.

S. c. crawshayi Ogilvie-Grant 1896 in northern Malawi, north-eastern Zambia and south-western Tanzania.

Description

- They are richer in colour than the Red-winged Francolin, with prominent rufous and white markings on the side and hind neck and a broad black-and-white collar but lack a black border to the white throat.
- *S. c. kikuyuensis* has no striping on the hind neck.
- They have a large bill with yellow near the base.
- Males have relatively small leg spurs.
- Juveniles resemble adults, but are duller, and the black-and-white barring on the lower neck and upper breast is less distinct.
- Downy chicks are rufous-brown above, with dark brown streaks on the crown and mid-back, the latter flanked by buffy streaks.
- The sides of their head are buffy, with multiple black-and-white stripes above and below the eye.
- The underparts are buffy, but somewhat darker on the breast.

Distribution and habitat

- *S. c. crawshayi* is localised on the Nyika Plateau in north-eastern Zambia, northern Malawi and western Tanzania.
- *S. c. kikuyuensis* is disjunctly distributed with populations in the highlands of Angola ranging into southern DRC, north-western Zambia and separately in Uganda, Rwanda, Burundi, and the western highlands of Kenya and north-western Tanzania.
- They are ecologically similar in behaviour and habitat use to the Red-winged Francolin.
- They inhabit open grassy woodland, grasslands often with scattered scrub and patchy cultivation from 600–3 000 m above sea level.

Habits

Although relatively common locally in Tanzania, Uganda and Burundi (*S. c. crawshayi*), their abundance elsewhere, particularly in Angola and north-western Zambia (*S. c. kikiyuensis*) is not well known. They occur in relatively small coveys of 4–8 birds. They roost on the ground in their covey group. Their call is similar to the call of the Red-winged Francolin, starting with a repeated sharp '*kik-kik-kik-kik*' followed by repeated '*kik-ker-ri-ku*'.

Food and feeding

They feed primarily on the bulbs or corms of iris and sedge plants, scraping with their heavy bill between grass swards and leaves around rocky outcrops and wetland fringes. Their diet is supplemented with insects, spiders and millipedes during the breeding season.

Breeding

Peak breeding largely follows the early rains, during April in south-western Angola but during the dry season July–December in the DRC (*S. c. kikuyuensis*), and November–January in Malawi (*S. c. crawshayi*). The nest-site is usually well concealed in rank moist grassland. The nest is a shallow scrape between grass tufts lined with live and dead grass. The clutch of 5–8 creamy-yellow eggs, usually faintly spotted with dull brown, measure 40.1 x 32.3 mm. Incubation by the female lasts 22 days. Chicks are precocial and are cared for by both parents.

Status and conservation

Their population status is uncertain, and they are sensitive to frequent burning and overgrazing by domestic livestock.

Crawshay's Francolin subspecies *S. c. kikuyuensis* at the Kwando River source lake, Angola (photo by Maans Booysen)

Finsch's Francolin
Francolin de Finsch
Scleroptila finschi

Francolinus finschi (Barboza du Bocage, 1881),
Caconda, Benguella, Angola

Finsch's Francolin in eastern Cuanza Sul Province, Angola (both photos by Antonio Martins)

Finsch's Francolin near Lekoni in eastern Gabon (photo by David Hoddinott)

FRANCOLINS & PARTRIDGES

Classification

Finsch's Francolin are most closely related to Shelley's Francolin *S. shelleyi* and Rufous-throated Francolin *S. whytei*.

They are monotypic with no subspecies recognised.

Description

- They can be considered the localised counterpart of the red-winged francolin group, with duller, less patterned plumage.
- They are the only Red-winged Group member with no black-and-white stripe patterning on the face or neck, and they have a grey breast and belly.
- They have a broad pale orange band on the side of the face and neck.
- The centre of their belly is buff with chestnut blotching and it is essentially unbarred.
- The sides of the face and border of the throat are ochre as in Red-winged Francolin *S. levaillantii* but this is less extensive on the hind neck.
- This species is also long-billed like the Red-winged Francolin.
- They are distinguished from the Coqui Francolin *Campocolinus coqui* by their larger size and Red-winged Group head pattern.
- They differ from the other grassland francolins by their yellowish legs and black bill.
- The primaries and outer secondaries are only slightly rufous in flight.
- They are sexually monomorphic.
- Both the juveniles and downy chicks are undescribed.

Distribution and habitat

- The most extensive population is in west-central Angola, with localised, patchy populations in south-eastern Gabon, the Republic of the Congo and south-western Democratic Republic of the Congo.
- They are regularly found on birding trips to the Lèkoni grasslands on the Bateke Plateau in eastern Gabon.
- They inhabit mainly short-grass savannas, *Brachystegia* woodland, forest edges and bare grassy slopes with mesic seeps above the timberline in mountainous terrain.
- They have also been recorded feeding in recently burnt areas.

Habits

They are usually seen in pairs. They are typical grassland francolins, being shy and elusive in the grass sward and sitting tight when approached. Their call is a loud '*wit-u-*

wit' duet, usually heard at dusk, somewhat similar sounding to the call of the Shelley's Francolin.

Food and feeding

Their diet includes corms, tubers and seeds, supplemented mostly during the breeding season with beetles and insect larvae.

Breeding

Probably monogamous, they breed during January, March and July in the DRC and during June and July in Angola. The nest is placed within secluded vegetation on the ground. Their clutch consists of, on average, 5 eggs which are plain light brown. Their incubation biology is unknown.

Status and conservation

Although the bulk of their range is in Angola, they are sparsely distributed and uncommon to rare. There is little known about their potential threats, but similar to most grassland francolins, habitat degradation by frequent grassland burning and excessive grazing will play a role.

Moorland Francolin
Francolin montagnard
Scleroptila psilolaema

Francolinus psilolaemus (Gray, GR, 1867), Shoa, Ethiopia

Moorland Francolin on the Sanetti Plateau, Bale Mountain National Park, south-central Ethiopia (photo by Merid Gabremichael)

Moorland Francolins in the Bale Mountain National Park, Ethiopia (photo by Maans Booysen)

Moorland Francolins in the Bale Mountains, Ethiopia (photo by Adam Riley)

Moorland Francolin in the Bale Mountains, Ethiopia (photo by Nigel Redman)

FRANCOLINS & PARTRIDGES

Classification

They are closely related to Grey-winged Francolin *S. afra*.

They are monotypic with no subspecies recognised.

Specimens from the Arussi Plateau south of the Ethiopian Rift '*ellenbecki*' are merely slightly larger and have darker, more richly coloured plumage but do not warrant separate taxonomic status.

One previous subspecies of Moorland Francolin has been elevated to full species status: Elgon Francolin *S. elgonensis* Mandiwana-Neudani *et al.* 2019, *Ostrich* 90(3): 191–221.

Description

- The Moorland Francolin is one of the montane red-winged francolin group.
- They are generally darker than the Archer's Francolin *S. gutturalis*, with a buff variably spotted or streaked, not white, throat similar to that of the Grey-winged Francolin and more rufous underparts suffused the buff and grey, with small black spots across the upper breast.
- They have a rather plain, buffy belly, not barred like that of the Shelley's Francolin *S. shelleyi*.
- The wings show relatively extensive rufous in flight, approaching that of the Red-winged Francolin *S. levaillantii*.
- They are the only member of the red-winged francolin group with black bars at the tips of their primaries.
- Juveniles and downy chicks are undescribed.

Distribution and habitat

- They are localised to north-eastern Africa, occurring as an endemic in the montane areas of central and south-eastern Ethiopia.
- Their preferred habitats are montane heath moorland and grasslands, adjacent livestock pastures and moist grassy areas sometimes near ponds, rarely found below 2 400 m.

Habits

They are usually found in pairs or small coveys which are shy. Although they can be relatively confiding in reasonably vegetated habitat, they will otherwise run for cover when approached or flush with vigorous wing beats, landing in scrubby cover where they will sit tight. Calling coveys will repeatedly answer one another with the typical advertisement call. Their advertisement call is a repeated short and unhurried two elements *'trich-chi-che'e'* which is unique amongst the Red-winged Group of grassland francolins. They also utter a high-pitched squealing when flushed. They roost overnight in a tight covey group on the ground.

Food and feeding

Similar to the diet of the other grassland francolins of the Red-winged Group, they feed mostly on corms, bulbs and roots. They forage by excavating with their bill in damp grassy areas and amongst sedges, often around montane pools and sponges.

Breeding

They are monogamous and breed mostly in the first half of the year. The nest is a shallow scrape concealed in open grassland or heath. The clutch is usually 4–5 eggs. There is very little further information about their breeding biology.

Status and conservation

They are uncommon to rare and listed as Near Threatened (The IUCN Red List of Threatened Species v 2016-3) because they are suspected to be undergoing moderately rapid declines owing to the reduction and degradation of high-altitude moorland and grassland habitats through overgrazing and agricultural cultivation. The heather moorlands have the highest density of livestock in Ethiopia, and habitat loss and disturbance, including trampling and damage to nesting sites, are probably a real concern.

Elgon Francolin
Francolin du Mont Elgon
Scleroptila elgonensis

Francolinus psilolaemus (Gray, GR, 1867), Shoa, Ethiopia

S. p. elgonensis (Ogilvie-Grant, 1891), Mount Elgon

TOP-LEFT Elgon Francolins on Mount Kenya (photo by Callan Cohen)

RIGHT Elgon Francolin on Mount Kenya (photo by Stratton Hatfield)

LEFT Elgon Francolins on Mount Kenya (photo by Callan Cohen)

Classification

Recently elevated from Moorland Francolin *S. psilolaema elgonensis* Mandiwana-Neudani *et al.* 2019, *Ostrich* 90(3): 191–221.

They are closely related to Orange River Francolin *S. levalliantoides*.

They are monotypic with no subspecies recognised.

The putative subspecies '*theresae*', although paler and less richly coloured with chestnut, is synonymised with *S. elgonensis*.

Description

- Elgon Francolin is one of the montane Red-winged Group of francolins.
- They are larger than Ulu Francolin *S. uluensis* with a similar face pattern but the line behind the eye and throat are buffy-white or pale buff rather than white.
- The top of the head is black, each feather margined with pale rusty brown, the back of the neck is chestnut, with a black spot at the tip of each feather.
- The sides of the face and neck are buff, divided from the top of the head and from the throat by mixed black and white lines.
- The lower throat and chest are chestnut with the feathers tipped with one or two black spots.
- Their underparts are warm rufous buff with small black dots on the upper breast and lack barring on the belly.
- The wings show a fairly extensive rufous primary feather patch in flight, approaching that of the Red-winged Francolin *S. levaillantii*.
- The bill is blackish brown with the base of the lower mandible yellowish horn-colour and the legs and feet are dusky yellow.
- Juveniles and downy chicks are undescribed.

Distribution and habitat

- They are endemic to far eastern Uganda and western Kenya.
- They are localised and uncommon on Mount Kenya, the Aberdares and Mau Narok in Kenya, but more common on Mount Elgon in both Kenya and Uganda.
- Their preferred habitats are grassy montane heath moorland and open grasslands from 2 300–4 000 m above sea level.

Habits

They are usually found in pairs or small coveys of 3–6 birds which are shy and sit extremely tight when approached. When flushed they erupt from the grass with heavy flight. Their advertisement call is similar sounding to that of Archer's Francolin *S. guttularis*, Shelley's Francolin *S. shelleyi* and Ulu Francolin. They also utter a high-pitched squealing when flushed.

Food and feeding

Similar to the diet of other grassland francolins of the Red-winged Group, they feed mostly on corms, bulbs and roots. They forage by excavating underground plant parts with their bill in damp grassy areas and amongst sedges, often around montane pools and sponges. Their diet is supplemented with invertebrates during the breeding season.

Breeding

They are monogamous and breed mostly in the first half of the year. The nest is a well concealed scrape in open grassland or heath. The clutch is usually 4–5 eggs. Very little is known about their breeding biology.

Status and conservation

They are uncommon to rare in Kenya and locally more common on Mount Elgon in both Kenya and Uganda. However, they may be threatened by the reduction and degradation of high-altitude grassy moorland and grassland habitats through overgrazing by free-range livestock and activities related to patchy agricultural cultivation. Current threat levels have them listed as Near Threatened (The IUCN Red List of Threatened Species v 2016-3).

Ring-necked Francolin

Francolin à collier

Scleroptila streptophora

Francolinus streptophorus (Ogilvie-Grant, 1891), Mangiki, Mount Elgon, Kenya

Ring-necked Francolin in Murchison Falls National Park, Uganda (photo by David Hoddinott)

Ring-necked Francolin near Kipedo Savannah Lodge, Kipedo Game Reserve, North-eastern Uganda (photo by Victor Michelini)

FRANCOLINS & PARTRIDGES

Classification

Ring-necked Francolin is an evolutionary basal member of the red-winged francolin group.

Their closest relatives are Crawshay's Francolin *S. crawshayi* and Shelley's Francolin *S. shelleyi*.

They are a monotypic species with no geographic variation and thus no subspecies are recognised.

Description

- The Ring-necked Francolin is a distinctive, elaborately patterned member of the Red-winged Group of francolins.
- They have a striped head, a rufous nape, a white throat and a breast band of black-and-white stripes which join around the back of the neck.
- They are distinguished by their dark unpatterned crown, broad white supercilium, chestnut face and neck, contrasting white throat margined with rufous and characteristic finely barred black-and-white breast collar, with no barring on the breast and a mottled belly.
- Their primaries are brown with a hint of rufous rather than red in the wings in flight.
- Although mostly sexual monomorphic, females have a dark brown crown with a pale edge and rufous-brown barred upper parts, with broad pale shaft-streaks.
- The upper mandible is black with the lower yellowish and legs are yellow.
- They are somewhat similar in appearance to Coqui Francolin *Campocolinus coqui*, but larger, with a different pattern below: mostly plain with a few bold dark streaks on the sides of the belly.
- Also similar in appearance to Crawshay's Francolin, but with a cleaner white throat, lacking the large red patches in the wings, and a different pattern on the underparts.
- Juveniles and downy chicks are undescribed.

Distribution and habitat

- They have a patchy disjunct distribution in Uganda, Burundi, Rwanda, western Kenya and north-western Tanzania, with a further isolated population in the highlands of the Foumban area of Cameroon.
- They are a shy, poorly known, and highly localised species.
- They inhabit largely uninhabited countryside with open grasslands and lightly wooded areas on rocky hillsides.
- They are reported to also visit crop cultivation areas.

Habits

They usually occur in pairs or small coveys which keep well hidden in sparse grass and run swiftly between and over rocks. They are shy and skulking, running for cover when disturbed, and are possibly one of the least photographed gamebirds in Africa. They shelter beneath a bush in the hotter parts of the day. When flushed, they fly fast. They call mostly in the early morning and often from a prominent perch such as a termite mound. The call is a mournful fluty dove-like cooing, followed by a piping trill that first goes up, then descends. They also give a raucous alarm call in flight.

Food and feeding

Their diet consists of seeds and insects, but may also enter cultivated areas to feed on weeds, waste grains and insects.

Breeding

They are monogamous, breeding during the early rains (April) in Uganda and during the dry season (December–March) in western Kenya. The nest is a well concealed shallow scrape with little or no lining, often placed close to a rock. The clutch of 4–5 greyish buff eggs have dark speckled pores. Their incubation biology is unknown.

Status and conservation

They are generally uncommon but are relatively common in the Gulu and Choa districts of northern Uganda and in north-western Tanzania. Rarer than previously believed, they have apparently declined in both range and abundance in Kenya, north-western Uganda and Rwanda, and are now suspected to have a moderately small population. They have therefore been moved from a species of Least Concern to Near Threatened (The IUCN Red List of Threatened Species v 2016-3), but even this listing might still be conservative.

Forest Francolin
Francolin de Latham

Peliperdix lathami

Francolinus lathami (Hartlaub, 1854), Sierra Leone

RIGHT Male Forest Francolin in leaf litter (photo by Andy Pugh)

BELOW LEFT Male Forest Francolin (photo by Tasso Leventis)

BELOW RIGHT Typical Forest Francolin nest on dry leaves between buttress roots of a forest tree (photo by Nik Borrow)

Classification

The Forest (or Latham's) Francolin represents its own evolutionary trajectory from that of the other francolins and retains the genus *Peliperdix* as the type specimen for that genus.

Forest Francolin are most closely related to the *Campocolinus* species of the red-tailed francolin group, particularly Schlegel's Francolin *C. schlegelii* and Pale-bellied Francolin *C. spinetorum*.

There are two subspecies recognised:

P. l. lathami Hartlaub, 1854 in Sierra Leone to north-western Democratic Republic of Congo and Angola.

P. l. schubotzi Reichenow, 1912 in western DRC to south-western South Sudan, western Uganda and north-western Tanzania.

Description

- Also known as Latham's Forest Francolin, they are a small, dark forest species which are strikingly sexually dimorphic.
- They are best distinguished from Nahan's Partridge *Ptilopachus nahani* by their pale grey, not black, ear coverts and their yellow, not red, legs.
- They have a dark chestnut cap, black bill and a dark black throat.
- The male upperparts are dark brown with fine, pale streaks, while the underparts are black with distinct white spots.
- *P. l. schubotzi* males in the DRC have the black and white pattern extending down the bulk of the belly continuing to the undertail coverts, where the ground colour still predominates.
- Females are paler brown above than males, with buffy cheeks and supercilium, and pale mottled rufous and brown underparts with cream spots.
- Juvenile males have a mottled black and brown crown, with a white chin and throat, and the sides of the head and ear coverts are brownish.
- Juvenile females have broad, black tipped crown and nape feathers.
- Downy chicks have dark chestnut brown crown and back, a buff face with chestnut eye-stripe from behind the eye to the nape.

Distribution and habitat

- They are distributed in equatorial lowland forest from Sierra Leone to Cameroon, Gabon and the Congo with an eastern population in the eastern Democratic Republic of the Congo, western Uganda and South Sudan.

- It is unclear if this disjunct distribution and the two small separated populations in central and northern DRC are a consequence of sparse sampling.
- They inhabit the undergrowth of primary and occasionally secondary forest.

Habits

They are secretive and difficult to observe in their dense habitat, although they will venture into glades during wet weather. They are difficult to flush, sitting tight or running through the undergrowth. If flushed, they fly fast for a short distance. Their call, often heard at night, is a low frequency dove-like '*kwee, coo, coo …*' or '*krook-kroo-kroo-kroo …*' cooing, often repeated, as well as various whistles and clucking contact calls.

Food and feeding

They forage by scratching through the leaf litter, sometimes even at night. Their diet consists mostly of invertebrates, including termites, ants, snails, beetles and other insects and their larvae. They will also consume fruits, seeds and green leaves.

Breeding

Most of their breeding records are for December to April. The eggs are laid on the open ground, amongst dry leaves between projecting forest tree root buttresses. The clutch of 2, rarely 3, elongate-ovate, thick-shelled dark buff or light rusty brown eggs measure 38.3 x 26.5 mm. Their incubation biology is unknown.

Status and conservation

They may be unsustainably harvested by baiting with termites and grains to areas where they are trapped with snares or shot. They are also threatened by forest destruction.

Barbary Partridge
Perdrix gambra
Alectoris barbara

Perdix barbara (Bonnaterre, 1790), Morocco

Barbary Partridge (photos by Bill Baston above and Sergio Bianchi left)

Classification

Four subspecies of the Barbary Partridge are recognised:

A. b. koenigi Reichenow, 1899 in north-western Morocco and introduced to the Canary Islands;

A. b. spatzi Reichenow, 1895 in southern Morocco to central and southern Algeria and southern Tunisia;

A. b. barbara Bonnaterre, 1790 in north-eastern Morocco to northern Tunisia;

A. b. barbata Reichenow, 1895 in north-eastern Libya and previously north-western Egypt.

Description

- Similar to the other *Alectoris* partridges, their most distinctive features are their chestnut brown crown, grey throat, and broad chestnut-and-white speckled lower neck band, which expands backwards.
- They also have an extended grey supercilium, which runs down the back of the neck.
- Juveniles are pale yellow and lack the grey throat and neck band.
- Downy chicks are pale buff with a dark rufous crown and hind-neck stripe, and dark streaks above and through the eye.

Distribution and habitat

- They are a North African and Sardinian species extending from Morocco through northern Algeria, Tunisia and coastal Libya.
- There is a gap in their range in the central Libyan coast and a separate population occurs in the Ajjer Mountains in the south-eastern Algeria section of the Sahara Desert.
- They commonly inhabit rocky or stony hillsides and deserts up to 3 300 m, with dry grass, sparse scrub or open woodlands from coastal dunes up to the top of the Atlas Mountains during the boreal summer.
- They also inhabit cultivated lands and groves of palm, citrus, olives and *Eucalyptus* species.

Habits

They occur in pairs or small groups. When approached, they prefer to run rather than flush, particularly where they can run between vegetation. If flushed they fly fast, direct and far before landing. Their alarm call when flushed is a rapid '*ckukachew-chew-*

chew-chew' and the advertisement call is a harsh '*kakalik*', similar to that of the Chukar Partridge *A. chukar*. When calling, males stand erect on the tips of their toes. They roost on the ground, often under the shelter of rocks or vegetation. They are not dependent on fresh water.

Food and feeding

They forage in the early morning and evening, sometimes into the night. Their diet consists of seeds, the fruits of *Euphorbia* species, the succulent leaves of *Sosola*, *Lycium* and *Asparagus* species, which provide moisture. They also eat insects, particularly ants, and will take the waste grains in agricultural fields.

Breeding

They are monogamous and breed mostly from March to June. The nest is a shallow scrape, often in the shelter of a bush, sometimes lined with vegetation. The clutch of 6–20 eggs, usually 11, smooth, slightly glossy buff, with fine brown speckles measure 40.5 x 30.4 mm. Incubation is by the hen and lasts for 24–25 days, similar to other *Alectoris* species.

Status and conservation

Although they are common to abundant in remote or protected areas, there is evidence of localised declines due to hunting and habitat loss to agriculture. The population in north-western Egypt is almost certainly extinct because of hunting.

Sand Partridge
Perdrix de Hey

Ammoperdix heyi

Perdix heyi (Temminck, 1825), Desert of Akaba, Arabia

ABOVE AND BELOW LEFT Male Sand Partridges (photos by Tasso Leventis)

BELOW Photo by Yael Shiff

Classification

Four subspecies are recognised:

A. h. heyi Temminck, 1825 in Israel and Jordan south to the Sinai Peninsula, Egypt and western Saudi Arabia;

A. h. nicolli Hartert, 1919 in northern Egypt east of the Nile River south to central Egypt;

A. h. cholmleyi Ogilvie-Grant, 1897 in central Egypt also east of the Nile River south to north-eastern Sudan;

A. h. intermedia Hartert, 1917 in southern Arabia and southern Oman.

Description

- This is a small partridge weighing about 180 g.
- They have rufous outer tail feathers which are conspicuous in flight.
- Males are pinkish-buff with a dark head, chestnut throat and boldly barred rufous and black flanks.
- They have a distinct white patch behind the eye, and orange-yellow bill and legs.
- Females are sandy greyish-brown, with pinkish bars on the sides of the neck and subtle vermiculation.
- Juveniles are similar to adult females.
- Downy chicks are pale buff above and whitish below.

Distribution and habitat

- In Africa, they are distributed from north-eastern Egypt east of the Nile River south to north-eastern Sudan.
- Their preferred habitats are the slopes of broken rocky or stony hills with minimal scattered vegetation and lightly vegetated valleys with shrubs and sparse grass.
- They seldom venture into open stretches of dry, flat sandy desert.

Habits

They are usually in small groups of 2–5 individuals. When approached they prefer to squat motionless and are very cryptic. If disturbed, they run fast between vegetation and rocks. They rest in shade during the heat of the day. Although they are known to drink, they can go for extended periods without water. They are mostly silent, but at dawn and dusk will utter their loud '*kew-kew-kew*' call, and their wings make a rattling sound in flight.

Food and feeding

Their diet consists of berries, particularly of *Salvadora persica* and *Commiphora* species, grass seeds, corms, bulbs, green leaves and insects.

Breeding

They are monogamous and their laying season peaks in April. The nest is a shallow scrape typically placed next to a bush or rock and often lined with grass. Their clutch is usually 5–7 hard-shelled eggs which are pale buff and measure 37.0 x 26.7 mm.

Status and conservation

Little is known about their population status in Africa, but they are abundant in Arabia. Their occurrence in Eritrea and northern Ethiopia is uncertain.

Udzungwa Forest Partridge
Xénoperdrix de Tanzanie

Xenoperdix udzungwensis

Xenoperdix udzungwensis (Dinesen, Lehmberg, Svendsen, Hansen and Fjeldså, 1994), Ndundulu Mountains in the Udzungwa Highlands in Tanzania

Male Udzungwa Partridges, immature (above) and adult (right), from the Udzungwa Ndundulu Forest (photos by Louis André Hansen)

Classification

The Udzungwa Forest Partridge was only discovered in 1991, first noticed as a pair of strange feet in a cooking pot in a Tanzanian forest camp by scientists who were invited to dinner by local villagers (See Dinesen *et al.* 1994 in the Bibliography).

The Rubeho Forest Partridge *X. obscuratus* is treated as a separate species. They gave rise to the Eurasian and North American gamebirds. Their closest relatives are the Asian Hill Partridges of the genus *Arborophila*.

Description

- They are small, approximately 29-cm-long (230 g), boldly barred, brownish partridges with a rufous face and throat, black forehead, olive-brown crown with orange-red supercilium, a narrow white necklace bordering the grey underparts blotched with black before the ochre vent.
- They have a diagnostic bright red bill, brown iris and yellow legs.
- Both sexes are similar, except in that the black forehead is most pronounced in the males.
- Juveniles vary according to age with a brown forehead and a dark bill which progresses to orange and finally to red.
- Downy chicks are undescribed.

Distribution and habitat

- They are endemic to central Tanzania where they are scarce in the Udzungwa Mountains.
- They are restricted to montane evergreen forests, mostly on ridges and steep slopes, with a thick understory, and in sub-montane forests with scattered *Cyperus* sedges and ferns.

Habits

They have been encountered in coveys of up to 13 individuals. They spend most of the day skulking in the forest understory, roost in trees at night and call mostly during the early morning. Their call is a whistled '*teedli teedli*' with high peeping notes.

Food and feeding

They forage among the leaf litter of the forest floor, scratching and turning over leaves with their bill. Their diet consists mainly of beetles, ants, flies, woodlice and seeds.

Breeding

The only information available is that breeding takes place following rains, from October to December.

Status and conservation

Because of their limited distribution they are vulnerable to habitat loss and snaring, facing a high risk of extinction in the wild. Their conservation status is therefore listed as Endangered (The IUCN Red List of Threatened Species v 2015-4).

Rubeho Forest Partridge
Xénoperdrix des Rubeho

Xenoperdix obscuratus

Xenoperdix obscuratus (Fjeldså and Kiure, 2003), Mafwemiro Forest, northern Rubeho Mountains, central Tanzania

Illustration of Rubeho Forest Partridge (female left, male right) by Jon Fjeldså

Only available images of Rubeho Forest Partridges captured by a camera trap placed by Francesco Rovero, MUSE – Science Museum, Italy

Classification

The Rubeho Forest Partridge was formerly considered to be a subspecies of the Udzungwa Forest Partridge *X. udzungwensis* of the Udzungwa Mountains. However, genetic analyses suggest a lack of recent gene flow between the two populations, which are separated geographically by only 100 km. They also differ in details of ornaments and colours of the face and tail, which are likely to function as visual signals. They are therefore now recognised to be sufficiently distinct to be treated as a separate monotypic species (See Bowie & Fjeldså 2005 in the Bibliography).

Description

- The Rubeho Forest Partridge is a small, approximately 29-cm-long (150 g) partridge, with orange-brown upper plumage boldly barred and spotted black, a rufous face, grey underparts and an olive-brown crown.
- They have a red bill, brown iris and yellow legs.
- Both sexes are similar.
- They are smaller than Udzungwa Forest Partridge, lack the white necklace and ochre-coloured vent, and have a speckled face, less distinctly barred secondaries, and scaly-patterned wing-coverts.
- Juveniles and downy chicks are undescribed.

Distribution and habitat

- They are endemic to Mbugu Hill in the Mafwemiro Forest, northern Rubeho Highlands, Dodoma region in southern Tanzania, where they are scarce.
- They inhabit and are restricted to mature montane forests 1 700–1 900 m above sea level with yellowwood (*Podocarpus*) trees and a thick understory.

Habits

They are shy and largely remain concealed in the undergrowth of the forest floor. They have a whistled call with high peeping notes.

Food and feeding

Although little is known about their diet it is probably similar to that of the Udzungwa Forest Partridge, consisting mainly of beetles, ants, flies, woodlice and seeds.

Breeding

There is currently no information available on their breeding biology.

Status and conservation

Because of ongoing habitat loss, their small population size, limited range and overhunting, the Rubeho Forest Partridge is considered to be Endangered (The IUCN Red List of Threatened Species v 2015-4), facing a high risk of extinction in the wild.

Madagascan Partridge
Caille de Madagascar

Margaroperdix madagarensis

Tetrao madagarensis (Scolopi, 1786), Madagascar

Female Madagascan Partridge (photo by Werner Suter)

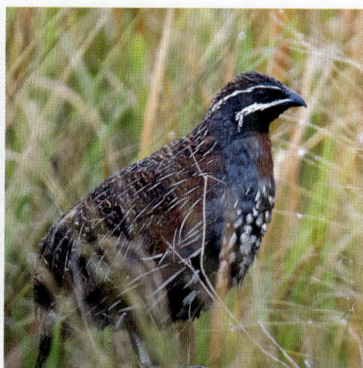

FAR LEFT Male Madagascan Partridge (photo by Markus Lagerqvist)

LEFT Male Madagascan Partridge (photo by Louise Jasper)

Classification

Madagascan Partridge are monotypic with no subspecies recognised.

Description

- Males have a reddish-brown crown with a diagnostic black-and-white mask and a black throat. The sides of the head and throat are dark grey, with a white stripe above the eye and along the sides of the throat.
- The upper breast is chestnut, while the lower breast and belly are black with distinct large oval white spots.
- The wings, flanks and tail are barred buff, chestnut and black.
- Females are tan-brown with black 'v' shaped barring on the back of the head and the throat down to the lower belly.
- The mantle, lower back and wings are dark brown with pale stripes similar to males.
- Juveniles are similar to but duller than females.
- Downy chicks are similar to those of *Coturnix* quails, being pale buffy-brown above, with dark brown lateral crown stripes and a broad dark brown stripe on the sides of the body, and dingy buff on the head with a blackish line below the eye.

Distribution and habitat

- They are an uncommon endemic across Madagascar, but absent from the extreme southern spiny forest.
- They are commonly seen near Perinet-Analamazaotra and between Toliara and Ihosy.
- They prefer grasslands, forest edges and forest clearings, weedy cultivated lands and heathlands in higher areas.

Habits

They are often found in pairs or small groups of 5–8 individuals, which run or fly to close cover when disturbed. They are mostly silent except for an occasional loud, repeated '*cou*' advertisement call and a short, throaty contact call.

Food and feeding

They forage while walking slowly, scratching the ground with their feet, picking at vegetable matter and occasionally lunging at insects. Their diet consists of seeds, berries, roots, green shoots and insects.

Breeding

Their breeding season is from March to June, possibly earlier as well. The nest is situated on the ground, well hidden in a tuft of grass or under a bush. The clutch is usually 8–15, possibly more, green-buff eggs with dark brown or black markings, and their incubation period is 18–19 days.

Status and conservation

Although they are not considered to be threatened, there is evidence of population declines, and they are sensitive to habitat degradation resulting from annual fires, which convert woody habitats to grassland. They are also heavily exploited through hunting with dogs, and are caught by trappers using rice-baited snares.

Stone Partridge
Poulette de rocher

Ptilopachus petrosus

Tetrao petrosus (Gmelin, JF, 1789), The Gambia

Stone Partridges subspecies *P. p. florentiae* in Kenya (both photos by Jacques Pitteloud)

Stone Partridges subspecies *P. p. petrosus* in Nigeria (photo by Tasso Leventis)

Stone Partridge in Nigeria (photo by Tasso Leventis)

Stone Partridge in Kenya (photo by Jacques Pitteloud)

FRANCOLINS & PARTRIDGES

Classification

The Stone Partridge is a sister species to Nahan's Partridge *P. nahani*, which in turn, are sister species to the New World quails. There are four subspecies recognised:

P. p. petrosus Gmelin, JF, 1789 from The Gambia and Senegal to Cameroon

P. p. brehmi Neumann, 1908 in southern Chad to Sudan

P. p. major Neumann, 1908 in northern Ethiopia

P. p. florentiae Ogilvie-Grant, 1900 in South Sudan and southern Ethiopia to north-eastern Democratic Republic of the Congo, northern Uganda and central Kenya

Description

- The Stone Partridge is a small, plain, dark, bantam-like partridge weighing about 190 g with a stout body, long tail usually held cocked, short neck, red facial skin and relatively short dull red legs with no spurs.
- At close range they show barred flanks and a creamy-white belly patch, which is paler in the females.
- Juveniles are similar to adults, but with distinct barring on the back, underparts, rump, tail and inner secondaries.
- Downy chicks have a blackish chestnut forehead, crown and back, and are dark brown with black speckles below.

Distribution and habitat

- They are distributed in a broad band from The Gambia and Senegal across to Sudan, South Sudan, northern Uganda and north-western Kenya, with isolated populations in Ethiopia.
- A large part of their range is in the Sudanian savanna.
- They are locally common and prefer dry rocky hillside scrubland, steep dry river courses, lightly wooded rocky areas and sandy plains with scattered vegetation.

Habits

They have a characteristic behaviour of cocking and fanning their tail as they move. Usually seen in pairs or small coveys, they scamper over and around boulders between which they roost at night. They typically scatter and run from any disturbance, seldom flushing, but fly fast and direct if flushed. Small groups often call together, with some duetting at dawn and dusk. The call starts abruptly and is a continuous, high pitched, far-carrying piping or flute-like '*oo-wirr*'*oo-wirr*'*oo-wirr* …', rising and falling in intensity, while other individuals utter soft trilled churrs. They are not dependent on fresh water.

Food and feeding

They forage mostly during the cooler parts of the day, resting in shade during midday. Their diet consists of grass and herb seeds, fruits, green leaves and buds, and insects during the breeding season.

Breeding

They are probably monogamous and breed following the onset of the rainy season in dry areas and during the dry season in wet areas. The nest is a simple scrape, sometimes lined with grass and invariably well concealed among rocks or vegetation. The clutch of 4–6 eggs are pale ochre-yellow, slightly pointed at one end, and measure 33.3 x 24.8 mm.

Status and conservation

Although considered to be a species of Least Concern by the IUCN, Stone Partridges including their eggs are used at significant levels for food, in magical rituals and for traditional medicine by local human communities in West Africa, particularly in Benin. A loss of their habitat and hunting have caused them to be locally threatened.

Currently the Stone Partridge has no protected status and is sourced primarily from wild populations for human use. Furthermore, ornithological studies that inform their population and ecological requirements are lacking in West Africa, and there is a need for further fieldwork to inform conservation action.

Nahan's Partridge
Francolin de Nahan

Ptilopachus nahani

Francolinus nahani (Dubois, AJC, 1905), Popoie, Aruwimi River, Zaire (DRC)

Nahan's Partridges among dense forest undergrowth (photos by Robert Tizard)

Classification

Nahan's Partridge is a sister species to the Stone Partridge *P. petrosus*, which in turn are sister species to the New World quails, thus the change of English common name and genus and the assignment to the family Odontophoridae.

Description

- Nahan's Partridge is small with a mottled and streaked black-and-white belly, not barred, with bare red skin around the eye and a mostly white throat.
- Their legs are red with no spurs.
- Both sexes are very similar.
- Latham's Francolin *Peliperdix lathami* has a barred belly, no red skin on the face and yellow legs.
- Juvenile Nahan's Partridge are darker than adults with grey legs.
- Downy chicks are not described.

Distribution and habitat

- This monotypic partridge is localised in north-eastern Democratic Republic of the Congo, far western and southern-central Uganda.
- They are only found in the thick understory of dense primary forest, preferring riverine or swampy areas with drier banks, up to 1 400 m.

Habits

They are most often seen in pairs, or small groups up to 8 individuals, and cock their tail similar to that of the Stone Partridge. They are very shy, preferring to remain concealed within thick undergrowth of dense primary rainforest. Their call is a rising-falling '*keh keh*' wave, similar to that of the Stone Partridge, and most often heard in the early morning. Coveys also erupt into a series of rapid growls followed by complex whistles, which grow louder and then stop abruptly.

Food and feeding

They forage by scratching on the forest floor in leaf litter. Their diet consists of seeds, bulbs, green shoots, insects and small molluscs.

Breeding

They are probably monogamous and possibly breed throughout the year. They nest in unlogged primary forest. One record of a nest was located in the hollow of a tree trunk about 1 m off the ground. The four eggs in that clutch were smooth, glossy buff to pinkish, with pale brown and purple speckles, and measured 36.0 x 26.0 mm.

Status and conservation

They are more rare than Latham's Francolin and they may be vulnerable to hunting pressure and forest degradation due to timber extraction. Their conservation status is therefore listed as Endangered (The IUCN Red List of Threatened Species v 2015-4).

PART 3
Spurfowls

SPURFOWLS

Classification

- Recent research has elevated two previous spurfowl subspecies to full species status: Cranch's Spurfowl *P. cranchii* and Schuett's Spurfowl *P. schuetti* and decreased the number of subspecies from 59 to 16 (Mandiwana-Neudani *et al.* 2019, *Ostrich* 90(2): 145–172).
- The 26 African spurfowl species are all placed in one genus *Pternistis* Wagler, 1832.
- They are grouped into four sub-groups according to diagnostic plumage or habitat preference features: bare-throated, montane, scaly or vermiculated (see Table 2).

The recent spurfowl taxonomy and phylogeny research employed a Consilience Species Concept that assessed evidence to find several congruent sources of evidence with regards to morphology, behaviour, calls, genetics and ecology. That approach tends to recognise more species than Mayr's Biological Species Concept (BSC) that places heavy evidence on inter-taxon reproductive compatibility and fewer species than Cracraft's Phylogenetic Species Concept (PSC) that merely seeks 'diagnosable' entities, placing heavy evidence on 'differences' between populations.

PREVIOUS PAGE Male Swainson's Spurfowl calling from a conspicuous perch (photo by Dayne Braine)

Table 2: Recognised spurfowl species groups (*Pternistis* spp.)

Bare-throated	Scaly
Red-necked	Ahanta
P. afer	*P. ahantensis*
Cranch's	Scaly
P. crachii	*P. squamatus*
Swainson's	Schuett's
P. swainsonii	*P. schuetti*
Yellow-necked	Grey-striped
P. leucoscepus	*P. griseostriatus*
Grey-breasted	
P. rufopictus	

Montane	Vermiculated
Erckel's	Double-spurred
P. erckelii	*P. bicalcaratus*
Djibuti	Heuglin's
P. ochropectus	*P. icterorhynchus*
Chestnut-naped	Clapperton's
P. castaneicollis	*P. clappertoni*
Black-fronted	Hilderbrandt's
P. atrifrons	*P. hilderbrandti*
Jackson's	Natal
P. jacksoni	*P. natalensis*
Handsome	Hartlaub's
P. nobilis	*P. hartlaubi*
Mount Cameroon	Harwood's
P. camerunensis	*P. harwoodi*
Swierstra's	Red-billed
P. swierstrai	*P. adspersus*
	Cape
	P. capensis

Description

- Spurfowls are generally larger than francolins weighing 340–950 g.
- They have black, red or orange legs, and the adult males have long, sharp leg spurs, generally two spurs on each lower leg, one above the other.
- They have streaked or vermiculated back feathers.

Natural history

Their distribution is restricted to sub-Saharan Africa, with only Double-spurred Spurfowl *P. bicalcaratus* extending into Morocco, North Africa, and no species occurring in Asia. They live in bushy and wooded habitats, regularly take refuge or sometimes roost overnight in trees, and prefer to run, rather than flush, to escape danger. Courting males will typically circle and approach a female with wings bowed and feathers puffed to induce her to pair with him. The hen is protective of her brood and will confront any threat with wings spread and raised. Their advertisement calls are raucous and grating or cackling, much more like those of pheasants and chickens than like francolins, and they tend not to react to tape recordings. Their chicks have a more extensive crown patch than those of the francolins and only one broad eye stripe.

Evolutionary placement

- As mentioned in the introduction to the francolins and partridges, spurfowls (and francolins) were previously classified with partridges in the tribe Perdicini within the family Phasianidae, although the only anatomical feature that supports this grouping unambiguously is that they both have 14 tail feathers.
- Until recently, all 41 species (36 African, 5 Asiatic) of spurfowls and francolins were lumped into a single genus, *Francolinus*, but divided among seven groups, at least one member of which may be found in all habitats throughout sub-Saharan Africa outside of true desert.
- However, many birders, farmers and wing-shooters divided these groups into two assemblages:
  - francolins (of the vermiculated and bare-throated spurfowl groups); and
  - partridges (making up the red-tailed, red-winged and striated francolin groups).
- Scientifically, there is no problem in naming them, because the generic name *Pternistis* (Greek for 'one who trips with the heel', referring to double spurs of males) has frequently been used for many spurfowls and is therefore available.
- Since 'partridges' is a taxonomic mosaic, 'partridge' is probably not an acceptable common name for the quail-like francolins.

Indeed, even 'the' Partridge *Perdix perdix* is grouped with the 'true' pheasants (for example *Phasianus* species), family Phasianidae.

The common name 'spurfowls' is therefore supported for this group because it has already been used for the Yellow-necked Spurfowl *Pternistis leucoscepus* of East Africa, which is a member of the Bare-throated Group and is a close relative of the Swainson's Spurfowl *P. swainsonii* and the Red-necked Spurfowl *P. afer*. Indeed, there is evidence that these species can interbreed.

The use of Pseudofrancolin as the French common name for the spurfowls is proposed.

Conservation

Another important reason to have separate common names for spurfowls and francolins is the fact that, at least some populations of various spurfowls can withstand sustainable utilisation, whereas with the exception of the Grey-winged Francolin *Scleroptila afra*, African francolins tend to occur at densities that cannot withstand sustained wing-shooting. In some regions, nesting and cover vegetation structure and forage plants are managed to sustain or increase spurfowl numbers for sustained wing-shooting. General threats that impact on the stability of spurfowl populations are the injudicious use of fire, overgrazing by livestock and forest degradation.

While 17 spurfowl species are listed as of Least Concern, only 4 of the 26 species are threatened; Mount Cameroon Spurfowl *Pternistis camerunensis* and Black-fronted Spurfowl *P. atrifrons* are listed as Endangered, Djibouti Spurfowl *P. ochropectus* is listed as Vulnerable, and Harwood's Spurfowl *P. harwoodi* is listed as Near Threatened (The IUCN Red List of Threatened Species v 2016-3).

Red-necked Spurfowl
Pseudofrancolin à gorge rouge

Pternistis afer

Tetrao afer (Statius Müller, PL, 1776), Benguella, Angola

Red-necked Spurfowl subspecies *P. a. afer* at the Kunene River, northern Namibia (photo by Ian White)

Red-necked Spurfowl subspecies *P. a. afer* at the Kunene River, northern Namibia (photo by Per Holmen)

Red-necked Spurfowl subspecies *P. a. castaneiventer* in the East Cape Province, South Africa (photo by Maans Booysen)

Red-necked Spurfowl subspecies *P. a. castaneiventer* in the Western Cape Province, South Africa (photo by Davide Gaglio)

LEFT Red-necked Spurfowl subspecies *P. a. humboldtii* at Gorongoza, Mozambique (photo by Maans Booysen)

RIGHT Black faced form of subspecies *P. a. humboldtii* in the Mikumi National Park, Tanzania (photo by Per Holmen)

Hybrid zone subspecies *P. a. humboldtii* in the Tarangire National Park, Tanzania (photo by Per Holmen)

Classification

They are most closely related to Cranch's Spurfowl *P. cranchii* and thereafter to Yellow-necked Spurfowl *P. leucoscepus*, Grey-breasted Spurfowl *P. rufopictus*, and Swainson's Spurfowl *P. swainsonii*, which all hybridise readily where zones of sympatric overlap occur.

Such a hybrid with Swainson's Spurfowl in north-eastern Zimbabwe was incorrectly described as a new 'species' *P. cooperi* during the 1940s.

With widespread geographical variation, as many as 20 subspecies have previously been described, but the latest suggestion is that three subspecies should be recognised:

P. a. afer Statius Müller, PL, 1776 in southern Angola and northern Namibia;

P. a. castaneiventer Gunning & Roberts, 1911 disjointly in southern Mozambique, north-eastern lowveld and south-eastern South Africa;

P. a. humboldtii Peters, 1854 from eastern South Africa and Zimbabwe through Mozambique, north-eastern Zambia to Tanzania and southern Kenya.

The previous Red-necked Spurfowl subspecies *P. a. cranchii* has been elevated to full species status: Cranch's Spurfowl *P. cranchii* Mandiwana-Neudani *et al.* 2019, *Ostrich* 90(2): 145–172.

Description

- They have bare red skin on the throat and around the eyes, as well as red legs and bill.
- In contrast to Cranch's Spurfowl, they have unvermiculated upperparts and are strongly patterned black and white on the face and underparts.
- On the crown and neck, the feathers may be brown with black streaks, or black with white, elongated markings.
- The throat feathers are mainly white, with chestnut and black markings along the shaft and on the outer edge.
- The breast and flank feathers are dark brown to black, with single, narrow, white, longitudinal streaks on either side of the shaft.
- *P. a. afer* has a white supercilium and white gular patches and broad black on white streaking on its flanks and underparts.
- *P. a. castaneiventer* has a relatively plain brown head with white and black streaking on the breast and flanks.
- *P. a. humboldtii* has a white face with a white jaw-beard and distinct black belly patch, except in the north in inland Tanzania, Malawi and eastern Zambia where synonymised '*melanogaster*' and '*loangwae*' have a black face.

- Males have long spurs, sometimes two on each leg.
- Juveniles resemble adults but have duller brown plumage and a white throat.
- The underparts are barred faintly with black and white.
- Downy chicks are rufous-brown above, with dark brown stripes on the crown and back.
- The sides of the head are buff, with a black stripe through the eye and extending downwards to the breast.
- The throat is buff, grading to yellowish-buff on the belly, flecked with dull black.

Distribution and habitat

- They occur from coastal Kenya in the north through south-eastern Tanzania, north-eastern Zambia, Malawi down to eastern Zimbabwe, Mozambique and South Africa with the nominate race along the western Cunene River in southern Angola and northern Namibia.
- The hybrid zone in Zambia is a narrow strip along the Luangwa Valley with Cranch's Spurfowl to the west and Red-necked Spurfowl (*P. a. humboldtii*) in the east.
- Those two taxa also meet at the Mikumi National Park in east-central Tanzania.
- They prefer dense cover and moist habitats, most frequently occurring on the edges of evergreen forests, or in riparian thickets or marsh edges.

Habits

They occur in pairs or small groups of 3–6 individuals. They are shy and reluctant to fly when disturbed, preferring to run into dense cover. When flushed, they fly fast and often perch in a tree. At night, they roost in trees. Although territorial and apparently seasonally monogamous, males that have an incubating hen will court other females that enter his territory. Males do not assist with care of their offspring. They are easily overlooked and their harsh '*krr krr krr korWA, korWA, korWA*' call, usually uttered at dawn and dusk, is similar to but more regular in volume than that of Swainson's Spurfowl.

Food and feeding

The diet consists primarily of small tubers, bulbs, roots, seeds, fruits and other vegetable material during the winter, and insects, termites and molluscs such as snails during the summer. They will also take waste commercial grains such as maize, sorghum and cereals.

Breeding

Their breeding season is variable from April–August in KwaZulu-Natal and the Eastern Cape, January–July (mainly April), November–December (mainly December) in Zimbabwe, and January–September (mainly February–June) in Malawi. The nest, lined with grass and feathers, is constructed by the female, and is often placed in dense grass at the base of a tree or bush. The clutch of 3–7, rounded to oval, creamy-white or creamy-brown, thick-shelled eggs measure 45.0 x 35.9 mm. Incubation lasts 23 days. Chicks can fly at 10 days and are almost fully grown at 3–4 months.

Status and conservation

They are impacted by the degradation and removal of forest and woodland edge by burning, heavy grazing and extensive cultivation. Numbers have reportedly declined in north-eastern Zimbabwe. They also respond to droughts by moving from a dry area to moister sites.

Cranch's Spurfowl
Pseudofrancolin de Cranch

Pternistis cranchii

Tetrao afer (Statius Müller, PL, 1776), subspecies cranchii (Leach, 1818)

P. afer cranchii (Leach, 1818), in western Congo eastward to East Africa and south to northern and eastern Angola, north-eastern Zambia, northern Malawi and western Tanzania

LEFT Male Cranch's Spurfowl in the Lake Mburo National Park, Uganda (photo by Cliff Dorse)

RIGHT Female Cranch's Spurfowl in the Kafue National Park, Zambia (photo by Salim Lee)

Cranch's Spurfowls in the Vwaza Marsh Wildlife Reserve, northern Malawi (photo by Maans Booysen)

Juvenile Cranch's Spur in the Masai Mara National Reserve, Kenya (photo by Washington Wachira)

Classification

Recently elevated from Red-necked Spurfowl *P. afer cranchii* Mandiwana-Neudani *et al.* 2019, *Ostrich* 90(2): 145–172.

They are a sister species to Red-necked Spurfowl *P. afer* and Grey-breasted Spurfowl *P. rufopictus.*

P. cranchii are reported to hybridise with *P. a. humboldtii* in a narrow strip in eastern Zambia east of the Langwa River and with *P. a. afer* in southern Angola.

Cranch's Spurfowl are monotypic with no subspecies recognised.

Previous putative subspecies and 'hybrid' forms *cunenensis, nyanzae, punctulatus, mackenziei, harterti, intercedens, benguellensis, itigi* and *boehmi* have minimal genetic divergence and are synonymised with *P. cranchii*.

Description

- Cranch's Spurfowl is differentiated from Yellow-necked Spurfowl *P. leucoscepus* and Grey-breasted Spurfowl *P. rufopictus* by being generally darker and by preferring more moist habitats.
- They are characterised by having no white on the head, but rather a black and grey facial pattern.
- The underparts are brown, heavily and finely vermiculated with grey with broad rufous streaks.
- Their belly feathers are plain grey-brown with buff central streaks vermiculated with blackish grey and margined with broad chestnut streaks (the degree of chestnut colour varies geographically).
- Populations from the Ruzizi Valley, north of Lake Tanganyika, are darker overall and the streaking on the abdomen is maroon rather than chestnut.
- The bare facial skin, bill, legs and feet are red.
- They are sexually monomorphic in plumage, although females may have less bare red skin on the face and throat.
- Males have sharp leg spurs.
- Juveniles resemble adults but have duller brown plumage and dark, not red, bills.
- Their underparts are buffy, with faint black barring.
- Downy chicks are rufous-brown above, with dark brown stripes on the crown and back.
- The sides of the head are buff with a black stripe through the eye and extending downwards to the breast.

Distribution and habitat

- They have highly geographically variable, but not taxonomically distinct populations.
- They are widely distributed from the southern Democratic Republic of the Congo, northern and eastern Angola, north-western and central Zambia, northern Malawi, western Tanzania, Rwanda, Burundi, south-western Uganda and the shores of Lake Victoria.
- The hybrid zone in Zambia is a narrow strip along the Luangwa Valley with Cranch's Spurfowl to the west and Red-necked Spurfowl (*P. a. humboldtii*) in the east.
- Those two taxa also meet in a band between the Tarangire and Mikumi National Parks in east-central Tanzania.
- They inhabit rough broken grassy plains and grassland savanna with dense woody patches and riparian strips with good bush cover, including tall grassland with *Acacia gerrardii* and *A. seyal*, and in *Brachystegia–Combretum–Terminalia* woodlands.
- They are fairly tolerant of human occupation and will venture into relatively open areas and agricultural lands to feed, particularly where dense escape cover is nearby.

Habits

They occur singularly, in pairs or small family groups of up to 8 individuals. They are less shy than Red-necked Spurfowls but also reluctant to fly when disturbed, preferring to run into dense cover. When flushed they will land in trees or bushes where they also roost overnight. Their call is a harsh rhythmical *ker-ker-kek ... kekekek* which increases before fading away and is similar to that of the Yellow-necked and Grey-breasted Spurfowls. They often call from a prominent perch and the frequency of calling is greatest approaching the breeding season but drops off once incubation starts.

Food and feeding

Their diet consisting of small tubers, bulbs, roots and seeds during the dry season and invertebrates, including insects and their larvae, termites and ticks, and grass shoots in the wet season. They will also take advantage of fallen waste grain. They are often seen near standing water where they drink.

Breeding

Breeding can occur during most months of the year but is mostly during the rainy season. Breeding in Angola is from March–June, November–August (mainly February–May) in Zambia, with peaks in December–January in Uganda and in February–April in Tanzania. The nest is a shallow hollow in dense cover lined by the female with grass, leaves and feathers. The clutch is 3–6 oval plain cream thick-shelled eggs measuring

43.4 x 33.9 mm with some racial variation in size. Incubation by the hen lasts for 23 days with the eggs hatching synchronously.

Status and conservation

There is no evidence that the distribution of this species has changed significantly in recent times. Potential threats are changes in woodland cover as a result of too frequent fires, continuous grazing by livestock and cultivation for crops. Generally reported to disappear from heavily populated cultivated areas.

Swainson's Spurfowl
Pseudofrancolin de Swainson

Pternistis swainsonii

Perdix Swainsonii (Smith, A, 1836), Kurrichane (Zeerust), North West Province, South Africa

Male Swainson's Spurfowl on a conspicuous territorial perch (photo by Ian White)

Female Swainson's Spurfowl with two juvenile chicks (photo by Hugh Chittenden)

ABOVE Male Swainson's Spurfowl calling from a prominent perch (photo by Andre Botha)

BOTTOM RIGHT Female Swainson's Spurfowl (photo by Ian White)

GAMEBIRDS

Male Swainson's Spurfowl (photo by Ian White)

Male Swainson's Spurfowl (photo by Andre Botha)

Calling Swainson's Spurfowl (photo by Hugh Chittenden)

Classification

They are most closely related to Cranch's Spurfowl *P. cranchii*, Red-necked Spurfowl *P. afer*, Grey-breasted Spurfowl *P. rufopictus*, and Yellow-necked Spurfowl *P. leucoscepus*.

A new 'species', *P. cooperi*, described during the 1940s was later correctly identified as a hybrid with Red-necked Spurfowl.

Swainson's Spurfowl is monotypic with no subspecies recognised.

The putative subspecies *P. s. lundazi* White, CMN, 1947 in north-western Zimbabwe to southern Mozambique is synonymised with *P. swainsonii*.

Description

- They are sexually dimorphic in size, dark brown overall, and have bare red skin on the throat and around the eyes, but have black legs and upper bill.
- They lack any distinct white, rufous or grey patterning on the breast and flanks.
- Males have large black leg spurs.
- Juveniles resemble the adults, but are paler and duller overall and the throat has white feathers.
- The belly is white, finely barred with black.
- Downy chicks are dark brown above, with darker streaks on the crown and back.
- The sides of the head are buffy, with a single black eye stripe.

Distribution and habitat

- They occur in southern Africa, extending into southern and central Zambia.
- They have expanded their range into maize-growing areas in KwaZulu-Natal, Mpumalanga, Lesotho and parts of Zimbabwe, where they exploit crops and the associated weeds and introduced alien trees.
- At least part of this range expansion, particularly into KwaZulu-Natal, the Limpopo Province and Eastern Cape, has been assisted by deliberate introductions.
- They are common in most savannas and tall grasslands adjacent to cultivation and water, except in the arid western South Africa and Namibia.

Habits

They occur in pairs and small groups. Although bold, they are wary as a rule. During the morning and late afternoon, they venture from cover into open ground to forage and dust-bathe. In the heat of the day they rest in the shade of scrub and brush. They feed at night in open lands during full moon, particularly following hot days. Although fond of cultivated lands, they favour weedy land edges and contour strips when these are adjacent to tall grass and trees. They also favour river banks and rank growth of sponges and marsh edges. When disturbed, they run into cover or flush and fly to the closest cover. A flushed bird will fly into grass or scrub cover, from which it is difficult to re-flush, or will perch in a tree. They roost overnight in low trees and bushes, and sometimes remain perched on wet mornings. The call is a harsh '*krrraa, krrraa, krrraa*', sometimes rendered as '*kwahli, kwahli*', repeated several times and descending in pitch and volume towards the end. It is similar to that of the Red-necked Spurfowl, whose call is more even in pitch and volume. Calling is most frequent at dawn and dusk, and calling males perch conspicuously on a termite mound, fence post or tree stump. They also have an extended high-pitched mewing contact call.

Food and feeding

The winter diet consists of the seeds of grass and agricultural weeds, bulbs, tubers, roots and berries. In summer they eat termites, worms, beetles and grasshoppers, ticks, spiders and small molluscs. They also exploit waste grains such as maize, sorghum, barley and cereals. They are accused of digging out crop seedlings. Although the amount of pioneer weed and grass seeds and seedlings consumed, along with the high intake of agricultural pest invertebrates ingested, make up for any perceived damage that they may cause. Prior to roosting, groups move to water to drink. However, water does not limit their distribution, with populations flourishing in semi-arid environments where watering points are few and well out of reach of the majority of the birds.

Breeding

Their extended breeding season peaks during February–May. They are monogamous and territorial while breeding. Their nest is a shallow bowl lined with grass and leaves, usually concealed within dense cover of weeds or shrubby vegetation. They will also nest among crops or in old lands. The clutch of 4–6, sometimes up to 12, rounded to oval pinkish-cream or buff eggs measure 43.9 x 35.7 mm. Incubation, by the female only, starts after the clutch is complete and lasts 21–24 days. Chicks can flutter-fly at 14 days and are almost adult size at 3 months.

Status and conservation

They are tolerant of human-transformed habitats, increasing population sizes to levels above those of natural populations in parts of Zimbabwe, Gauteng, Limpopo, KwaZulu-Natal and the Northern Cape, where they can support commercial wing-shooting. Habitats are often modified, by adding water points and plants suitable for food and cover, especially along the interface between croplands and natural habitats, to encourage the growth of their populations. However, repeated hunting on the same property within one season can reduce populations to levels that cannot be hunted sustainably. Hunting of this species should also be delayed until August to allow for completed breeding and full development of the chicks.

Yellow-necked Spurfowl
Pseudofrancolin à cou jaune
Pternistis leucoscepus

Francolinus leucoscepus (Gray, GR, 1867), Abyssinia, 'Ethiopia' probably Eritrea.

Yellow-necked Spurfowl
(photo by Lorenzo Barelli)

Yellow-necked Spurfowl from Kenya
(photo by Tasso Leventis)

Yellow-necked Spurfowl from Kenya
(photo by Tasso Leventis)

GAMEBIRDS

Female Yellow-necked Spurfowl with a brood of chicks from Tarangire National Park, Tanzania (photo by Ron Eggert)

Female Yellow-necked Spurfowl from Kenya (photo by Jacques Pitteloud)

Female Yellow-necked Spurfowl from Tarangire National Park, Tanzania (photo by Sergey Dereliev)

Classification

First described by Cretzschmar (in Ruppell 1826, p.44) under the name *Perdix rubricollis*. But this name was preoccupied by a species of hill partridge, eventuating in the later name change.

Ruppell's 'Ethiopian' expedition from which this taxon was described was apparently aborted and never made it beyond Massawa, Eritrea.

The Yellow-necked Spurfowl is most closely related to Cranch's Spurfowl *P. cranchii*, although they are also sister to Red-necked Spurfowl *P. afer*, Grey-breasted Spurfowl *P. rufopictus* and Swainson's Spurfowl *P. swainsonii*.

There are two subspecies recognised:

P. l. leucoscepus Gray, 1867 nominate race in Eritrea and far northern Ethiopia;

P. l. infuscatus Cabanis, 1868 the southern race in East Africa, type locality Lake Jipe on the Kenya/Tanzania border.

Other putative subspecies (*holtemülleri, keniensis, kilimensis, tokora, muhamed-ben-abdullah*) are synonymised with *P. l. infuscatus*.

They are known to hybridise with Grey-breasted Spurfowl.

Description

- They are the most morphologically and ecologically differentiated Bare-throated Group species.
- They are dark brown with a characteristic bright yellow bare-skin throat, red bare-skin face and black bill and legs.
- The upper back plumage is dark brown with white shaft streaks and the underparts are streaked with white and chestnut with narrow white edges and a triangular white patch at the tip, tapering up the shaft.
- *P. l. infuscatus* differs in having more chestnut than white on the underparts in contrast with the dominant white over chestnut in the nominate *P. l. leucoscepus*.
- In flight they have a conspicuous whitish buff patch in the wing primaries.
- Juveniles are less well marked with a dull yellow throat.
- Downy chicks have a dark brown forehead, a light brown crown with a dark brown crown stripe and a single eye stripe from behind the eye to the nape.
- Their back is dark brown with two buff and brown stripes on each side.

Distribution and habitat

- They are distributed across southern and northern Somalia, west-central Ethiopia,

south-eastern South Sudan, far north-eastern Uganda, most of Kenya and northern Tanzania (*P. l. infuscatus*) with the *P. l. leucoscepus* population in eastern Eritrea and far northern Ethiopia.
- Whether the two subspecies are contiguous or allopatric needs further confirmation.
- Their preferred habitats are arid open savanna, subdesert scrub and adjacent cultivated lands.
- They generally avoid tall grass.

Habits

They are usually seen in pairs or small groups but will congregate at sites with good food availability. They roost overnight in low trees, emerge to forage and dust-bathe during the early morning, and rest in scrub shade for most of the rest of the day. When disturbed, they prefer to run into cover, but when flushed will often fly to perch in a tree. Their advertisement call is similar sounding to that of the Grey-breasted Spurfowl but is slower. They often call from a conspicuous, elevated perch. The call is a repeated raucous descending '*kerak*' or '*ko-warrrk*, mostly at dawn and dusk.

Food and feeding

Most foraging is done during the early morning. Their diet consists mainly of corms and tubers, including those of the sedge *Cyperus rotundus*, the fruits and seeds of herbs and grasses, plants parts and insects – mostly termites. They will also eat waist grains in cultivated lands. A common foraging behaviour is to scratch through rhinoceros (Rhinocerotidae) and African Elephant *Loxodonata africana* dung for undigested seeds, insects and their larvae.

Breeding

They are monogamous, breeding at any time of the year, but mostly during the first half of the year. The nest is a scrape in the ground, usually unlined. The clutch of 3–8, usually 5, eggs are oval with a slight point and are cream to pale buff with darker speckles and white pore marks, and measure 45.2-x-35.5 mm. Incubation is for 18–20 days, and chicks can fly short distances at two weeks.

Status and conservation

Although previously abundant throughout most of their range, numbers have declined dramatically where human populations have increased. Noose snaring is a common technique for hunting of this species, particularly along fence lines adjacent to cultivated lands.

Grey-breasted Spurfowl
Pseudofrancolin à poitrine grise
Pternistis rufopictus

Pternistis rufopictus (Reichenow, 1887), Wembere Steppe, Tanzania

ABOVE AND LEFT Male Grey-breasted Spurfowls from Serengeti National Park, Tanzania (photos by Adam Riley above & Dalton Gibbs left)

Classification

They are most closely related to Cranch's Spurfowl *P. crachii* and Red-necked Spurfowl *P. afer*, followed by Yellow-necked Spurfowl *P. leucoscepus* with which they are reported to hybridise, and Swainson's Spurfowl *P. swainsonii*.

They are monotypic with no subspecies recognised.

Their evolutionary origin may be from hybridisation between the various taxa of the bare-throated spurfowl group.

Description

- The Grey-breasted Spurfowl is a medium-sized dark brown spurfowl (average male mass 848 g, average female mass 588 g) with broad chestnut streaks on their back.
- The upper back plumage is grey-brown with dark vermiculations and dark shaft streaks, grading posteriorly to black, white and chestnut streaking.
- The eye-stripe and sides of the face are black and white with a white chin-stripe on either side of the bare throat.
- The breast is grey with black shaft streaks and the belly is streaked black and white with narrow central black streaks and rufous chestnut margins.
- They differ from Yellow-necked, Cranch's and Red-necked Spurfowls by having an orange bill, dark grey-brown legs, orange-pink skin on the throat and around the eye, and white moustachial stripes.
- In flight, they show pale bases to the primary feathers.
- Juveniles are similar in appearance to adults, but their upperparts are grey-black with white central shaft streaks and barring and grey-buff margins.
- Downy chicks have a dark crown with rufous-brown margins and two dark brown eye-stripes above and below the eye.

Distribution and habitat

- They are endemic to the dry plains, thickets and savannas from the south-eastern shores of Lake Victoria to the Wembere River in north-western Tanzania.
- They are relatively common in the ecotones of grasslands, Umbrella Thorn *Vachellia tortilis* scrub and woodlands, and riverine thickets from the southern Serengeti west to Mwanza.

Habits

They usually occur in territorial pairs and small coveys of 5–7 individuals but may congregate into comparatively large groups in their favoured feeding areas. They often venture into open grasslands at dawn and dusk. They call mostly at dawn and dusk, usually from an elevated mound or stump, particularly at the start of the rainy season. Their crowing call '*ka-waaaark, ka-waaaark, ka-waarrrk*' or '*koarrrk-koarrrk-karrkkrrk-krrk-krr*' descending towards the end is very similar to that of the Yellow-necked Spurfowl but is much faster. Their alarm call when flushed is a high-pitched cackle.

Food and feeding

Their diet consists mainly of sedge *Cyperus* spp. corms and tubers, grass and weed seeds and insects, including grasshoppers and termites. They will also eat waste cereal grain and legume seeds and the seeds of crop weeds in scattered cultivated lands.

Breeding

They are monogamous, breeding mostly from February–April, but can be as late as July. The nest is a scrape amongst long grass, often lined with grass and feathers. The clutch of 4–5 buff or pale brown eggs with chalky white pore spots measure 43.4 x 35.2 mm.

Status and conservation

Although still relatively common, they have been impacted by habitat degradation and transformation by extensive crop agriculture and overgrazing.

Erckel's Spurfowl
Pseudofrancolin d'Erckel

Pternistis erckelii

Perdix erckelii (Rüppell, 1835), Taranta Mountains, Ethiopia

ABOVE Female Erckel's Spurfowl (photo by Marvin Hyett)

RIGHT Male Erckel's Spurfowl (photo by Dick Daniels)

Classification

They are most closely related to their sister species the Djibouti Spurfowl *P. ochropectus* and thereafter to Chestnut-naped *P. castaneicollis* and Black-fronted *P. atrifrons* Spurfowls.

They are a monotypic spurfowl with no subspecies recognised.

The putative subspecies '*pentoni*' in the Red Sea Hills is regarded as a local variant and is synonymised with *P. erckelii*.

Description

- The Erckel's Spurfowl is a large, grey and chestnut striped spurfowl with a striking head pattern, including black forehead and supercilium, chestnut crown, grey ear coverts and a white throat.
- The lower neck is grey like the upper belly but has greyish brown margins and a thin central buff streak, whereas the upper belly feathers have central greyish-black streaks.
- The lower belly feathers have a broad buff central streak constricted in the middle and expanded distally into a tear drop, margined with rufous.
- They have no bare facial skin and have a black bill and yellowish legs.
- They are more olive-brown above than Chestnut-naped, Black-fronted and Djibouti Spurfowls.
- Where they are sympatric with Clapperton's Spurfowl *P. clappertoni*, they are distinguished by the dark face and bare red skin around the eye, lacking an eye-stripe.
- Females are similar in appearance but smaller than males.
- Juveniles are paler grey above with quail-like streaks and bars on the back.
- Downy chicks have a dark stripe from the forehead down the centre of the crown.
- The sides of the head have a buff and black moustachial stripe, through the eye down the side of the neck.
- The upper body is dark brown and black with a buff lateral stripe on each side.

Distribution and habitat

- They occur in the highlands of central and northern Ethiopia and Eritria north and west of the Rift Valley, with another small population in the Red Sea Province of north-eastern Sudan.
- They are locally common between 2 000–3 500m above sea level in giant heath *Erica arborea*, on scrub-covered hill slopes and cliffs, and in forest edges and remnants.
- They will venture out of forests for short forays into adjacent heath and grassland.

Habits

They are shy and sedentary and more often heard than seen. They mostly occur in pairs or small groups of up to 8 individuals which largely remain within dense cover. When disturbed they will run, often uphill, for cover or flush and fly downhill. They forage during the early morning within scrub and forest edges, sometimes entering cultivated lands to feed on waste grain. They are generally quiet, calling occasionally from a conspicuous perch at dawn and dusk. Their call is an extended harsh cackling crow '*errk-erkk-erk-erk-rkkuk-kuk-ku*', ending in a descending chuckle-like rattle.

Food and feeding

They often forage on sheer cliffs by flying from ledge to ledge. Their diet consists of grass seeds and shoots, berries and seeds of shrubs and herbs, and some fallen grain and insects. They drink in the late afternoon before roosting overnight in a tree.

Breeding

They are monogamous, breeding mostly during the rainy months of April and May in Sudan, and September–November in Ethiopia. Their nest is a typical scrape on the ground. The clutch of 4–10 hard-shelled dirty white to pale brown eggs measure 46.2 x 36.5 mm. Their incubation biology is not known.

Status and conservation

They are heavily impacted by widespread deforestation, particularly resulting in reduced populations in northern Ethiopia.

Djibouti Spurfowl
Pseudofrancolin des Somalis
Pternistis ochropectus

Francolinus ochropectus (Dorst & Jouanin, 1952), Plateau du Day, near Tadjoura, Djibouti

Djibouti Spurfowl
(photo by Callan Cohen)

Djibouti Spurfowls
(photos by Nik Borrow)

Classification

They are most closely related to Erckel's Spurfowl *P. erckelii*, followed by Chestnut-naped Spurfowl *P. castaneicollis* and Black-fronted Spurfowl *P. atrifrons*.

It is a monotypic species with no subspecies recognised.

Description

- The Djibouti Spurfowl, also sometimes known as the Ochre-breasted Spurfowl, resembles a dark drab Erckel's Spurfowl, but it has a black face with a short white supercilium behind the eye, and their ranges do not overlap.
- They are similar in appearance to Chestnut-naped Spurfowl and Black-fronted Spurfowl, but do not occur in the same landscape as those species.
- Females closely resemble males but have a slightly more rufous tail.
- Juveniles are similar in appearance to adults with more buff and grey barring than streaking.
- Downy chicks are undescribed.

Distribution and habitat

- They are endemic to the dense evergreen forests of Djibouti where they are confined to the small area around Forêt du Day and the nearby Mabla Mountains, between 700 and 1 800m above sea level.
- They are mostly found in the undergrowth of juniper *Juniperus procera* forests and adjacent wadis, as well as in dry secondary woodlands and river courses.

Habits

They occur in pairs and family groups of 5–9 individuals that forage during the early morning and spend much of the day roosting in dense trees where they also roost overnight. They are shy and more often heard than seen. Their call is a loud accelerating '*Erk-erk-ka-ka-krrrr*' rattle, similar to that of the Erckel's Spurfowl. Foraging individuals also have a soft contact cluckle.

Food and feeding

When foraging, they search for food by raking over the ground, including in areas which have been disturbed by warthogs *Phacochoerus africanus*. Their diet consists mainly of berries, grass and other seeds, figs and termites.

Breeding

They breed in dense, lush wadi vegetation with palms and ferns at high altitudes. Breeding is during December–February. The only nest discovered to date was a shallow depression lined with grass on a mountain ledge. Their clutch is 5–7 eggs. Little more is known about their breeding biology.

Status and conservation

They are Vulnerable (The IUCN Red List of Threatened Species v 2016-3), and listed on CITES Appendix II, although Djibouti is not a signatory nation. With fewer than 500 individuals estimated in the population, they are threatened by habitat destruction due to deforestation for firewood, overgrazing by domestic livestock, including cattle, camels and goats, and possible climate change, droughts and fungal disease.

Chestnut-naped Spurfowl
Pseudofrancolin à cou roux
Pternistis castaneicollis

Francolinus castoneicollis (Salvadori, 1888), Lake Ciar-Ciar (= Chercher), Shoa (Hararghe), Ethiopia

ABOVE A pair of Chestnut-naped Spurfowls in the Bale Mountains, Ethiopia (photo by Maans Booysen)

LEFT Male Chestnut-naped Spurfowl (photo by Otto Schmidt)

Classification

Black-fronted Spurfowl *P. atrifrons* was recently split from Chestnut-naped Spurfowl, and they together form the sister group to a clade comprising Erckel's Spurfowl *P. erckelii* and Djibouti Spurfowl *P. ochropectus*.

Chestnut-naped Spurfowl is regarded as monotypic with no subspecies recognised.

The putative subspecies *P. c. bottega* and *P. c. ogoensis* are morphologically clinal variants, while *P. c. gofanus* and *P. c. kaffanus* are clinally less well defined. All four are synonymised with *P. castaneicollis*.

Description

- The Chestnut-naped Spurfowl is a large richly coloured spurfowl with conspicuous chestnut-coloured flanks and wing coverts.
- Black-fronted Spurfowl *P. atrifrons* are confined to the Mega region of southern Ethiopia, are smaller and paler with no chestnut on the flanks or neck and have a diagnostic single bald yellow skin-patch just above the ear.
- They are the same size as the Erkel's Spurfowl but are more brightly coloured with a chestnut head and neck, and bright red bill and legs.
- They lack the bare red face of the Harwood's Spurfowl *P. harwoodi* and differ further by having an overall rusty neck, breast and cap.
- Females are similar in appearance to males but are smaller.
- Juveniles are duller, have a black and buff barred and vermiculated rump and tail.
- Downy chicks are undescribed.

Distribution and habitat

- They are common to abundant above 2 800m above sea level in far northern Somalia through south-central Ethiopia.
- Their preferred habitats in Ethiopia are montane heath moorlands, juniper forests, *Hagenia-Hypericum* forests with rank moist undercover, forest glades and edges and *Erica* scrub.
- In Somalia, they inhabit arid juniper forests at lower altitudes 1 200–2 250m above sea level.

Habits

They generally occur in small groups of 4–8 individuals or pairs and emerge from cover to feed, particularly during wet weather. Although they are relatively tame, when disturbed they will flush in open cover, otherwise they will retreat to dense cover where they will remain. Where vegetation is sufficiently tall, they will roost overnight on elevated perches, but will also roost near or on the ground in *Erica* scrub. They call from dense cover, mostly during the early morning and evening, but will also call throughout the day. Their call is a noisy '*kek kek kek keraak*' crowing.

Food and feeding

They forage in small groups during the morning and evening, but will feed throughout the day, particularly during overcast wet weather. Their diet consists of seeds and insects, including termites. They seldom feed in croplands but will occasionally pick up waste grain such as barley.

Breeding

They are monogamous and breed mostly during the drier months, January–March and October–December in Ethiopia and from May–December in Somalia. The nest is a scrape under a bush or within dense cover. The clutch of 5–6 smooth round cream-coloured eggs measure 46.8 x 36.8 mm. Their incubation biology is unknown.

Status and conservation

Although they are easily snared in dense cover, they are relatively tame in some areas and are not heavily utilised.

Black-fronted Spurfowl
Pseudofrancolin à front noir
Pternistis atrifrons

Pternistis (castaneicollis) atrifrons (Conover, 1930), Boran (Mega), Ethiopia

Male Black-fronted Spurfowl (photo by Kai Gedeon)

LEFT Male Black-fronted Spurfowl in the Mega area, southern Ethiopia (photo by Nik Borrow)

RIGHT Black-fronted Spurfowl showing the absence of any chestnut on the flank and neck feathers (photo by Kai Gedeon)

Classification

During an expedition in 1929 to Ethiopia, a 'francolin' was collected from the Mega Mountains for the Field Museum Chicago which was described as a new species, the Black-fronted (or Ethiopian) Francolin.

Although later treated as a subspecies of the Chestnut-naped Francolin (Spurfowl) *P. castaneicollis*, this was regularly challenged.

Expeditions to this area during 2012 and 2013 by Till Töpfer and others (see Töpfer *et al.* in the Bibliography) concluded that the separate taxonomic status of *P. atrifrons* is warranted.

Most of the information in this species account is gleaned from their findings.

With Chesnut-naped Spurfowl, they form the sister group to a clade comprising Erckel's Spurfowl *P. erckelii* and Djibouti Spurfowl *P. ochropectus*.

Black-fronted Spurfowl is monotypic with no subspecies recognised.

Description

- They are smaller and paler than Chestnut-naped Spurfowl with much reduced or no chestnut-coloured flanks or chestnut neck feathers, and lack the red face of Clapperton's Spurfowl *P. clappertoni*.
- Males have bold black and buff scaly upperparts and a nearly plain off-white throat, breast and underparts.
- The characteristic black forehead and supercilium is separated by an ill-defined white line from the greyish-brown crown.
- The bill is coral-red and the legs orange-red with two equal-sized spurs.
- The eye-rings are yellowish with a diagnostic single bald yellow skin-patch just above the ear.
- Females are slightly smaller than males with no leg spurs, and have a smaller head with a weaker bill, much less black forehead and lack the pronounced black supercilium.
- Juveniles have a more streaky appearance with prominent whitish shaft streaks on the feathers of the lower neck and upper back and a bluish skin-patch above the ear, bluish eye-ring and orange legs.

Distribution and habitat

- This species is restricted to the moist mountainous areas of the Mega region in southern Ethiopia, and far northern Kenya.
- They occur in semi-open woodland with extensive low shrubs, interspersed by taller

trees and bushes and open rocky and grazed patches between 1 480 and 2 223m above sea level.
- Although previously reported to inhabit four different forest habitats (*Hagenia* forests, Highland bamboo *Arundinaria*, Juniper-*Podocarpus* forest and Olive-*Podocarpus*-Juniper forest), many of these habitats have been severely transformed, such that they are now largely found in scrubby woodland where juniper trees are largely missing.

Habits

They generally occur in small groups or pairs which are shy and tend to hide in low vegetation when approached. They prefer to escape on foot and fly only relatively short distances before landing on the ground, not in trees or bushes. Their advertisement call, similar sounding to that of the Chestnut-naped Spurfowl, is a harshly grating and fairly noisy cackle lasting about three seconds and consisting of four elements with pauses of about two seconds. This call is usually uttered from the ground, mostly at dawn and later during the day.

Food and feeding

Their diet includes seeds and insects, similar to that of other spurfowl inhabiting scrubby habits in mountainous terrain.

Breeding

The breeding behavior is probably very similar to that of the Chestnut-naped Spurfowl. Evidence suggests that the timing of breeding is closely aligned with the primary rainy season from October to March. The nest is a scrape concealed under a bush or in undergrowth, and the clutch is probably 5 or 6 eggs.

Status and conservation

Their range may be smaller and more fragmented than previously thought, making localised populations highly threatened and listed as Endangered (The IUCN Red List of Threatened Species v 2016-3). Their habitats may already be degraded, resulting mainly from grazing pressure, agricultural expansion, and commercial firewood and timber exploitation. Hunting, largely by young people using nooses for trapping, appears to be the main direct threat to these isolated populations. They should probably be considered an endangered range-restricted species like the Djibouti Spurfowl.

Jackson's Spurfowl
Pseudofrancolin de Jackson

Pternistis jacksoni

Francolinus jacksoni (Ogilvie-Grant, 1891), Kikuyu, Kenya

Jackson's Spurfowl (photo by Lorenzo Barelli)

Jackson's Spurfowl in the Mount Kenya National Park, Kenya (photo by Per Holmen)

Juvenile Jackson's Spurfowl (photo by Jacques Pitteloud)

Classification

Although considered with the montane spurfowl group, they are most closely related to the Grey-striped Spurfowl *P. griseostriatus* of the Scaly Group.

Their closest Montane Group relative is the Swierstra's Spurfowl *P. swierstrai*.

They are a monotypic spurfowl with no subspecies recognised.

The subspecies '*pollenorum*' from Mount Kenya is not supported.

Description

- The Jackson's Spurfowl is a large rufous spurfowl with red legs and bill, and narrow red eye-rings.
- They are larger and more rufous than the Scaly Spurfowl *P. squamatus*.
- Males weigh over 1 kg.
- They have a buff throat and greyish lower neck with the upper part of the lower neck being similarly patterned to the rest of the belly.
- The lower neck feathers are chestnut-coloured edged with buffish to white, but the degree of chestnut and buff and white varies.
- They have white-streaked chestnut underparts.
- Females are similar in appearance to males but are smaller.
- Juveniles are duller, with dark barring above and on the belly.
- Downy chicks are undescribed.

Distribution and habitat

- They are endemic to the montane forests and Afro-alpine zone of the western and central Kenyan mountains, especially in the Aberdare range, Mount Kenya, the Mau Escarpment and Cherangani Mountains, as well as marginally into Uganda.
- They are locally common in montane moorlands, bamboo patches, *Podocarpus* and *Juniperus* forests, and montane giant heath, from 2 200 to 3 700m above sea level.
- They usually prefer dense shrubby thickets and moribund bamboo stands rather than primary forest.

Habits

They are particularly sedentary, usually confined to dense vegetation where they are more often heard than seen. However, they do occasionally emerge onto short grassy patches and dust-bathe on sandy roads, particularly during the early morning and during wet weather. Where they have become accustomed to humans, such as at picnic places and lodges, they do become tame and confiding. If flushed, they will perch in a tree or bush and they roost overnight in low trees, tall montane heath or scrub. Their call is a raucous high-pitched deliberate '*kirr-kee-kik*' crowing at dawn and dusk, similar sounding to that of the Scaly Spurfowl and Hildebrandt's Spurfowl *P. hildebrandti*. They also utter a low clucking contact call while foraging in dense vegetation.

Food and feeding

Their diet consists of bulbs and tubers, bamboo seeds, grass shoots, berries, insects and small snails.

Breeding

They are monogamous and breed during the drier months of the year from October–February. Little is known about their breeding biology, but their clutch size is 3–7 eggs which are glossy pale brown and measure 46.5 x 36.0 mm.

Status and conservation

Although they are abundant in some national parks, they are dependent on appropriate park management for their future stability. They are also vulnerable to habitat degradation in lower forest edges throughout their range.

Handsome Spurfowl
Pseudofrancolin noble
Pternistis nobilis

Francolinus nobilis (Reichenow, 1908), Virunga Volcanoes, Zaire

Handsome Spurfowl from the Bwindi Impenetrable Forest, Uganda (photo by Nik Borrow)

Male Handsome Spurfowl in the Bwindi Impenetrable Forest, Uganda (photo by Per Holmen)

A pair of Handsome Spurfowl from Rwanda (photo by Tasso Leventis)

Classification

They are most closely related to their sister species the Mount Cameroon Spurfowl *P. camerunensis*.

They are a monotypic spurfowl with no subspecies recognised.

The putative subspecies '*chapini*' from the Ruwenzori Mountains is regarded as a localised variant and is synonymised with *P. nobilis*.

Description

- The Handsome Spurfowl is medium-sized: average male mass 877 g, average female mass 624 g.
- They are dark reddish-brown, particularly in the wings, back and underparts, with a greyish-brown head, primaries and rump.
- The wing coverts and the lower neck are deep maroon, with light grey scalloping on the lower neck.
- The throat is buff-white with the rest of the belly being chestnut with grey edges varying to broad buff or white edges.
- They have a bare red eye-patch, as well as a red bill and red legs.
- Females are smaller and somewhat duller than males.
- Juveniles are similar in appearance to adults, but the upperparts are barred with dark grey and rufous buff, while the underparts are paler.
- Downy chicks are undescribed.

Distribution and habitat

- They are endemic to the highlands of the Albertine Rift of the far western mountain forests of the Democratic Republic of the Congo, south-western Uganda, and border areas between Rwanda and Burundi.
- They are locally common in dense undergrowth and moist bamboo thickets from the lower edge of the montane forests, through the bamboo thicket zone, up to the Afro-alpine heath zone, especially near water or in swampy areas, mainly at altitudes from 1 850–3 700m above sea level.

Habits

They are sedentary and difficult to see in the dense undergrowth, although most easily seen in small groups or pairs, in early mornings and at dusk, in clearings and on tracks. They are shy and elusive, more often heard than seen, and when disturbed they will run through thick undergrowth. If flushed, they fly a short distance before dropping back into dense cover. They roost overnight in low trees or bushes. They are very vocal, particularly at dusk before roosting. Their call is a noisy musical crowing '*chuk ker-ack*' repeated 4–5 times or a squealing '*ker-ack*' repeated 6–8 times at dawn and dusk.

Food and feeding

They forage along roads in the early morning and late afternoon. Their diet consists largely of seeds.

Breeding

They are known to breed from May–September in the eastern Democratic Republic of the Congo, but little is known about their breeding biology.

Status and conservation

Although common to locally abundant, they are trapped with snares for food by local people. They are locally dependent on stable bamboo patches which are prone to disturbance and destruction by heavy harvesting.

Mount Cameroon Spurfowl
Pseudofrancolin du Mont Cameroun
Pternistis camerunensis

Francolinus camerunensis (Alexander, 1909), Cameroon Mountain, Cameroon

RIGHT Male Mount Cameroon Spurfowl (photo by Hadoram Shirihai)

BELOW LEFT Incubating hen Mount Cameroon Spurfowl (photo by Ashute Essebi Marcel)

BELOW Mount Cameroon Spurfowl nest and clutch (photo by Ashute Essebi Marcel)

Classification

The Mount Cameroon Spurfowl is most closely related to its sister species the Handsome Spurfowl *P. nobilis*.

They are a monotypic spurfowl with no subspecies recognised.

Description

- They are a sexually dimorphic dark brown spurfowl with a red bill, facial eye patch and legs.
- They are darker than the similar Scaly Spurfowl *P. squamatus*, with red facial skin, but do not share the same distribution range.
- Males have extensive red periorbital skin, unmarked dark brownish-grey upperparts, darker brown on the crown and nape, greyer throat and neck with pale feather fringes, while underparts are dark grey, darkest on under-tail coverts, with all of the feathers having darker centres and blackish shaft-streaks.
- The flight feathers and tail are dark brown.
- Females are distinctive, with mottled upper- and underparts vermiculated with black, dark brown and buff, and some off-white U- to V-patterning on the belly and U-patterning on the lower neck.
- Juveniles are similar in appearance to adult females but have white barring below, black and white tips to the flank feathers, less extensive or no bare skin around eyes, and have a dull red bill and legs.

Distribution and habitat

- They are endemic to the south-east slopes of Mount Cameroon between 850 and 2 100m above sea level.
- They are confined to primary and secondary montane forest provided there is dense undergrowth, along forest edges and in old fields adjacent to the forests.
- They avoid montane grasslands on the upper slopes of Mount Cameroon, but have been observed in savanna-scrub habitats following forest burning.

Habits

They mostly occur in pairs, foraging among leaf litter. They are territorial and shy, will fly to trees to escape dogs, but otherwise run to the safety of thicket cover when alarmed. Their call is a short high-pitched, 3-noted '*Kilu kilu kilu*' or slower '*Kee-ku kee-ku kee-ku*' whistle usually given from a concealed perch at dusk.

Food and feeding

Their diet consists of berries, grass and legume seeds, and insects.

Breeding

They breed during the dry season, laying their clutch from October–December. Nests which are a relatively deep scrape are usually located on the ground amongst vegetation in the savannas or grasslands adjacent to forest edges. One nest was lined with leaves and had a clutch of four plain creamy buff eggs. No further information on their breeding biology is available.

Status and conservation

They are reportedly locally common, especially on the southern slopes of the mountain down to 850m above sea level. There is no evidence of marked population declines. Although much of the forests on Mount Cameroon have suffered damage, the species appears to be able to tolerate secondary forests. However, because of their limited range they are classified as Endangered (The IUCN Red List of Threatened Species v 2016-3). They may be adversely affected by deliberate burning, by man and/or volcanic activity, which causes the retreat of forest edges, and by excessive hunting.

Swierstra's Spurfowl
Pseudofrancolin de Swierstra
Pternistis swierstrai

Francolinus swierstrai (Roberts, 1929), Mombolo, south-western Cuanza Sul district, Angola

ABOVE Male Swierstra's Spurfowl (photo by Dayne Braine)

LEFT Female Swierstra's Spurfowl (photo by Dayne Braine)

Classification

Swierstra's Spurfowl is an early diverging lineage of the spurfowls.

Like *P. hartlaubi,* their closest relative is Schuett's Spurfowl *P. schuetti*, with Erckel's Spurfowl *P. erkelli* being its closest montane spurfowl group relative.

The Swierstra's Spurfowl is monotypic with no subspecies recognised.

Description

- They are a small sexually dimorphic brown-backed montane spurfowl with a diagnostic broad black breast band, white throat and broad white supercilium.
- The bill is orange-red in the male, brown in the female, and the legs of both sexes are red.
- The male's black breast contrasts with the light throat while the white belly has broad buff central streaks with blackish margins.
- Females have a paler, more rusty back, mantle and upper wings.
- Their underparts are buff with irregular black or brown blotches or bars which are concentrated on the upper belly to form a mottled band and are sparse on the lower belly.
- Juveniles are similar in appearance to the adult female but their throat and supercilium are pale buff, and the upperparts are streaked and barred with rufous buff.
- Downy chicks are undescribed.

Distribution and habitat

- This uncommon Angolan endemic is resident in the highlands of western Angola, in Mountains Moco and Soque, the Bailundu Highlands and the Mombolo Plateau along the escarpment, and with isolated populations on the Chela escarpment and Tundavala in the Huila district and at Cariango in the Cuanza Sul district.
- They are restricted to the undergrowth and forest edges of a few relict patches of evergreen montane forests, such as on Mount Moco and Mount Soque.
- They also occur on the grass- and bracken-covered rocky slopes of mountain sides and in tall grass savannas on mountain tops and gullies.

Habits

They are secretive and usually remain secluded in dense undergrowth, shrubbery and large ferns. When disturbed, they will run deeper into cover, or flushed individuals will fly into a tree. The call is shrill and harsh, increasing in volume then fading away, similar sounding to that of the Jackson's Spurfowl *P. jacksoni*.

Food and feeding

They forage among fallen leaves in the undergrowth. Their diet includes the seeds of legume and grass species, as well as insects.

Breeding

Very little is known about the breeding habits of this species. They are suspected to breed during the drier months of May–July.

Status and conservation

Their habitat has been reduced by forest destruction, due to the extraction for timber and by clearing and burning for subsistence agriculture. As a consequence of these ongoing threats, their populations are small and vulnerable to fragmentation. Hunting may be a further problematic threat. They are Vulnerable (The IUCN Red List of Threatened Species v 2015-4) and listed on CITES Appendix II.

Ahanta Spurfowl
Pseudofrancolin d'Ahanta
Pternistis ahantensis

Francolinus ahantensis (Temminck, 1854), Ahanta, Gold Coast (Ghana)

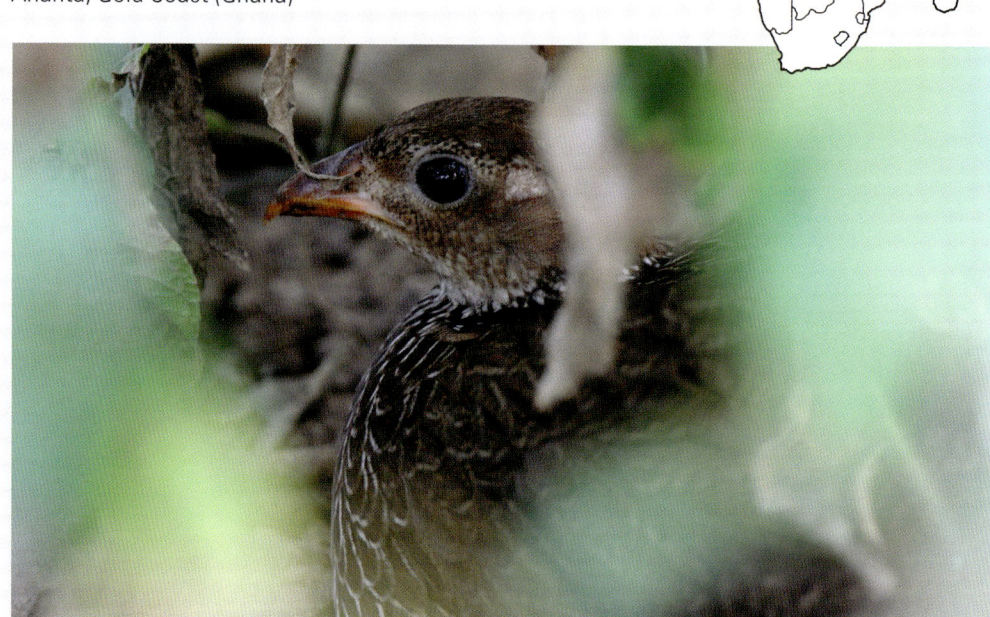

Ahanta Spurfowl in dense cover in the Bunso Arboretum, Ghana (photo by David Hoddinott)

Male Ahanta Spurfowl in the Kakum National Park, Ghana (photo by Nik Borrow)

Male Ahanta Spurfowl from Abuko Forest Reserve, The Gambia (photo by Bjarne Skov)

Classification

They are most closely related to their sister clade, Scaly *P. squamatus* and Schuett's *P. schuetti* Spurfowls.

Ahanta Spurfowl are monotypic with no subspecies recognised.

The western subspecies *P. a. hopkinsoni* (Bannerman, 1934) in western Senegal, Gambia and Guinea-Bissau, although paler overall, do not warrant separate taxonomic status and is synonymised with *P. ahantensis.*

Description

- The Ahanta Spurfowl replaces the Scaly Spurfowl in West Africa and is the only orange-billed spurfowl in its range.
- It is a medium-sized, dark brown spurfowl, with an orange-red bill and orange legs and feet.
- It is the most patterned scaly spurfowl group member.
- It has a white throat with white edges and darker centres to the feathers of the hindneck, back and underparts, appearing streaked at close range.
- The belly feathers are richly coloured and streaked with dark brown chestnut edged buff.
- Juveniles are similar in appearance to adults but have arrow-shaped black streaks above.
- Downy chicks have a dark rufous-brown crown, nape and broad stripe down the middle of the back.
- The sides of the head are buffy-rufous with a rufous-brown eye-stripe extending back from the eye.

Distribution and habitat

- They are an endemic of West Africa, with three separate populations: coastal areas of southern Senegambia and northern Guinea-Bissau; southern Guinea, Sierra Leone and western Liberia; north-eastern Ivory Coast and Ghana through central Togo and central Benin to south-western Nigeria.
- Their preferred habitats are dense secondary vegetation at forest edges and in gallery forest, old plantations and cultivated patches.

Habits

They occur in pairs and small groups, and are generally shy and secretive. If flushed, they will typically fly to perch in a tree. They are most active and vocal at dawn, but will call at any time of the day and during moonlit nights. Their call is a loud raucous, squealing '*kee-kee-keree*', which is repeated several times and is higher pitched than that of the Scaly Spurfowl.

Food and feeding

Their diet consists mostly of seeds, small beans, cassava and large fruits, as well as insects, including termites.

Breeding

They breed from September–January in Senegambia and in late December in Ghana. Their nest is a scrape in the ground under thick cover and lined with leaves. The clutch of 4–6 eggs, sometimes as many as 12, are cream to pinkish-buff and measure 42.0 x 33.0 mm. Little is known about their incubation and chick rearing.

Status and conservation

They are most common in north-eastern Ivory Coast and Ghana through central Togo and central Benin to south-western Nigeria, and rare and localised in the coastal areas of southern Senegambia and northern Guinea-Bissau.

Scaly Spurfowl
Pseudofrancolin écaillé
Pternistis squamatus

Francolinus squamatus (Cassin, 1857), Cape Lopez, Gabon

A wet female Scaly Spurfowl perched on an elevated tree branch in Gabon (photo by Paul van Giersbergen)

Classification

They are phylogenetically a sister taxon of Schuett's Spurfowl *P. schuetti*, however they are genetically most closely related to Grey-striped Spurfowl *P. griseostriatus*.

The taxonomic and ecological separation of the two sister taxa requires further testing by analysing specimens along a transect across their inferred 'ranges' to test levels of difference with regards to morphology, behaviour and genetics.

Scaly Spurfowl are monotypic with no subspecies recognised.

P. squamatus Cassin, 1857 in south-eastern Nigeria to the Democratic Republic of Congo.

One previous subspecies of Scaly Spurfowl has been elevated to full species status: Schuett's Spurfowl *P. schuetti* Mandiwana-Neudani *et al.* 2019, Ostrich 90(2): 145–172.

The putative subspecies '*whitei*' is synonymised with *P. squamatus*.

Description

- They are a smallish dull olive-brown spurfowl, characterised by pale buff-brown feather edges giving a scaly effect, particularly on the lower neck.
- They are generally more reddish tinged above, more mottled and blotched dorsally and paler ventrally than Schuett's Spurfowl.
- The belly is plain brown with a scaly pattern and ill-defined dark shaft streaks margined buff.
- They have conspicuous orange-red legs and a red bill.
- Males may have one or two tarsal spurs.
- Juveniles are similar in appearance to adult females but are more rufous with black arrow-shaped markings on the upperparts and lightly barred black and white below, with a duller bill than adults.
- Downy chicks have a dark rufous-brown crown, hind neck and broad mid-dorsal stripe.
- Their face and sides of the head are buffy white, with a single dark brown eye-stripe.

Distribution and habitat

- Their distribution is across a belt of equatorial African forest between 10°N and 10°S, and between 800 and 3 000m above sea level; from south-central Nigeria, southern Cameroon down to Gabon, the Congo, southern Central African Republic, western and northern DRC and southern South Sudan.
- It is uncertain whether Scaly Spurfowl are contiguous or allopatric with Schuett's Spurfowl.

- The location of an assumed contact zone of Scaly Spurfowl and Schuett's Spurfowl in southern South Sudan, northern DRC or indeed western Uganda is uncertain and needs further clarification.
- They prefer evergreen forests with dense undergrowth, forest clearing and the dense understory of bamboo patches and old plantations.
- They are rarely found away from forest belts, or thick bush bordering the forests.

Habits

They are usually encountered in pairs or small groups which are secretive and skulking. When disturbed, they prefer to squat and then run to cover. If flushed, they fly with heavy wing beats and will land in a tree. They are active and vocal from before dawn and again at dusk, often into the evening and on moonlit nights. They call from a prominent perch, such as a termite mound. The call is a high-pitched, grating '*ke-rraak*' repeated 4–12 times, and increasing in volume to a crescendo.

Food and feeding

Their diet consists mostly of vegetable material including seeds and fruits, as well as snails, millipedes, termites, ants and other small insects. They will also take cultivated crops including cassava, sweet potato, peanuts and rice.

Breeding

They do not have a peak breeding season, but mostly lay from October–March, except for Gabon where they breed during June–August, and with a second peak during May and June in the DRC. Their nest is a shallow scrape under a tuft of grass or bush lined with grass, leaves and feathers. The clutch of 3–8, usually 6, oval very hard-shelled pinkish-buff pitted white eggs measure 41.9 x 33.6 mm. Their incubation biology is unrecorded.

Status and conservation

Although widely distributed in most equatorial forests, including forest reserves and national parks, and locally common in places, even sometimes more common than Double-spurred Spurfowl *P. bicalcaratus* in Nigeria, forest destruction and trapping may lead to local extinction.

Schuett's Spurfowl
Pseudofrancolin de Schuett

Pternistis schuetti

Francolinus squamatus (Cassin, 1857), Cape Lopez, Gabon

P. s. schuetti (Cabanis, 1880) in eastern DRC, Uganda, Ethiopia, Kenya, Tanzania and Malawi

Male Schuett's Spurfowl in the Arusha National Park, Tanzania (both photos by Per Holmen)

 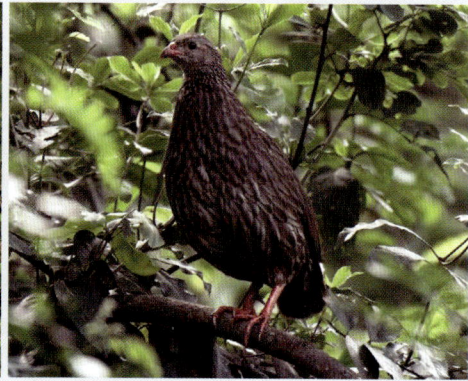

Female Schuett's Spurfowl in typical forest edge habitat in Kibale National Park, western Uganda (photo by Nik Borrow)

Male Schuett's Spurfowl at the Wondo Genet College of Forestry and Natural Resources, central Ethiopia (photo by Merid Gabremichael)

Female Schuett's Spurfowl in Kenya (photo by Jacques Pitteloud)

Female Schuett's Spurfowl at Lake Langano, Oromia, Ethiopia (photo by Guido Keijser)

Classification

Recently elevated from Scaly Spurfowl *P. squamatus schuetti* Mandiwana-Neudani *et al.* 2019, *Ostrich* 90(2): 145–172.

They are phylogenetically a sister taxon of Scaly Spurfowl *P. squamatus*, however they are genetically most closely related to Grey-striped Spurfowl *P. griseostriatus*.

The taxonomic and ecological separation of the two sister taxa requires further testing by analysing specimens along a transect across their inferred 'ranges' to test levels of difference with regards to morphology, behaviour and genetics.

Two subspecies are recognised:

P. s. schuetti Cabanis, 1880 in southern South Sudan, eastern DRC to Uganda, Rwanda, Burundi, Ethiopia, Kenya, Tanzania and Malawi;

P. s. maranensis Mearns, 1910 in south-east Kenya and north-eastern Tanzania.

Previously recognised subspecies *P. s. usambarae* Conover, 1928, *P. s. uzungwensis* Bangs & Loveridge, 1931, and *P. s. doni* Benson, 1939 are synonymised with *P. schuetti*.

However, they are clinal or idiosyncratic variants of *P. schuetti* which may warrant subspecific status should they exhibit significant genetic divergence.

Description

- Resembles Scaly Spurfowl but is more drab and darker with less vermiculation overall and the scaly pattern on the lower neck is less clearly defined.
- Each feather has a deep red-brown centre.
- They have orange-red legs and a red bill.
- Males have one or two tarsal spurs.
- Populations west of the Rift Valley in Kenya south towards Kilimanjaro, Monduli and Mt Meru in north-eastern Tanzania become clinally increasingly darker and greyer (more readily seen in males) and tend to have less white on the belly.
- Birds further east ('*maranensis*') on Mt Kilimanjaro (up to 2 000 m), Monduli, Mt Meru and in the Chyulu Hills are also darker and less patterned.
- About 240 km southeast of Kilimanjaro, birds ('*usambarae*') from the Usambara Mountains have the area around their eyes and cheeks freckled with black and white instead of uniform brown.
- Another isolated population from the forests on the Vipya Plateau between 900–2 800 m ('*doni*') in Malawi have more reddish-brown upper and underparts with some white streaking on the underparts.

- Juveniles are similar to adult females but are more rufous-brown with black arrow-shaped flecks on the upperparts, lightly barred black and white below and have a duller bill.
- Downy chicks have a dark rufous-brown crown, hind-neck and broad mid-dorsal stripe.
- Their face and sides of the head are buffy white, with a single dark brown eye-stripe.

Distribution and habitat

- Their distribution is from southern South Sudan, the eastern DRC, across to Uganda, Rwanda, Burundi, south-western Ethiopia, central Kenya, the highlands of northern and eastern Tanzania and northern Malawi.
- It is uncertain whether Schuett's Spurfowl are contiguous or allopatric with Scaly Spurfowl.
- The location of an assumed contact zone of Schuett's Spurfowl and Scaly Spurfowl in southern South Sudan, northern DRC or indeed western Uganda is uncertain and needs further clarification.
- Their occurrence in north-western and north-eastern Zambia is not confirmed, although there is reportedly a putative sound recording from Mwinilunga in the north-west.
- They prefer montane and lowland secondary and riverine forests with dense undergrowth from 800–3 000 m.
- Rarely found away from thick bush or forest edges but will frequent dense undergrowth plantations and abandoned plantations.

Habits

They are most often seen in pairs or small groups of up to 5 individuals which are secretive and skulking. When disturbed, they prefer to squat and then run fast to cover seldom flushing. If flushed, they fly with heavy wing beats and will land in a tree. They are active and vocal in the early morning and in the evening when they leave the thick cover to feed in the 'shambas' or on fallow lands. Their call begins with soft, rising and grating churrs and ends in a rasping repeated *'kerrak'* crescendo.

Food and feeding

Their diet consists mostly of seeds, fruits and crop plants, as well as snails, millipedes, termites, ants and other small insects. They will take advantage of crops such as cassava, sweet potatoes, ground nuts and rice.

Breeding

They do not have a peak breeding season, but mostly breed during October–December in Ethiopia and August–September in Malawi. Their nest is a shallow depression under cover lined with grass and feathers. The clutch is 3–8, usually 6, oval, very hard-shelled pinkish buff, pitted white eggs which measure 41.9 x 33.6 mm.

Status and conservation

Although locally common in places and generally not threatened, forest destruction and trapping may lead to reduced local numbers. Once plentiful in the forest bordering the lake at Entebbe they have been trapped in considerable numbers. Hunting by local villagers has also reportedly caused declines in the Tugen Hills, Baringo County, Kenya.

Grey-striped Spurfowl
Pseudofrancolin à bandes grises

Pternistis griseostriatus

Francolinus griseostriatus (Ogilvie-Grant, 1890), Quanza River, northern Angola

LEFT, ABOVE & BELOW LEFT Grey-striped Spurfowls in dense forest thickets (photos by Sean Braine)

RIGHT A roosting Grey-striped Spurfowl (photo by Tony Dowd)

Classification

They are most closely related to Schuett's Spurfowl *P. schuetti*.

They are also sister to four southern vermiculated species: Hilderbrant's *P. hiderbrandti*, Natal *P. natalensis*, Red-billed *P. adspersus* and Cape *P. capensis* Spurfowls.

They are a monotypic species with no subspecies recognised.

Description

- The Grey-striped Spurfowl is medium- to small-sized and has rufous-chestnut-streaked plumage, a pale throat, unmarked face, and red-orange bill and legs.
- They are sexually monomorphic.
- The lower neck feathers and wing coverts are chestnut broadly vermiculated with grey as in the Scaly Spurfowl and the Ahanta Spurfowl, but the belly is plain and the upper belly and flank feathers are chestnut, edged with greyish or creamy buff.
- They are paler than the Scaly Spurfowl, which they replace in north-eastern Angola.
- They are differentiated from the Red-necked Spurfowl *P. afer* by lacking bold black and white underparts and a bare red face and throat.
- Juveniles are rich cinnamon, with each feather having a blackish, not chestnut, centre and with black triangular-shaped markings above and below.
- Downy chicks are undescribed.

Distribution and habitat

- They are endemic to the escarpment zone and northern coastal plain of western Angola.
- There are two separate populations: one in southern Cuanza and western Milanje (Ndalo Tando, Punga Andongo, Dondo, Cuanza Basin and Cuanza Gorge), and another on the escarpment in the southern Benguela District and far north-eastern Huila District (Chingoroi and Caxito).
- They inhabit dense thicket undergrowth of vestigial patches of gallery and secondary forests and in riverine forests between 800 and 1 200m above sea level.

Habits

They venture from dense cover to forage in grasslands and fallow cultivation lands, mostly former cotton fields, during the morning and late afternoon. When disturbed, they flush back to the forest edge. If disturbed, they flush back to the cover of the forest edge. They roost overnight in the cover of leafy trees. They make a duetting '*shwiii ke-ke-ke-ke*' advertisement call, as well as a softer '*fifififif*', repeated rapidly towards a crescendo. Their flight and alarm calls are a raspy '*kerak kerak*'.

Food and feeding

Their diet consists mostly of seeds and green shoots, as well as insects and other small arthropods.

Breeding

While they are assumed to nest in a well-concealed shallow scrape like other spurfowls, their timing of breeding and breeding habits are unknown.

Status and conservation

Little is known about their population status, and although they can be locally common, they are still regarded as vulnerable, being potentially impacted by forest destruction, including the clearance of undergrowth.

Double-spurred Spurfowl
Pseudofrancolin à double éperon
Pternistis bicalcaratus
Tetrao bicalcaratus (Linnaeus, 1766), Senegal

Double-spurred Spurfowls from Nigeria (photos by Tasso Leventis)

Classification

They are most closely related to their sister vermiculated species Heuglin's Spurfowl *P. icterorhynchus* and thereafter to Clapperton's Spurfowl *P. clappertoni* and Harwood's Spurfowl *P. harwoodi*.

Three subspecies are recognised:

P. b. bicalcaratus Linnaeus, 1766 from Senegal to south-western Niger and Benin;

P. b. ayesha Hartert, 1917 in northern and south-western Morocco;

P. b. adamauae Neumann, 1915 in Nigeria and Cameroon.

The putative subspecies *P. b. ogilvie-granti* Bannerman, 1922 in north-western Cameroon is not recognised as a separate taxon and is synonymised with *P. b. adamauae*.

Description

- Double-spurred Spurfowls are sexually monomorphic and have an olive-green bill and legs and lack any bare facial skin.
- They have a chestnut crown and nape, black frons and eye-stripe, a conspicuous white supercilium, streaked back and chestnut black and white tear-drop-marked breast and underparts.
- All three subspecies are similarly patterned above and below, differing in the degree of colouration and vermiculation, and the size of the arrow-shaped buff marks in the centre of the belly feathers.
- *P. b. ayesha* in Morocco is paler above with slightly more rufous on the lower neck, with small arrow-shaped buff marks on the belly feathers.
- *P. b. adamauae* is the darkest form with very little rufous on the lower neck, and the underparts are more buff with extremely reduced chestnut and larger arrow-shaped buff marks along the belly feather shafts.
- Females are similar in appearance to males but have smaller spurs.
- Juveniles are generally duller and the underparts are buff blotched with black.
- Downy chicks have a rufous brown crown with dark brown eye-stripes.
- They have a dark rufous-brown stripe down the mid-back, flanked with a buff stripe on either side.

Distribution and habitat

- They are common to abundant in drier areas of West Africa from Senegal to northern Cameroon and southern Chad.
- There are also two isolated populations of the subspecies *P. b. ayesha* which is endemic to central and northern Morocco.
- They are the commonest spurfowl in West Africa outside of forests.

- Their preferred habitats are open dry grasslands, lightly wooded savanna and woodlands, shrubby pastures, dense riparian cover, palm groves, cultivation clearings, including oil-palm, cassava and cocoa plantations, and croplands including maize, rice, cereals, groundnuts and cotton.
- In Morocco, they occur in the zone surrounded by the agglomerations of Sidi Yahia des Zaër, Sidi Bettache and Ben-Slimane where they inhabit cork oak forests with a low density of large trees, moister coastal open heath areas, palm groves and active and fallow cultivated cereal lands between forests and woodlands.

Habits

They are usually found in groups of 2–12 individuals, or larger flocks of up to 40 individuals. They feed in relatively open areas during the day, often seen on road tracks, particularly during the rainy season. They will seek cover in thickets and forest edges where savannas are burnt and when disturbed they run to cover. Large trees are used for overnight roosting. They often call from a prominent perch such as a termite mound. The advertisement call is a series of loud, raucous '*ke-rraak, ke-rraak*' repeated crowing, mostly at dawn and dusk.

Food and feeding

Their diet consists largely of fruits and berries, roots, green leaves and seeds. Agricultural cereals, including millet, maize, rice and groundnuts are also taken, particularly during spring and summer. Animal food items include termites, caterpillars, ants, beetles, grasshoppers, small molluscs and frogs.

Breeding

They are monogamous and their breeding season is variable geographically, but mostly related to water availability and the rainy season. In Morocco breeding peaks during May and June, August–May in Senegambia, October–February in Sierra Leone and Nigeria, and October–December in Cameroon. The nest is a shallow scrape sometimes lined with grass and feathers in patchy cover or in fallow cereal croplands. The clutch of 5–7 smooth oval sandy or yellowish-buff eggs, sometimes with darker spots, measure 42.0 x 33.0 mm. Their incubation behaviour is not recorded.

Status and conservation

Although common, they are susceptible to hunting pressures, particularly in Ivory Coast and in Morocco where they are regarded as critically endangered. They are also vulnerable to displacement by habitat destruction and frequent burning. The population of *P. b. ayesha* at Souss in south-western Morocco has declined dramatically in recent times. A captive bred reintroduction programme has been initiated in Morocco to halt and reverse their population decline.

Heuglin's Spurfowl
Pseudofrancolin à bec jaune

Pternistis icterorhynchus

Francolinus icterorhynchus (Heuglin, 1863), Bongo, Bahr-el-Ghazal, Sudan

Female Heuglin's Spurfowl (photo by Nik Borrow)

Hueglin's Spurfowls in recently burnt open woodland in the Central African Republic (photo by Andy Pugh)

Male Heuglin's Spurfowl in Murchison Falls National Park, Uganda (photo by Maans Booysen)

Classification

Heuglin's Spurfowl is most closely related to their northern vermiculated sister-taxon Double-spurred Spurfowl *P. bicalcaratus*, followed by Clapperton's Spurfowl *P. clappertoni* and Harwood's Spurfowl *P. harwoodi*.

They are monotypic with no subspecies recognised.

Description

- They are a medium-sized sexually monomorphic spurfowl.
- They are easily distinguished by their yellow-orange bill and legs, and a yellow-brown bare facial skin patch behind the eye.
- They have a chestnut crown, brown back and pale cream underparts, which are heavily marked with brownish-black V-shaped chevrons.
- Females are similar in appearance to males but are slightly smaller.
- Juveniles are more heavily barred above.
- Downy chicks have a rufous-brown crown with a dark border.
- The sides of the head are buffy with a dark brown eye-stripe.
- Their back has a broad dark brown stripe down the middle, with a buff stripe on either side.

Distribution and habitat

- They are localised to the Central African Republic, northern Democratic Republic of the Congo, South Sudan and western Uganda.
- They are common in open or scrubby grasslands, open woodlands and adjacent agricultural fields.

Habits

They are usually encountered as pairs or small groups of up to 5 individuals. They can be difficult to see and when approached will run into cover or flush with heavy frantic wing beats, often into a nearby tree. Calling males will often perch on a prominent site such as a tree branch or termite mound and may be joined by the female. Adjacent territory males may answer the advertisement call. Their call is a harsh, slow '*kerak-kerak-kek*' or faster '*kerak-kerak-kerak-kerak-kerr*', similar sounding to that of the Double-spurred and the Clapperton's Spurfowls, and mostly given just after sunrise and late afternoon.

Food and feeding

Their diet consists mainly of seeds and berries, as well as beetles, bugs, millipedes, termites and ants. They also occasionally feed on waste grains such as millet.

Breeding

They are monogamous and have an extended breeding season from April–November. The nest is a scrape under a bush or in thick vegetation. The clutch of 6–8 pale greyish buff eggs measure 42.0 x 33.3 mm. Little is known about their incubation or chick rearing.

Status and conservation

Similar in population status to the related spurfowls of the Vermiculated Group, they are common to abundant in most of their range, but are probably vulnerable to hunting, habitat destruction and frequent habitat burning.

Clapperton's Spurfowl
Pseudofrancolin de Clapperton

Pternistis clappertoni

Francolinus clappertoni (Children & Vigors, 1826), Bornu, (Chad/Nigeria)

Clapperton's Spurfowl calling from an elevated mound (photo by Tasso Leventis)

Perched Clapperton's Spurfowls (Left photo by Tasso Leventis, right photo by Nik Borrow)

Classification

They are most closely related to their sister species Harwood's Spurfowl *P. harwoodi*, followed by Natal Spurfowl *P. natalensis*.

Two subspecies are recognised:

P. c. clappertoni Children & Vigors, 1826 in north-eastern Nigeria and southern Niger across to western Ethiopia. *P. c. clappertoni* includes *P. c. heuglini* Neumann, 1907 in South Sudan and *P. c. gedgii* Ogilvie-Grant, 1891 in South Sudan to north-eastern Uganda;

P. c. sharpii Ogilvie-Grant, 1892 in north-eastern Sudan, northern and central Ethiopia and Eritrea. *P. c. sharpii* includes *P. c. nigrosquamatus* Neumann, 1902 in eastern Sudan and western Ethiopia and *P. c. koenigseggi* Madarász, 1914 in eastern Sudan.

Description

- Clapperton's Spurfowl are easily distinguished from Double-spurred Spurfowl *P. bicalcaratus*, Heuglin's Spurfowl *P. icterorhynchus* and Chestnut-naped Spurfowl *P. castaneicollis* by their red facial skin and red legs.
- They have a fairly extensive white throat and neck, and white edges to the feathers giving a scaled appearance to the back and underparts.
- They differ from Harwood's Spurfowl by having a white supercilium, mostly black bill with a red base, and a variable black moustachial stripe.
- The subspecies *P. sharpii* in the east has streakier marks on the belly.
- Juveniles are duller overall than adults and are less distinctly marked.
- The downy chick is undescribed.

Distribution and habitat

- Their distribution is widespread across north-central Africa from southern Niger, far north-eastern Nigeria, Chad, Sudan, northern South Sudan, north-eastern Uganda, western Ethiopia to Eritrea.
- They are generally patchily distributed but can be locally common to abundant from sea level up to 2 300 m above sea level.
- Their preferred habitats are within dry sandy grasslands, semi-arid bushy savanna, rocky hillsides and often in adjacent agriculture fields and near water.

Habits

They are mostly seen singly or in pairs, seldom in small groups, which are most active during the late afternoon. Males call from a conspicuous site such as a tree branch or termite mound. They roost overnight in tall trees. Their call is a loud raucous '*kerrak*' crowing repeated 4–6 times, with variations, at dawn and dusk, similar to the calls of the Double-spurred and Heuglin's Spurfowls.

Food and feeding

Their diet consists of seeds, berries, insects and small molluscs.

Breeding

They are monogamous and their breeding season peaks during February and March in Nigeria, July–September in Mali, Chad and Sudan, and April–December in Ethiopia. The nest is a well-concealed scrape. The clutch of up to 9 thick-shelled yellowish-brown eggs have distinct pores and measure 43.0 x 33.0 mm. Little is known about their clutch size, incubation or chick rearing.

Status and conservation

They are locally common to abundant and probably are vulnerable to hunting, habitat destruction and frequent habitat burning.

Hildebrandt's Spurfowl
Pseudofrancolin de Hilderbrandt
Pternistis hildebranti

Francolinus hildebranti (Cabanis, 1878), Voi, Teita district, Kenya Colony

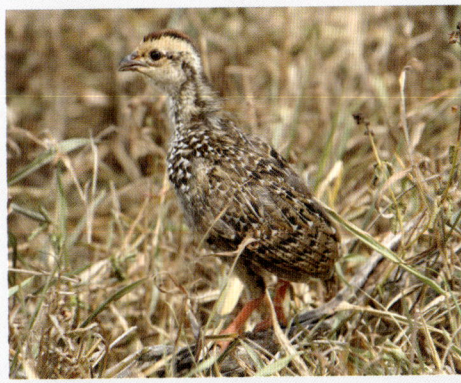

Juvenile Hilderbrandt's Spurfowl (photo by Ian Little)

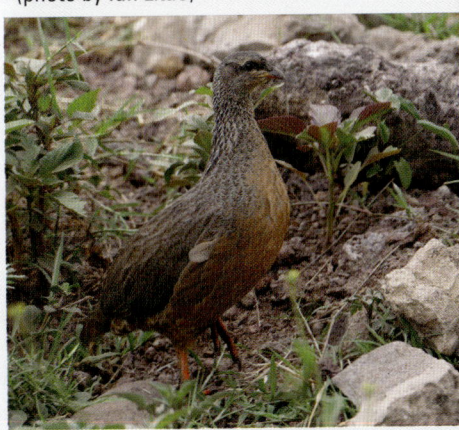

Female Hilderbrandt's Spurfowl at the Ngorongoro Crater, Tanzania (photo by Nik Borrow)

Male Hilderbrandt's Spurfowl in scrub habitat in Tanzania (photo by Tasso Leventis)

Classification

They are most closely related to Natal Spurfowl *P. natalensis* with which they are known to interbreed.

Two subspecies are recognised:

P. h. hildebrandti Cabanis, 1878 in eastern and central Kenya, northern and western Tanzania, south-eastern Democratic Republic of the Congo, northern and eastern Zambia;

P. h. johnstoni Shelley, 1894 in south-eastern Tanzania, Malawi and northern Mozambique.

The putative subspecies *P. h. altumi* and *P. h. fischeri* are synonymised with *P. h. hildebrandti*.

Description

- They are a member of the vermiculated spurfowl group and their rufous-buff underparts are distinctive.
- They have a yellow ear-patch and eye-ring.
- Males are greyish brown with vermiculations. The hind and lower neck are streaked black with white margins and the belly plumage has marked black blotching.
- Males are similar in appearance to the Heuglin's Spurfowl *P. ichterorhynchus* and Natal Spurfowl but have paler underparts which are clearly marked with large black spots.
- Males are also somewhat similar in appearance to the Clapperton's Spurfowl *P. clappertoni*, but they lack the red facial skin and the obvious white supercilium.
- Females have distinctive plain, rusty underparts.
- Female *johnstoni* is smaller than nominate *hildebranti* and lacks the white on the mantle and the black mottling on the breast or nape.
- Both sexes have red legs, with a reddish mandible and brown culmen with a yellow base.
- Juveniles are similar in appearance to adult females but are more heavily barred blackish above and below.
- Downy chicks have a rufous-brown crown with dark stripes and a dark brown stripe from the front of the eye back to the nape which is more pronounced than in other spurfowl chicks.

Distribution and habitat

- They are endemic to East Africa where they are thinly distributed from Kenya through

most of Tanzania, south-eastern Democratic Republic of the Congo, northern and eastern Zambia and Malawi, and marginally into northern Mozambique.
- They prefer extensive dense thickets and scrub on grassy hill slopes, acacia woodlands, as well as bracken-briar edges of evergreen forest and montane heath.

Habits

They usually occur in pairs or small groups and are wary, sitting particularly tight when approached. They perch and roost overnight in trees. More often heard than seen. Their raucous crowing '*KEK kek kek kerak*' call, with the first note the loudest, is similar sounding to that of the Natal Spurfowl, and is more often heard than they are seen.

Food and feeding

Their diet consists of seeds, bulbs, tubers, as well as insects and their larvae.

Breeding

Although their breeding season can extend from March–November, peak breeding is during June and July. The nest is a small scrape, lined with grass and leaves, usually well concealed in vegetation. The clutch of 4–8 creamy white to pale brown eggs measure 39.8 x 31.9 mm. Their incubation behaviour is not recorded.

Status and conservation

Because of their localised, uncommon occurrence, little is known about their population status, potential threats and conservation needs.

Natal Spurfowl
Pseudofrancolin du Natal

Pternistis natalensis
Francolinus natalensis (Smith, A, 1834), Durban, Natal, South Africa

Courting male Natal Spurfowl in the Kruger National Park, South Africa (photo by Jessie Walton)

Female Natal Spurfowl with chicks (photo by Ian White)

Perched Natal Spurfowl (photo by Ian White)

Juvenile Natal Spurfowls (photo by Ian White)

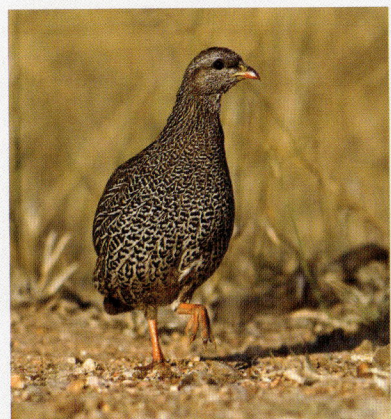
Female Natal Spurfowl (photo by Andre Botha)

Conspicuous calling territorial male Natal Spurfowl (photo by Andre Botha)

Classification

They are most closely related to their sister species Hildebrandt's Spurfowl *P. hildebrandti*, particularly *P. h. johnstoni*.

Natal Spurfowl are monotypic with no subspecies recognised.

The putative subspecies *P. n. neavei* Mackworth-Praed, 1920 in southern Zambia and western Mozambique, although slightly sexually dimorphic, is synonymised with *P. natalensis*.

They are reported to hybridise in the wild with Swainson's Spurfowl *P. swainsonii* and Red-necked Spurfowl *P. afer*.

Description

- The size difference between the appearing similar sexes is marked, and the larger males have stout leg spurs.
- Their overall plumage is dark brown, with white and dark brown vermiculations across the breast and flanks.
- The crown and sides of the head are brown, grading downwards into black and white.
- The restricted white on the throat is less conspicuous than that of the Cape Spurfowl *P. capensis*.
- They lack bare skin on the face and throat.
- Their legs are bright orange, particularly during the breeding season.
- Their bill is also orange with a dull greenish base.
- Juveniles resemble adults but are paler, with greyish-brown upperparts with dense vermiculations and indistinct rufous-buff barring.
- The underparts are buffy with faint black barring, with each feather having a conspicuous white shaft streak.
- Downy chicks are rufous-brown above, with prominent darker streaks on the crown and back.
- The sides of the head are buffy, with a dark brown eye-stripe extending from the back of the eye.
- The underparts are buffy, with light rufous-brown on the breast.

Distribution and habitat

- They occur across north-eastern South Africa, Swaziland, inland Mozambique, Zimbabwe, eastern Botswana, and south-central Zambia. Although most common in the lowveld and drier savannas, they also venture into riverine bush among escarpment grasslands.
- They inhabit savannas and woodlands with scrub thickets, riverine vegetation and montane forest edges to coastal forest.
- They have expanded their range along watercourses invaded by the alien Black Wattle *Acacia mearnsii*.
- They also use modified habitats, including cultivated land edges adjacent to good cover, and firebreaks cut through commercial plantations.

Habits

Although sometimes in groups of up to 10 birds, they are usually encountered as scattered individuals because coveys are loose and individuals disperse when disturbed.

They will congregate where food is abundant, such as in livestock feedlots where waste grain is available. When disturbed, they normally run into thicker cover, or flush as individuals rather than as a covey, flying a short distance before falling back into cover. A flushed bird will also often land on a perch, and freeze, hoping to avoid detection. Like most other spurfowls, they often fly to their over-night roosting site, thus avoiding being tracked by predators. Where cohabiting with humans, such as at conservation area camp sites, they will become tame, keenly accepting or even soliciting food items. Their advertisement call '*kak-keek, kak-keek, kak keeeeek*' at dawn and dusk is similar to that of the Cape Spurfowl and is often the only evidence of their presence in the area. They also have a high-pitched, mewing contact call when individuals are separated.

Food and feeding

They usually feed during the early morning and late afternoon, and tend to forage under the cover of vegetation where they scratch in leaf litter and loose soil to detect food items. Bulbs, roots, seeds, berries and fruits are their main diet, but they also take fallen grains such as sorghum, cowpeas and maize. During the austral summer they feed on beetles, termites, grasshoppers and caterpillars. They also scratch through rhinoceros (Rhinocerotidae) and African Elephant *Loxodonata africana* dung for undigested seeds, insects and their larvae.

Breeding

The breeding season is extended, particularly in the northern parts of its range, where breeding has been recorded during all months of the year. Peak breeding is from December–February in South Africa and March–May in Zimbabwe. The nest is a shallow scrape lined with roots and grass and is concealed beneath dense entanglements of scrub. The clutch of 5–7 rounded cream or buff-coloured eggs measure 41.9 x 34.2 mm. Incubation by the female lasts 20–22 days. Chicks can flutter-fly at 10–14 days.

Status and conservation

There are no reasons for concern regarding the conservation of this species. Potential threats are habitat modification and fragmentation by woodland removal and frequent burning, which has led to declines in their numbers in parts of South Africa. They are sustainably hunted in many parts of their range, along with Helmeted Guineafowl *Numida meleagris* and Swainson's Spurfowl.

Hartlaub's Spurfowl
Pseudofrancolin de Hartlaub

Pternistis hartlaubi

Francolinus hartlaubi (Barboza du Bocage, 1869), Huila, southern Angola

Male Hartlaub's Spurfowl (photo by Cliff Dorse)

Pair of Hartlaub's Spurfowl, female on the right (photo by Dayne Braine)

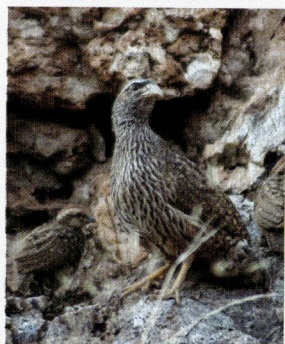

Male Hartlaub's Spurfowl parenting chicks at Hobatere Lodge, northwestern Namibia (photo by Dayne Braine)

Male Hartlaub's Spurfowl (photo by Maans Booysen)

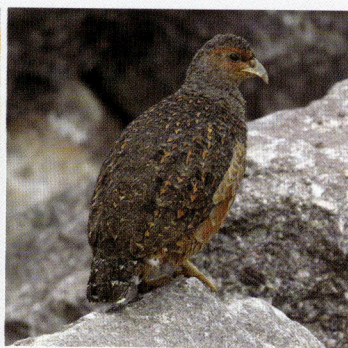

Female Hartlaub's Spurfowl (photo by Cliff Dorse)

SPURFOWLS

Classification

Hartlaub's Spurfowl is not closely related genetically to any other spurfowls.

However, they are relatively distantly related to Schuett's Spurfowl *P. schuetti*, and closest in the Vermiculated Group to Harwood's Spurfowl *P. harwoodi*.

Previous suggestions for any subspecies are not supported, thus there are no subspecies recognised.

A case might be made to elevate Hartlaub's Spurfowl to generic status, with the generic epithet *Chapinortyx* Roberts, 1928 being available.

Description

- Hartlaub's Spurfowl is the smallest spurfowl.
- They are sexually dimorphic with a relatively small head and an unusually large down-curved beak.
- The upper mandible is horn coloured with the lower yellowish and their legs are dull yellowish-brown.
- Males have a dark greyish-brown crown, a conspicuous white over black eye-stripe and chestnut ear coverts.
- They have contrasting dark brown and faintly barred back plumage, with pale belly feathers, heavily streaked with brown.
- The lower surface of the male's tail feathers is blackish brown, distinctly barred black and white, which is conspicuous in flight and during the courtship display.
- Females have a grey-brown head, and orange-brown eye-stripe, cheeks, chin and belly, with dark grey-brown, boldly marked back plumage.
- Neither of the sexes has leg spurs, only small, rounded bumps.
- Juveniles have a buffy forehead and a brown crown tinged with rufous.
- The side of the head is buffy with a faint greyish stripe behind the eye.
- The upperparts are buffy-grey, vermiculated with black and white, with each feather having a white shaft streak.
- The breast is barred black and white, grading to buffy-grey on the belly, with each feather also having a white shaft streak.
- The plumage of the chick has not been described.

Distribution and habitat

- This near-southern African endemic is scattered in central and northern Namibia, particularly on the Namibian escarpment, and slightly into south-western Angola.

- They are confined largely to mixed grass-shrub cover on boulder-strewn slopes and rocky outcrops in hilly and mountainous granite and sandstone outcrops in semi-desert open savanna.
- The vegetation within and immediately adjacent to these outcrops is invariably dense, mixed grass-scrub, with heavy undergrowth, on sandy soils.

Habits

They are sedentary and territorial. They are not easily flushed, preferring to seek refuge in gaps between boulders. If flushed, they fly quickly, often uttering a rapid, 3–5-second chattering '*krak*'. Pairs are difficult to observe as they dart between rocks and among vegetation. They remain monogamous throughout the year, and the pair-bond assists with conflicts with conspecifics which are resolved by call contests and postural displays rather than by physical confrontation. Each partner helps to demarcate the territory with a complex, raucous, antiphonal (duet-like) advertisement call initiated by the female. They have a complex and elaborate courtship ritual, thereafter the bond is maintained by interactive vocal contact. Their ventriloquial daily advertisement calls are uttered at sunrise and comprise a closely synchronised, antiphonal duet by the male and female alternating rapidly, '*wiich ter wideo, wiich ter wideo, wiich ter wideo…*'

Food and feeding

The pair ventures from the security of boulder outcrops to feed in openings adjacent to their refuge. The powerful bill is used to scrape out corms and bulbs, and large areas of soil can be upturned while foraging. They eat mainly corms, bulbs and rhizomes of small sedges, particularly 'uintjies' *Cyperus edulis*, as well as seeds, fruits, beetles, grubs, larvae and land molluscs.

Breeding

Most breeding records are from May–August. The nest scrape is well hidden between boulders. Clutch size is relatively small, with only 2–4, usually 3, rounded plain cream eggs, measuring 41.6 x 30.2 mm. Incubation lasts for 23 days. Also unusual in gamebirds is that the chicks are cared for by the male. Chicks can flutter-fly at 3 days and fledge at 12 days. Sexual dimorphism begins to show after 100 days.

Status and conservation

Because of their low population densities and confinement to suitable habitat, the local population size and distribution might fluctuate according to droughts or due to overgrazing and are probably influenced by predators. Their habitats might be further threatened by granite-mining activities. However, there is no evidence that distribution patterns have changed to any large degree in recent times.

Harwood's Spurfowl
Pseudofrancolin de Harwood

Pternistis harwoodi

Francolinus harwoodi (Blundell & Lovat, 1899), Aheafeg (= Ahaia Fej & Haiafegg), Shoa, Ethiopia

Male Harwood's Spurfowl (photo by Nik Borrow)

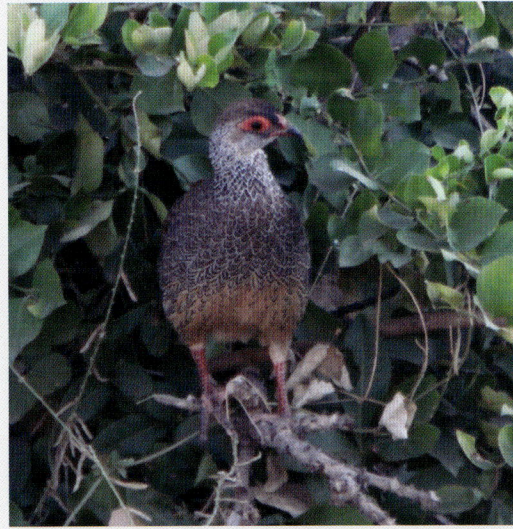

Male Harwood's Spurfowl (photo by Nik Borrow)

Male Harwood's Spurfowl (photo by Adam Riley)

Classification

They are most closely related to Clapperton's Spurfowl *P. clappertoni*.

They are monotypic with no subspecies recognised.

Description

- The Harwood's Spurfowl is a medium-sized grey-brown spurfowl with bare red eye-rings, a red bill with a black tip and red legs.
- The upperparts are grey speckled and finely barred with blackish and buff.
- The hind and lower neck, sides of face, throat and breast are speckled with black and pale buff.
- They have irregular double-V-shaped patterning on the underparts, which tends to be scattered on the buff lower belly.
- Although not sympatric, they are most similar in appearance to the Natal Spurfowl *P. natalensis* and the lack of a white eye-stripe sets them apart from other vermiculated spurfowls.
- They are darker than the Clapperton's Spurfowl, with less red skin around the eyes and largely red, not mostly black, bill.
- They are also differentiated from the Erckel's Spurfowl *P. erckelii* with which they do have range overlap by their reddish, not black, bill, red, not yellow, legs, and vermiculated, not streaked, underparts.
- Females are similar in appearance to males but are slightly paler and browner below with a less streaked belly.
- Juveniles resemble adults and the downy chick is undescribed.

Distribution and habitat

- They are an endemic range-restricted species in the gorges of the Jemmu Valley, the Blue Nile River, and its tributaries in the highlands of central Ethiopia.
- They prefer dense and extensive *Typha* reedbeds along streams, semi-arid scrub and thickets along rivers and on scrubby hill slopes, foraging on adjacent fields, often near the reeds.

Habits

They are not overly shy, but, when disturbed, they will fly back into reedbeds, which they also use for shade during the heat of the day. They roost overnight in trees within the reedbed or in the reedbed itself. Their call is a harsh, raucous '*ko reek*' crowing, usually given in sets of three well-spaced calls at dawn and dusk, similar sounding to that of the Clapperton's Spurfowl.

Food and feeding

They will venture out into open agricultural lands, such as sorghum, to forage. Their diet consists of tubers, berries, grass and sorghum seeds, as well as worms and termites. Although they consume agricultural seeds, they are not considered to be a pest.

Breeding

Very little is known about their breeding biology, with the breeding season possibly being from November–February, and the clutch size being between 3 and 10 eggs.

Status and conservation

Although they are classified as Near Threatened (The IUCN Red List of Threatened Species v 2016-3), and are range restricted, they are locally common at several sites. Habitat destruction by clearing for agriculture and timber harvesting for fuel and construction, and the injudicious use of fire, may affect their local range. They are also trapped using leg snares, as they are reported to be good to eat, as well as for their reputed medicinal properties.

Red-billed Spurfowl
Pseudofrancolin à bec rouge

Pternistis adspersus

Francolinus adspersus (Waterhouse, 1838), upper Kuiseb River, Namibia

ABOVE Group of Red-billed Spurfowls (photo by Michael Poliza)

FAR LEFT Male Red-billed Spurfowl (photo by Eric Stockenstroom)

LEFT Male Red-billed Spurfowl (photo by Yathin S Krishnappa)

SPURFOWLS

Calling male Red-billed Spurfowl
(photo by Ian White)

Female Red-billed Spurfowl
(photo by Ian White)

Red-billed Spurfowl portrait
(photo by Ian White)

Classification

They are most closely related to their sister species Cape Spurfowl *P. capensis* and thereafter to Natal Spurfowl *P. natalensis*.

Red-billed Spurfowl is monotypic with no subspecies recognised.

The putative subspecies *P. a. mesicus* Clancey, was recognised in 1996 in two isolated populations in mesic areas of the Waterberg plateau, north-central Namibia and in the eastern Caprivi, western Zimbabwe and south-western Zambia is synonymised with *P. adspersus*.

Description

- Although in the Vermiculated Group of spurfowls, their feathers are not flecked, but rather have pale white bars.
- They are medium sized, with conspicuous and distinctive yellow eye-rings and finely barred underparts.
- The bill and legs are orange-red, and adult males have formidable spurs.
- Females are smaller than males, with smaller blunt spurs.
- Juveniles are lighter brown, with buff bars and streaks, and do not have the yellow skin around the eye.
- Downy chicks have a rufous-brown crown with a darker stripe.
- The sides of the head are buffy, with a dark stripe extending backwards from the eye.
- A broad dark stripe extends down the mid-back, flanked by narrower buff stripes.
- The rest of the underparts are pale yellowish-buff, darker on the breast.

Distribution and habitat

- They are common in the drier, sandy Kalahari and Zambezian areas of south-western Africa, extending marginally into southern Angola and south-western Zambia.
- They are abundant throughout central and northern Namibia, the western corner of Zimbabwe, and throughout Botswana, except for the drier south-western Kalahari region and far eastern Botswana.
- Although they generally inhabit relatively dry savannas, they are also abundant on floodplains in the Okavango Delta and in the fossil-like beds of the Makgadikgadi Pan.
- Typical savanna habitats are *Baikaiea, Senegalia* and mixed woodlands, low scrub, thickets interspersed with open ground, and edges of woodlands on Kalahari sand, usually not far from water, and frequently along watercourses.
- There has been a southward extension of their distribution, during the late 1900s, into southern Botswana and the Northern Cape in South Africa.

Habits

They are usually seen in pairs or groups of up to 12 birds. Although often shy and elusive, they can be bold at sites in association with humans. They are known to venture into smaller rural villages, where they free-range feed with domestic poultry. When disturbed, they run rapidly into nearby cover or flush with a harsh alarm call, often seeking a perch to avoid intruders. They are most active at dawn and dusk, resting under the shade of broad-leafed scrub during the heat of the day. Often, their scratching for food items in leaf litter under scrubby cover will disclose their presence. Their '*ka-wak-wak-wak, ka-krr-krr-krr*' call, heard mostly at dusk and dawn, and often well before daylight, is similar sounding to that of the Cape Spurfowl and the Natal Spurfowl, but slightly more strident.

Food and feeding

Their diet consists largely of bulbs and corms in the dry season, but they will also feed on fruits, berries and seeds. Their close association with relatively lush areas that are adjacent to water mean that they disperse or concentrate depending on seasonal rainfall. They often associate with large game, particularly at waterholes, where they scratch through droppings in search of undigested seeds and associated invertebrates.

Breeding

They are solitary nesters and are probably monogamous. Although they breed throughout the year, usually after substantial rainfall, peak breeding activity is from April–September in Namibia, Botswana, Zambia and Zimbabwe, and from November–January in the Northern Cape. The nest is a scrape in the ground, sparsely lined with dry vegetation and placed among grass tufts or under a bush. It is, however, often relatively poorly concealed compared to that of most other spurfowl nests. The average clutch is 5 eggs, ranging from 4–10 eggs, which measure 42.2 x 33.4 mm. The eggs are dull yellowish, dirtying as the incubation progresses, and are particularly thick shelled and pitted, resembling small guineafowl eggs. The incubation period is 22 days. Juveniles attain adult plumage at about 3 months and the male's spur develops at about 5 months.

Status and conservation

Their tolerance of human activity and preference for somewhat modified habitats, coupled with their general abundance, place them beyond consideration for conservation action. The only threat to the otherwise secure populations is degradation or clearing of habitat by and for livestock. They are hunted as an opportunistic addition to game mammals which can conflict with their breeding season, and the offtake levels should be carefully monitored to ensure that they can be sustained.

Cape Spurfowl
Pseudofrancolin criard

Pternistis capensis

Tetrao capensis (Gmelin, JF, 1789), Cape of Good Hope, South Africa

ABOVE Cape Spurfowl shaking off a dust-bath (photo by Jessie Walton)

LEFT Male Cape Spurfowl (photo by Davide Gaglio)

BELOW Cape Spurfowl in coastal fynbos habitat (photo by Davide Gaglio)

SPURFOWLS

Female Cape Spurfowl (photo by Maans Booysen)

Preening Cape Spurfowl (photo by Ian White)

Female Cape Spurfowl with a juvenile (photo by Davide Gaglio)

Classification

They are most closely related to their sister species Red-billed Spurfowl *P. adspersus* and thereafter to Natal Spurfowl *P. natalensis*.

The Cape Spurfowl is monotypic with no subspecies recognised.

Description

- Cape Spurfowl is the largest vermiculated spurfowl.
- They are dark overall, with white streaking and flecking, particularly on the breast and flank feathers.
- When alarmed, they raise their dark crown feathers.
- In flight, the tail appears blackish.
- The legs are dull orange-red and males have large spurs, often two on each leg, one above the other.
- The upper bill is dark brown with an orange-red base and the lower is dull orange.
- There is no bare skin on the face or throat.
- Juveniles are similar in appearance to adults, but are browner above and grey below, with less distinct markings.
- Downy chicks have a rufous-brown crown and nape, narrowly bordered with a darker stripe on each side.
- The sides of the head are buffy-white, with a blackish brown eye-stripe.
- The back is brown with a dark brown median stripe bordered by buffy stripes.
- The underparts are buffy, darker on the breast.

Distribution and habitat

They are endemic to southern African fynbos and karoo habitats, from the mouth of the Olifants River in the west to Alexandria near Port Elizabeth in the east. Isolated populations occur northwards into the Karoo, up the Western Cape coast and along the lower Orange River in the Northern Cape, from Upington to the Atlantic coast.

They inhabit scrubby heath, especially coastal fynbos (standveld and renosterbos), and in sheltered scrub along streams and rivers.

They are also fond of stands of introduced Australian acacias.

They rarely wander far from escape shelter and their densities are affected by the placement, size and connectedness of fragmented natural habitats and patches of alien bush.

Habits

They are conspicuous and occur in pairs or small groups, averaging 5 birds in the non-breeding season. When disturbed, they escape by running, flying only when pressed. Despite being alert to danger, where they are accustomed to human presence such as in camp sites and parks, they can be bold, regularly approaching humans and human dwellings to scavenge food. Overnight roosting sites are invariably in dense scrub patches, reed beds or patches of Palmiet *Prionium serratum* in wetland sponges, where they huddle together on the ground or, occasionally, perch in trees. Coveys fly across river estuaries at dawn and dusk, using the estuary as a barrier to terrestrial predators between their daily activity sites and their roost site. The advertisement call is a loud crowing '*kak-keek, kak-keek, kak-keeeeek*', with the second syllable accented, similar sounding to the call of the Natal Spurfowl, and is usually uttered in the early morning and late afternoon. Juveniles give a single long tonal whistle contact call, decreasing in frequency.

Food and feeding

Their diet is primarily bulbs, corms, seeds, berries and fallen grain during the non-breeding season, with small snails, termites, ants and insects also eaten during the breeding season. They also feed on fallen fruits, such as grapes, apples and pears.

Breeding

Breeding occurs from August–January, peaking during September and October. Pairing is characterised by males vigorously chasing each other to determine dominance. The nest is a scrape lined with grass and is usually well concealed in a patch of fynbos or under a bush. The clutch is 4–8 eggs, but can be as many as 14, possibly when two females contribute to the clutch. The round to oval eggs are brownish cream to pale pink and measure 47.0 x 37.0 mm. Incubation by the female lasts 22–23 days. Chicks can fly short distances at 12 days old.

Status and conservation

There is no evidence of recent population declines or range contraction. They benefit from habitat transformation by colonising alien vegetation patches and suburban parklands. However, in agricultural land, such as wheat, vineyard and deciduous fruit farms, they are dependent on roosting and nesting sites in connected patches of fragmented natural habitats.

PART 4
Quails

QUAILS

Classification

Old World quails occur widely throughout Africa, Europe, Asia and Australia and belong to the Tribe Coturnicini. The three African quail species belong to the family Phasianidae and to two genera:

Coturnix Garsault, 1764, containing two species:

- Common Quail *C. coturnix* of Africa, Europe and central Asia
- Harlequin Quail *C. delegorguei* of Africa and southern Arabia

Synoicus (Excalfactoria) (Linnaeus, 1766), containing one species:

- Blue Quail *S. adansonii* are widespread through sub-Saharan Africa and are a sister species of the King or Blue-breasted Quail *E. chinensis* of Asia, New Guinea and north-eastern Australia.

Description

- The back plumage of quails is characteristically rufous-chestnut, strongly marked with a white, longitudinal shaft streak and transverse white and black bars.
- Their tail has, depending on the species, 8–12 feathers (normally 14 in partridges, francolins and spurfowls, and 16 or more in pheasants and grouse).
- Their legs are yellow and lack spurs.
- Males of the three African species have musical, three-note advertisement calls, which are used presumably to notify each other of their territorial domains and to attract mates.

Natural history

The natural history of the three African quails is relatively poorly understood. The biology of even the most common species, the Common Quail *Coturnix coturnix*, in the wild is still not fully understood, making conservation and management of the species relatively challenging. In fact, much of the information on their biology is derived either from anecdotal observations or from observations of birds reared and kept in captivity.

These quails have complex movement and spatial occurrence patterns. Furthermore, the geographical ranges of all three species, unlike those of most other African gamebirds, extend outside of the borders of Africa.

PREVIOUS PAGE **Male Harlequin Quail (photo by Hugh Chittenden)**

Again, unlike Africa's other gamebirds, excluding sandgrouse, all of which venture no more than a few kilometres from the area where they were hatched, quails move or migrate within, and in some cases outside, of Africa. Some nomadic African populations of Common Quail move thousands of kilometres, from as far north as Kenya down to the Western Cape in South Africa.

Evolutionary placement

- Anatomically, quails are the smallest of the African gamebirds, yet their skeleton is remarkably similar to that of the Wild Turkey *Meleagris gallopavo*, which is the largest gamebird, being more than a hundred times the size of the Common Quail.
- Genetic studies suggest that the nearest relative of the three African quails is the Madagascan Partridge *Margaroperdix madagarensis*.
- The quails form a genetically distinct branch, well up in the evolutionary tree for galliform birds, along with the Madagascan Partridge, the African spurfowls *Pternistis* species, the Bush Quails *Perdicula* species of India, and the Sand and See See Partridges *Ammoperdix* species of northern Africa and the Middle East.
- They are very distantly related to the New World quails (Family Odontophoridae), which are genetically closer to the guineafowls (Numididae).
- Some other Asiatic partridges (for example, *Rollulus* spp. and *Arborophila* spp.) and the Udzungwa Forest Partridge *Xenoperdix udzungwensis* and Rubeho Forest Partridge *X. obscuratus* from Tanzania branch off near the base of the gamebird evolutionary tree.
- They are the relicts of the ancestral phasianine galliform from which the balance of pheasants, partridges and Eurasian quails are derived.
- They and other galliforms are not related to the buttonquails (Turnicidae), with which they co-occur in Africa, and which are, in turn, genetically closest to the shorebirds (Charadriiformes).

Conservation

Common Quail and Harlequin Quail are extensively hunted or netted for food by humans. Common Quail are also farmed in large numbers for table meat or to produce eggs. Where hunted, they are often artificially stocked on game farms or to supplement wild populations.

Common Quail
Caille des blés

Coturnix coturnix

Tetrao coturnix (Linnaus, 1758), Sweden

Common Quail (photo by Maans Booysen)

Common Quail subspecies *C. c. africana* in Dullstroom, eastern South Africa (photo by Ian Little)

Common Quail subspecies *C. c. erlangeri* in Kenya (photo by Lorenzo Barelli)

Classification

Five subspecies are recognised:

C. c. coturnix Linnaeus, 1758 in the British Isles and north-western Africa, east to east-central Russia and east-central India, possibly to Bangladesh;

C. c. conturbans Hartert, 1917 and *C. c. inopinata* Hartert, 1917 on the Azores and Cape Verde Islands, respectively;

C. c. africana Temminck & Schlegel, 1849 in sub-Saharan Africa, from Ethiopia, Democratic Republic of the Congo (DRC) and Uganda to southern Angola and South Africa, and also on Madagascar;

C. c. erlangeri Zedlitz, 1912 in eastern Zimbabwe and adjacent Mozambique to Malawi, north-eastern Zambia (Nyika Plateau), Tanzania, eastern DRC, Uganda, Kenya, Sudan and Ethiopia.

Description

- They are the plainest of the African quails.
- Their back plumage is rufous-brown, mottled with black.
- Each feather has a lance-shaped, buffy-white streak and two or more similarly coloured bars.
- The flanks are broadly streaked with black and buff, the breast is pale rufous-brown and the belly is dull grey.
- They have no bold facial or throat markings and there is relatively little difference in colour and plumage pattern between the sexes.
- Males have a narrow black, anchor-shaped throat patch compared with the white throat of females.
- Juveniles resemble adult females, but the flanks are less heavily streaked and the breast has brownish spots.
- Downy chicks are rufous-brown above, with two dark streaks on the crown which merge to form a single streak down the back. This streak is flanked by two additional dark streaks that merge with it on the rump.

Distribution and habitat

- Their distribution and movements are complex and variable.
- Northern populations are largely migratory.
- In south-eastern Africa, some populations are nomadic residents, whereas others migrate within the subcontinent, only rarely venturing into the Northern Hemisphere.
- The winter migration of the southern African population is into southern DRC,

Angola, western and northern Namibia and western Zambia.
- It is uncertain if any proportion of the Northern Hemisphere population regularly visits southern Africa.
- Favoured habitats are grasslands, usually less than 50 cm tall, agricultural crops (particularly cereals), fallow weedy fields, and pastures (such as lucerne, clover, Eragrostis, Kikuyu and rye grass).
- Habitat attractiveness is determined by the abundance of insects in summer and seeds in winter, and by the type of cover afforded.
- Grasslands that are seldom burnt or grazed, or that are burnt too frequently and/or overgrazed, are not favoured.
- They also avoid the drier, hotter parts of Africa and areas with heavy bush and tree cover.

Habits

The proportion of the population which is migratory, nomadic or resident is uncertain. Changing local conditions may affect the faithfulness of birds to a particular area, and movement patterns may vary from place to place and from year to year. Their advertisement call is a ventriloquial '*whit wit-wit*', uttered repeatedly from within cover, which is slower and less evenly spaced than that of Harlequin Quail *C. delegorguei*. The flush call is a '*crwee-crwee-crwee*' trill. Unless flushed, they run swiftly through the grass in a hunched position when approached. Flocks of migrating birds usually fly on dark, moonless nights, and their passage can usually only be detected by the constant fluttering sounds of their wings.

Food and feeding

Their diet includes seeds (mostly of grasses, grains and weeds), flower buds, green leaves, and some smaller fruits, rhizomes and tubers (e.g. Cyperaceae). During the summer the diet is supplemented with invertebrates, particularly caterpillars and grasshoppers.

Breeding

C. c. erlangeri is a summer-breeding intra-African migrant resident in East Africa, while *C. c. coturnix* is a non-breeding Palearctic migrant. The nest is a scrape in the ground, lined with grass and rootlets, usually well concealed in dense herbaceous or grassy cover, sometimes in crops. The clutch size is 5–8 eggs, but can be as many as 12. The pointed oval eggs, which measure 30.3 x 23.4 mm, are smooth creamy-yellow with bold spotting and blotches of olive, dark brown and black. Incubation by the female lasts for 17–20 days.

Status and conservation

Because of the uncertainty of their movements, it is difficult to develop an effective conservation strategy for Common Quail. However, they have benefited from crop farming in some regions. They are prized as quarry by wing-shooters when they gather in high concentrations. Unfortunately, because they concentrate to breed during summer in eastern and southern Africa, hunting coincides with their breeding season. Therefore, hunting should be delayed to allow successful completion of breeding. Elsewhere in Africa, migrating flocks are heavily exploited for food by netting. Other landscape issues affecting the habitat availability for this species are expanding commercial afforestation, overgrazing and expanding rural human settlement.

Harlequin Quail
Caille arlequine
Coturnix delegorguei

Coturnix delegorguei (Delegorgue, 1847), Oury, upper Limpopo River, Limpopo Province, South Africa

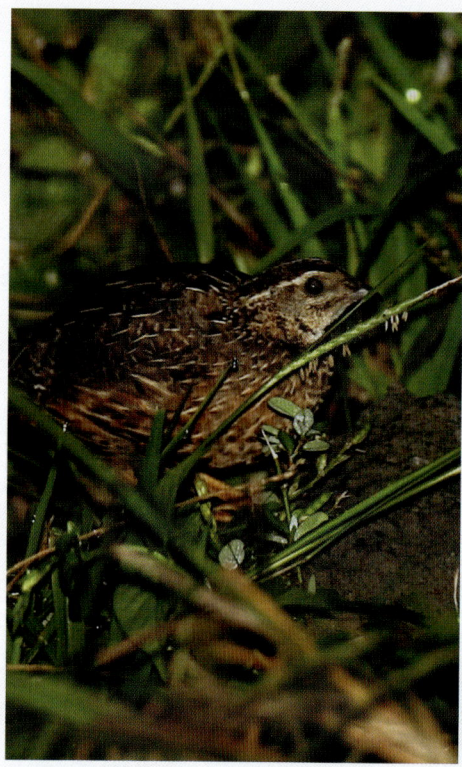

Female Harlequin Quail from São Tomé (photo by Tasso Leventis)

Calling male Harlequin Quail (photo by Richard Grant)

Classification

Three subspecies are recognised:

C. d. delegorguei Delegorgue, 1847 found from the Ivory Coast to Ethiopia (and is apparently the only migrant quail to West Africa) and south to South Africa and western Madagascar;

C. d. histrionica Hartlaub, 1849 on São Tomé in the Gulf of Guinea;

C. d. arabica Bannerman, 1929 in southern Arabia.

Description

- They are smaller and more sexually dimorphic than Common Quail *C. coturnix*, but not as striking as in Blue Quail *Synoicus adansonii*.
- The white throat and thin white collar of the male are as conspicuous as those of male Blue Quail, but differ in having a white stripe above the eye.
- The black on the throat of males is anchor-shaped, with the shaft running down the centre of the throat and the hooks curling up behind each eye.
- Males are darker overall than male Common Quail and have chestnut and black underparts which are distinctive.
- Females are paler overall than males and are similar to female Common Quail, but lack any dark marking on the throat and their underparts are darker.
- Juveniles resemble adult females, but have a light brown crown with a pale streak and a light brown nape. Their underparts are pale grey, with the breast spotted and barred with dark brown, and each feather has a white shaft streak at its tip.
- Downy chicks have a brownish crown and nape with a buff streak. Their back is also brown, with a darker stripe down the mid-back that is flanked by narrower stripes of buff and black. The belly is buffy yellow.

Distribution and habitat

- They are widespread and locally common to abundant throughout south-central and eastern Africa, excluding forest belts and arid south-western Africa, and are scattered and less common in north-central and West Africa.
- They are both a nomadic resident and an intra-African migrant.
- They are uncommon migrants to western Madagascar.
- Rainfall plays a role in determining their movements. They can be irruptive in their presence locally during a summer, and then may fail to return there for several years.
- They prefer short (<30 cm), rank wooded and flooded grasslands, occasionally with scattered bush cover, and are not as common in highland grasslands as Common Quail.

Habits

They are gregarious, often found in coveys of 6–20 individuals during the non-breeding season. Large migrating flocks sometimes move on foot during both the day and night. High adult mortalities during migration occur where birds are killed or injured on roads by cars, or when birds fly into the windows of buildings. They are secretive, spending most of the day concealed within cover. They are reluctant to flush, preferring to sit tight until approached and then bursting into fast, low flight before dropping back into cover. Their three-note call is repeated monotonously, similar to Common Quail, but is less connected, a more deliberate '*wit, wit, wit*'. Calling males stand erect, displaying chestnut underparts and a distinct throat pattern. Most calling is during the morning and late afternoon, and after rain or when a storm is looming. The flush call is a squeaky '*kree-kree-kree*'.

Food and feeding

They usually forage within cover, but sometimes at the edges of roads or tracks. Their diet includes the seeds of grasses, weeds and some agricultural crops, e.g. Goose Grass *Eleusine* sp., bristle grasses *Setaria* spp. and Sorghum *Sorghum purpureosericum*. The breeding season diet is supplemented with grasshoppers, caterpillars, termites, ants, beetles and small molluscs.

Breeding

The breeding season is variable, linked to heavy rainfall. They may nest in loose colonies and the males may be polygynous. The nest is a small bowl with sparse lining, usually located in grasslands with well-spaced tufts or weedy fields. They lay 4–8 creamy eggs, and occasionally up to 20 eggs are probably laid by more than one hen, which are creamy, speckled, spotted and blotched with dark brown. They measure 29.2 x 22.4 mm. Incubation by the female lasts 14–18 days.

Status and conservation

Although locally abundant in some years, the relative absence of this species in some regions indicates a restriction of its historic distribution. In general, the status, movements and habitat requirements are uncertain. They are captured by aviculturists and trapped heavily for food, using decoy individuals, in some areas.

Blue Quail
Caille bleue

Synoicus adansonii

Coturnix adansonii (Verreaux, JP & JBÉ, 1851), Gabon

Male Blue Quail from Zimbabwe (photo by Peter Ginn)

Pair of Blue Quails, female on the right, from Uningi Pans, northern Zambia (photo by Derrick Wilby)

Classification

Although closely related to Harlequin Quail *Coturnix delegorguei* and Common Quail *C. coturnix*, their closest relative is the Chinese Painted, Blue-breasted or Asian Blue Quail *Synoicus chinensis* of south-eastern Asia. The African Blue Quail, formerly placed in the genus *Excalfactoria*, is monotypic with no subspecies recognised.

Description

- This is the smallest quail in Africa.
- They are sexually dimorphic.
- Males have a black-and-white throat, a brown back and rufous upper wings, which are distinctive in flight, and a slate-blue breast and belly. The central throat is black, with bold white moustache patches and an extended white bib. They do not have the white stripe above the eye of the male Harlequin Quail and, although less conspicuous, of the Common Quail.
- Females are pale brown, with a streaked back and barred breast and flanks. They are difficult to distinguish from female Common Quail and Harlequin Quail, except for the barred, rather than streaked, breast and flanks.
- Both sexes have bright yellow legs and feet.
- Males have a black bill while the female's bill is pale brown.
- Juveniles resemble adult females, but have pale shaft streaks on the rump, upper tail and wings.
- Downy chicks have brown upperparts with a buff crown streak and three strong, darker longitudinal streaks on the back that converge with one another on the rump.

Distribution and habitat

- They occur widely across Africa, from Sierra Leone and southern Mali, eastwards to western Kenya, and southwards to south-central Angola, Zimbabwe and Mozambique.
- They are nomadic residents in West Africa.
- Outside of forests and dry areas, they are widespread across southern Gabon, southern DRC, north-western Angola and Zambia.
- They are rare in southern Africa, confined to north-eastern Zimbabwe and the coastal plain of Mozambique. Although occasionally recorded during winter in Zimbabwe, usually following above-average summer rains, they are largely a summer nomadic visitor to southern Africa.
- They prefer dense, grassy habitats, such as thick grass along watercourses and around swamps, the edges of cultivated lands and rice fields.

- They usually occur in wetter flooded grasslands and in more wooded areas than sites frequented by Harlequin Quail.
- Prolonged droughts and the degradation of wetlands and grasslands may impact the occurrence of this quail.

Habits

They are seldom as numerous as Common Quail or Harlequin Quail, usually occurring singly, in pairs or small, loose groups. They are reluctant to flush and fly direct and fast for a short distance (20–40 m) when flushed. They are seen most often in the early morning when they emerge into the open to feed. Their call is a piping, three-note whistle, '*ki-kew-yu*', with the first note being the loudest. They are less vocal than the other two African quails. The flush call is also high pitched and three-noted.

Food and feeding

Their diet consists of the seeds of grasses and weeds, and some green plant parts, as well as invertebrates, including termites. The availability of preferred food types may be determined by good rainfall, since local movement often follows rainfall patterns.

Breeding

Breeding in southern Africa is mostly during January to April and in East and West Africa during April to July. The nest is a grass-lined scrape within dense sedges or grass. The clutch of 6–9 thick-shelled eggs are pale yellowish-brown to olive and measure 24.9 x 19.5 mm. Incubation is probably by the female and lasts for 16 days.

Status and conservation

Concern about their stability is associated with increasing transformation and degradation of African wetlands. The only modification of wetlands which favours this species is the establishment of rice paddies. The Asian Blue Quail is a popular aviary bird, but the conservation implications of that species interbreeding with local wild African Blue Quail are probably minimal because of the small chance of any escapees of domesticated foreign birds surviving in the wild.

PART 5
Sandgrouse

SANDGROUSE

Classification

Sandgrouse form the family Pteroclidae, consisting of 16 species distributed across the arid areas of Africa, south-western Europe, and central and southern Asia. They have been associated variously with terrestrial gamebirds (Galliformes), pigeons (Columbiformes) and waders (Charadriiformes). There are two sandgrouse genera:

- *Pterocles* Temminck, 1815, with 14 species, all occurring in warm to hot deserts.
- *Syrrhaptes* Illiger, 1811, which contains two species, both confined largely to cold deserts. The fused three forward toes that characterise the two *Syrrhaptes* species form a 'sand-shoe' that may help the birds walk more easily through sand. *Syrrhaptes* species also lack a hallux (fourth, hind toe), which is typically present in other birds, including *Pterocles*.

Description

Their short bill and legs, seed-eating habits and overall external appearance are all reminiscent of gamebirds. Linnaeus initially assigned sandgrouse to the genus *Tetrao*, which they shared with a range of grouse and spurfowls. However, their long, pointed wings are like those of some pigeons, which also have a short bill and legs, and feed predominantly on seeds.

Natural history

Of the 14 *Pterocles* species, six are endemic to Africa, six are shared between northern Africa and Asia, while India and Madagascar each have one endemic species. All *Pterocles* species have a thick skin, specialised foot sole scales and densely packed feathers with thick underdown, which help them to cope with the high temperatures of deserts. A lower-than-usual (based on body size) metabolic rate further helps to reduce the production of body heat, which is another way they have adapted to cope with a hot environment. The most charismatic desert-related adaptation of sandgrouse is the capacity of their belly feathers to absorb water. During the breeding season, male sandgrouse soak up water in this way to transport the water to flightless chicks in the desert. 'Belly-wetting' behaviour can be an indicator of whether the chicks in a population have begun hatching and of what proportion of the males at a watering site are tending chicks. Chicks are precocial, leaving the nest and feeding themselves on seeds soon after hatching. However, they rely on the female for shelter from the sun,

PREVIOUS PAGE A leopard ambushes Burchell's and Namaqua Sandgrouse at a drinking site in the Kalahari, South Africa (photo by Matt Prophet)

and for the supply of drinking water by the male, for up to 6 weeks before they can fly and are independent of their parents.

Sandgrouse can be choosy about where they drink, preferring sites which are less suitable for ambush by raptors, and generally avoiding relatively saline water. They are dependent on water, often flying long distances daily to water sources. They drink by dipping the bill into the water, taking a couple of sips and tilting the head back to swallow. Sandgrouse are also adapted to exploit the often ephemeral availability of huge quantities of protein-rich seeds produced by annual plants within semi-arid ecosystems, and from hatching they feed exclusively on hard seeds, especially those of legumes (Fabaceae). Their oesophagus is enlarged to form a crop, within which thousands of tiny seeds may be stored. Grit is also eaten to assist with grinding up the seeds in the gizzard. The only other group of birds that feed exclusively on seeds from the time of hatching are the seed-snipes of South America, members of the wader family Thinocoridae.

Sandgrouse are nomadic or migratory and often gregarious. They can occur at high densities, particularly when they gather daily to visit their traditional drinking sites. However, once they take to the ground, sandgrouse can be difficult to find. They appear to actively seek soil types that allow them to blend into the background, and tend to skulk within patchy vegetation rather than seek open ground. Adults may perform injury-feigning distraction displays near eggs or young, giving a distraction call.

Evolutionary placement

- The appropriate evolutionary placement for the sandgrouse was settled in the mid-1960s by South African ornithologist Gordon Maclean, who noted that sandgrouse calling behaviour, nest architecture, clutch size, egg pigmentation, as well as chick plumage and development suggest a closer, albeit distant, relationship to the waders (Charadriiformes).
- Also, despite their short legs, sandgrouse can move around quite well on foot, another feature that links them with waders and not pigeons.
- This was subsequently supported by studies of their DNA, which suggested that they diverged evolutionarily from a wader-like ancestor about 80 million years ago.
- However, more recently comprehensive research on their DNA places them back among the pigeons.
- Despite this, sandgrouse are so distinct in terms of their anatomy, behaviour and genetics, that they are best placed in their own order, Pterocliformes.

Conservation

Sandgrouse have been exploited for food by humans for centuries. In southern Africa, Kalahari tribesmen prevented sandgrouse access to isolated watering sites until they dropped exhausted to the ground. African sandgrouse have also provided wing-shooters with sporting quarry for more than a century. In 1902, in his book *Bird Hunting on the White Nile*, wing-shooter Harry Witherby writes: 'Sandgrouse [in this case Chestnut-bellied Sandgrouse *P. exustus* and Spotted Sandgrouse *P. senegallus*] shooting along the banks of the White Nile afford such sport that millionaires would give untold gold for similar shooting were it to be had in England or Scotland.' More recently, commercial wing-shooting of Namaqua Sandgrouse *P. namaqua* and Burchell's Sandgrouse *P. burchelli* has been offered in the Northern Cape province of South Africa. This wing-shooting 'industry' significantly supplements the incomes of farmers in that semi-arid part of Africa.

Their occurrence in generally remote and relatively inhospitable environments render them largely free of any major threats which therefore allows the conservation status of all of the African sandgrouse to be listed as Least Concern (The IUCN Red List of Threatened Species v 2015-4).

Sandgrouse, in this case a male Burchell's Sandgrouse, belly-wetting to transport water to their flightless chicks in harsh arid environments (photo by Ian White)

Pin-tailed Sandgrouse
Ganga cata

Pterocles alchata

Tetrao alchata (Linnaeus, 1766), Spain

LEFT Male Pin-tailed Sandgrouse showing the pure white belly and underwing in flight (photo by Francois Mougeot)

BELOW LEFT Incubating male Pin-tailed Sandgrouse with a research telemetry transmitter (photo by Francois Mougeot)

BELOW Pair of Pin-tailed Sandgrouse, female on the left (photo by Francois Mougeot)

Classification

Pin-tailed Sandgrouse are a weakly supported sister species to Burchell's Sandgrouse *P. burchelli* at the base of the clade that comprises the Short-tailed and Long-tailed sandgrouse.

There are two subspecies recognised:

P. a. alchata Linnaeus, 1766 in the Iberian Peninsula and south-eastern France;

P. a. caudacutus Gmelin, SG, 1774 in northern Africa through the Middle East to southern Kazakhstan and Pakistan.

Description

- These are the only sandgrouse with a pure white belly and underwing.
- They have long needle-like tail feathers, similar to Spotted Sandgrouse *P. senegallus* and Chestnut-bellied Sandgrouse *P. exustus*.
- In flight, both sexes show a distinctive white wing-bar and white underwing with a black tip.
- Males have greenish-yellow upperparts mottled with yellow, orange-buff sides of the head, a black line through the eye and a maroon breast band and black throat.
- Females have a pale buff breast with three black bands and a distinctive white throat.
- Juveniles have black and buff concentrically marked upperparts and breast.
- Downy chicks have a rust-coloured crown with black edges and a whitish line down the mid-crown.
- The back has four whitish and rust-brown patches that form a double figure-eight pattern.

Distribution and habitat

- They are resident and nomadic north of the high Atlas Mountains in Morocco, Algeria, Tunisia and Libya, except the band of north-eastern plains.
- They inhabit arid and semi-arid steppes, including sparsely vegetated stony ground, dry plains and plateaus, mudflats and dry coastal river beds and depressions (*wadis*), but avoid open deserts.

Habits

They are gregarious even roosting as a flock. They drink in the early morning, 1–2 hours after sunrise. They rest in the heat of the day and gather to dust-bathe in the evening. Their flight call is a loud far-reaching ringing '*kata, kata*' uttered frequently.

Food and feeding

Their diet consists almost exclusively of small seeds, mostly of legumes and *Polygonum*, *Fagopyrum*, *Salicornia*, *Artemisia*, *Alhagi*, *Helianthemum* and *Asphodelus* species. They move onto farmlands in the early boreal summer to feed on wheat, oat grains, lentils and other cereals.

Breeding

They are monogamous and mostly solitary nesters, but sometimes nest in loose colonies. The breeding season is mostly from April to June, after the rains. The nest is a scrape sometimes close to a large stone or bush. The clutch of 2–4 long elliptical smooth eggs are slightly glossy buff, variably spotted, blotched or speckled with brown and grey. They measure 47.0 x 30.0 mm. Incubation by the male during the day and female during the night lasts for about 21 days.

Status and conservation

Their populations are suspected to be stable in the absence of evidence for any declines or substantial threats. They are common in Algeria and Morocco, except for western Morocco, where numbers have declined in recent decades.

Namaqua Sandgrouse
Ganga namaqua

Pterocles namaqua

Tetrao namaqua (Gmelin, JF, 1789) Namaqualand, Northern Cape Province, South Africa

Male Namaqua Sandgrouse in flight
(photo by Ian White)

Female Namaqua Sandgrouse
(photo by Eugene Vorster)

Incubating male Namaqua Sandgrouse
(photo by Penn Lloyd)

Pair of Namaqua Sandgrouse
with cryptic chicks
(photo by Penn Lloyd)

Classification

Namaqua Sandgrouse are a sister species to Chestnut-bellied Sandgrouse *P. exustus*, followed by Black-bellied Sandgrouse *P. orientalis*, which together comprise the Long-tailed Group that drink in the morning only, although Namaqua Sandgrouse will occasionally drink again in the afternoon.

Namaqua Sandgrouse are monotypic with no subspecies recognised.

Description

- They have long, pointed central tail feathers.
- Males have a plain olive-yellow head and neck, a white-and-chestnut breast band and a dark brown belly.
- Females have a yellow face and throat, mottled pale orange and grey on brown on the back and wings, barred on the belly and streaked on the breast.
- Juveniles resemble adult females but their back plumage is tinged with rufous, with darker barring.
- Each feather has a whitish border and the tail lacks the long central feathers.
- Downy chicks have a yellowish-brown crown and nape with irregular white bars, edged with black.
- The face is light brown, with a whitish stripe in front of the eye, which trails off down to the throat.
- The upperparts are also yellowish-brown, strongly marked with irregular white stripes and bars.

Distribution and habitat

- They are a southern African near-endemic, with a minimal extension into southern Angola.
- North-western populations are nomadic, while south-eastern populations are migratory, concentrating in the Northern Cape, South Africa, during the breeding season.
- During the austral winter non-breeding season, these populations migrate to the north and east into the southern Kalahari.
- They inhabit stone and gravel deserts and open semi-deserts with a sparse scattering of low shrubs or grass tufts, and occasionally arid sandy savanna with denser vegetation.

Habits

Flocks drink 2–3 hours after sunrise. In the evening, flocks fly to roosting sites in stony areas, where each bird makes a shallow roosting scrape. Favoured drinking sites have clear, fresh water with low salinity, gently sloping, open banks and limited tall vegetation, which might provide cover for predators, particularly raptors. They land several metres from the water, where they socialise and dust-bathe, then run down to the water to drink and belly-wet. They have a nasal, three-note flight call, '*ki-ki-vee*' or '*kel-kie-wyn*'. The take-off call is a rapid '*kip-kip-kip-kip*' and flocks mutter '*kip*' notes continuously while on the ground at water.

Food and feeding

They feed on the seeds of annual plants, including *Indigofera* species in the Nama Karoo, *Lotononis* species in the Succulent Karoo, *Tephrosia* species in Namibia and *Tephrosia* species and *Requernia sphaerosperma* in the southern Kalahari. Feeding birds walk slowly with head bent, pecking rapidly at the ground. They do not scratch with their feet, but flick the sand with their bill.

Breeding

They are monogamous solitary nesters. Namibian populations breed from January to August, peaking in May. South African populations breed from June to November in the Kalahari, August to January in the Nama Karoo, and September to February in Namaqualand and the south-western Western Cape. They nest on sparsely vegetated calcrete and sandy flats. The nest is a scrape in the sand, often placed next to stones or a tuft of grass, which act as disruptive camouflage. They have a 3-egg clutch, with each egg measuring 36.1 x 25.2 mm. The eggs are variable in appearance between clutches and in some cases within clutches, some being sparsely speckled with a light pigment over a cream background, while others are covered with heavy, dark speckles on a dark beige background, and still others have the speckling concentrated in a band around the thickest part of the egg. Females incubate during the day, while males incubate at night. Incubation lasts 21 days.

Status and conservation

Although there is no evidence of extensive changes in their distribution or numbers, large flocks at traditional watering sites in the Northern Cape have declined since the late 1940s. This may be due to increased dispersion in response to an increased number of artificial watering points. Nest predation is primarily by Yellow Mongoose *Cynictis penicillata* and Common Egg-eater *Dasypeltis scabra* snakes. Telephone lines and fences located in the flight path to and from favoured watering sites cause fatal collisions. Wing-shooting should only be during the non-breeding months.

Chestnut-bellied Sandgrouse
Ganga à ventre brun

Pterocles exustus

Pterocles exustus (Temminck, 1825), Senegal

LEFT Male Chestnut-bellied Sandgrouse subspecies *P. e. exustus* from Nigeria (photo by Tasso Leventis)

BELOW Two male and two female Chestnut-bellied Sandgrouse subspecies *P. e. ellioti* in the Doho Lodge area of Awash National Park, Ethiopia (photo by Maans Booysen)

GAMEBIRDS

ABOVE A male and two female Chestnut-bellied Sandgrouse flush from a drinking site (photo by Peter W Hills)

TOP RIGHT Male Chestnut-bellied Sandgrouse belly-wetting to carry water to his flightless chicks (photo by Tasso Leventis)

BOTTOM RIGHT A male Chestnut-bellied Sandgrouse scans the sky above for potential danger (photo by Tasso Leventis)

Classification

Chestnut-bellied Sandgrouse are a sister species to Namaqua Sandgrouse *P. namaqua*, followed by Black-bellied Sandgrouse *P. orientalis*, which together comprise the Long-tailed Group that drink in the morning.

There are six subspecies recognised:

P. e. floweri Nicoll, 1821, in Egypt;

P. e. exustus Temminck, 1825, in Mauritania, Senegal and Gambia to southern Sudan;

P. e. ellioti Bogdanov, 1881, in south-eastern Sudan, Eritrea, northern Ethiopia and Somalia;

P. e. olivascens Hartert, EJO, 1909 in south-western Ethiopia, Kenya and northern Tanzania;

P. e. erlangeri Neumann, 1909 in the western and southern Arabian Peninsula;

P. e. hindustan Meinertzhagen, R, 1923, in south-eastern Iran, Pakistan and India.

Description

- They have long, needle-like tail feathers, similar to Namaqua Sandgrouse, Spotted Sandgrouse *P. senegallus* and Pin-tailed Sandgrouse *P. alchata*.
- Males have a distinctive yellow head and wings, and although the belly and underwing appear black, it is actually dark chestnut.
- They have a narrow black breast-band, without black on the throat, which differentiates from Black-bellied Sandgrouse.
- Females have dark brown barred upperparts and belly, and the breast is flecked, not plain.
- Juveniles have yellowish upperparts, throat and breast with fine dark vermiculations, and no breast band.
- Downy chicks have a dark streak above the bill separated from the lores by a creamy white line, a golden buff patch around the eye which is edged black.
- They have a white line down the back, flanked by golden buff patch lines edged with black.

Distribution and habitat

- Their distribution stretches in a band from the Mauritanian coast across central West Africa to the Red Sea and Gulf of Aden in East Africa, along the lower Nile River basin in Egypt, and through Arabia to India.
- They prefer open semi-desert and sandy arid scrub, as well as cultivated or fallow fields and grasslands.

Habits

They are gregarious, gathering in large flocks to drink 2–3 hours after sunrise, and in the evening during hot weather. They approach the waterhole from height, circling and landing 20–30 m from the water. When disturbed, they crouch or creep silently away until hidden. They have a harmonious deep-toned '*kwit-gurut, kwit kwit-gurut*' flight-call and mutter a musical '*creen*' murmur at the waterhole.

Food and feeding

They forage mostly during the cooler morning and late evening. Their diet consists mostly of hard legume and grain seeds, *Trianthema*, *Indigofera* and *Heliotropium* species, as well as some plant shoots and insects, including ants.

Breeding

They are monogamous, solitary nesters. They breed during March to July in the west and during April to June in the east. The nest is a shallow unlined scrape in open desert. The clutch of three elongate, equally rounded eggs are creamy buff, greyish to light olive, heavily spotted and blotched with brown and pale purplish grey, and measure 36.1 x 25.2 mm. Incubation by the female during the day and by the male at night lasts 22–23 days.

Status and conservation

They are locally abundant, with large flocks in north-central Mali, Sudan, Somalia and the lowlands of Ethiopia, and are the commonest sandgrouse in central Chad.

Spotted Sandgrouse
Ganga tacheté
Pterocles senegallus

Tetrao senegallus (Linnaeus, 1771), Algeria

LEFT A flock of Spotted Sandgrouse at a drinking site (photo by Nik Borrow)

BELOW LEFT Female Spotted Sandgrouse (photo by Nik Borrow)

BELOW Male Spotted Sandgrouse (photo by Nik Borrow)

Classification

Spotted Sandgrouse are a weakly supported sister species of Namaqua Sandgrouse *P. namaqua* and Chestnut-bellied Sandgrouse *P. exustus* of the Long-tailed Group which drink in the morning.

They are monotypic with no subspecies recognised.

Description

- They are a rather pale yellowish-buff sandgrouse, with elongated needle-like tail feathers and less black on the belly than the short-tailed Black-bellied Sandgrouse *P. orientalis*.
- Males have mostly uniform upperparts, no black on the face or throat, an orange-yellow throat and a blue-grey crown and hind neck which meets the blue-grey breast band.
- In flight, they show black secondaries and a distinctive black line down the mid-belly.
- Females have spotted upperparts and a breast band.
- Juveniles have sandy upperparts with darker crescentic bars and somewhat vermiculated streaks.
- Downy chicks are light greyish brown with obscure mottling.

Distribution and habitat

- They are distributed in North Africa, Israel and Arabia to Afghanistan and Pakistan.
- In Africa, they are spread from southern Morocco and Mauritania across to Egypt, Eritrea, north-eastern Ethiopia and northern Somalia.
- They inhabit a wide range of dry open country from flat stony desert plains (*hammadas*) to sandy desert with isolated patches of vegetation.

Habits

They are resident, nomadic or partially migratory. Flocks of up to 60 individuals circle and land close to a waterhole each morning, and less so again in the evening during hot weather. They are very vocal and vigilant, approaching the water to drink and flushing at any disturbance. They roost in loose flocks, with each bird making a shallow roost scrape. Their call is a distinctive, liquid and musical '*cuito, cuito*' or '*wittoo, wittoo*'.

Food and feeding

They feed largely on small hard seeds, including those of *Euphorbia guyoniana* and *Asphodela tenuifolia*. In Egypt, they gather with Crowned Sandgrouse *P. coronatus* to feed on grain spilled from trucks transporting between Red Sea ports and Nile valley markets.

Breeding

They are monogamous solitary nesters, breeding mostly from March to July. The nest is a small unlined scrape on flat ground, sometimes placed among stones about the same size as the bird. The clutch averages 3 eggs, which are elliptical and equally rounded at each end. They are buff, sparingly spotted and scrawled with light brown, reddish brown and purplish grey, and measure 41.7 x 28.0 mm. Incubation by the female during the day and by the male during the night lasts for 29–31 days.

Status and conservation

They are common to abundant in most parts of their range, except Morocco where their distribution is patchy and they are less common.

Black-bellied Sandgrouse
Ganga unibande
Pterocles orientalis

Tetrao orientalis (Linnaeus, 1758), 'In Orient' = Anatolia, ex Hasselquist

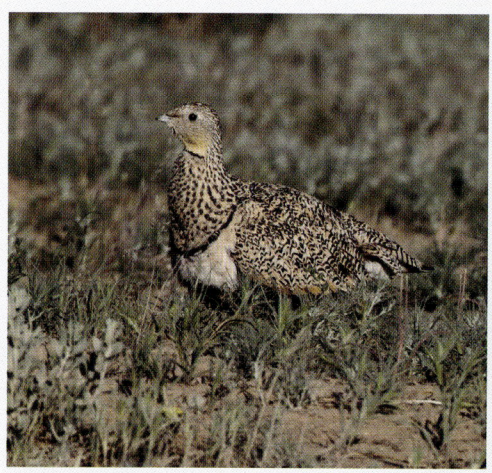

Female Black-bellied Sandgrouse (photo by Tasso Leventis)

Male Black-bellied Sandgrouse (photo by Tasso Leventis)

Black-bellied Sandgrouse at a drinking site (photo by Sergey Dereliev)

Classification

They are most closely related to Chestnut-bellied Sandgrouse *P. exustus* and Namaqua Sandgrouse *P. namaqua*.

There are two subspecies recognised:

P. o. orientalis Linnaeus, 1758 in the Canary Islands, Morocco to Libya, and the Iberian Peninsula to western Iran;

P. o. arenaruis Pallas, 1775 in Kazakhstan to southern Iran and Afghanistan east to north-western China.

Description

- They are a large sandgrouse with the average male weighing 514 g while the female weighs about 434 g.
- Their short tail, completely black belly and black-and-white underwing coverts are distinctive.
- Males are distinguished from Spotted Sandgrouse *P. senegallus* by a black throat, black band across the breast and contrasting yellow wings.
- Females have a dark band below their breast spots and an extensive black belly.
- They also have a pale throat, buff in the male and white in the female.
- Juveniles are similar to adults, but greyer.
- Downy chicks are ochre-tawny above with black tips to the down.
- They have a bold cross-shaped pattern of buffy white lines dividing the tawny back into a bold double figure-eight pattern.

Distribution and habitat

- They occur in north-western Africa from Morocco to Libya, the Canary Islands, southern Iberia, Cyprus, and the Middle East to south-central Asia.
- They are also a regular non-breeding migrant to Egypt.
- In north-western Africa, they prefer the semi-arid steppe north of the Atlas Mountains.
- They avoid open desert.

Habits

They are sedentary or nomadic in north-western Africa. Flocks drink at watering holes with no vegetation on the banks between 1–2 hours after sunrise. They are reluctant to fly during the heat of the day, often seeking shade. Their call is a gruff-mellow '*churr-rur-rur*' or '*tchourou*'.

Food and feeding

Their diet consists mostly of small seeds with a preference for legume species. They will also eat some agricultural grains and insects including termites, beetles and their larvae.

Breeding

They are monogamous solitary nesters. Breeding occurs from April to July in north-western Africa. The nest is a shallow unlined scrape. The clutch of 3 elliptical eggs are pale to deep buff or greyish, smudged, blotched and spotted with brown and grey, which measure 47.0 x 32.0 mm. Incubation by the female during the day and by the male at night lasts 21–22 days.

Status and conservation

They are common in Algeria and Libya, scarce in Tunisia, and absent from the north-east.

Yellow-throated Sandgrouse
Ganga à gorge jaune

Pterocles gutturalis

Pterocles gutturalis (Smith, A, 1836), Kurrichane (Zeerust), North West Province, South Africa

Male Yellow-throated Sandgrouse subspecies *P. g. saturatior* from Kenya (photo by Jacques Pitteloud)

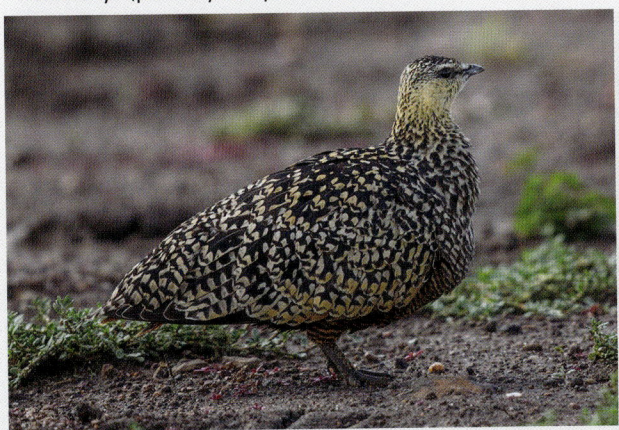

Female Yellow-throated Sandgrouse subspecies *P. g. saturatior* from Kenya (photo by Jacques Pitteloud)

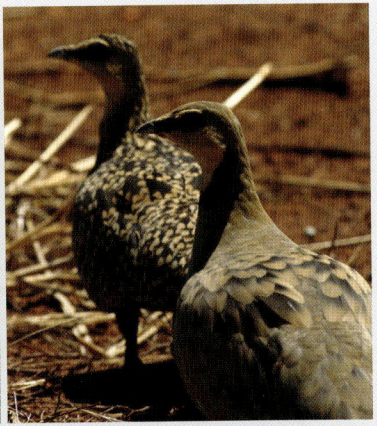

Pair of Yellow-throated Sandgrouse subspecies *P. g. gutturalis* from southern Africa (photo by Maans Booysen)

Classification

Yellow-throated Sandgrouse are a sister species to Madagascan Sandgrouse *P. personata* and thereafter to Crowned Sandgrouse *P. coronatus*, all of which comprise the Short-tailed Group which have a morning drinking peak and also regularly drink in the late afternoon.

Two subspecies are recognised:

P. g. gutturalis Smith, A, 1836 in South Africa, north-eastern Namibia, eastern and northern Botswana, western Zimbabwe and Zambia;

P. g. saturatior Hartert, EJO, 1900 in Ethiopia, Kenya, Tanzania and north-eastern Zambia;

The subspecies *P. g. tanganjicae* described for the population in Tanzania is not widely accepted.

Description

- They are a large sandgrouse with distinctive dark chestnut belly feathers that are conspicuous in flight, dark brown underwing plumage and a wedge-shaped tail.
- Both sexes have blue-grey, bare-skinned eye rings.
- Males have a pale creamy-yellow face and throat encircled by a black band, and a dull grey breast.
- Females also have a yellowish throat, but lack the black collar, and the back and breast are mottled with black and brown.
- Juveniles are similar to adult females, but the back is barred olive-buff and the mottling is finer.
- Downy chicks have a strongly marked crown and back with a network of rufous-brown patches, edged with black and separated by a matrix of white lines in a double figure-eight pattern.
- The sides of the head are dark buff, with a buffy-white stripe above the eye.
- The underparts are greyish-white, washed with brown on the breast.

Distribution and habitat

- They have a widespread but fragmented distribution throughout southern and eastern Africa, ranging from South Africa up through Zambia, Tanzania, Kenya and Ethiopia.
- They are variably resident or nomadic with some sub-regional migration.
- They prefer more mesic habitats than most sandgrouse, commonly frequenting short, open grasslands on deep, alluvial soils, often near swamps and rivers.

- In agricultural areas they will also forage in recently burnt grasslands and cultivated fields.

Habits

They drink during the mid-morning, and tolerate more shrubs and trees in the near vicinity of a watering site than open-country sandgrouse. They are found in flocks of 2 to 20 birds, but migratory flocks of up to a couple of hundred are sometimes encountered. When disturbed, they freeze before flushing with heavy, audible wing beats. The flight call is a loud, guttural, two-syllable '*aw aw*'. The take-off call is a harsh '*glock-glock-glock*'.

Food and feeding

Because they inhabit relatively moist habitats, they have a diet of more varied seed types than dry-country sandgrouse. They also use manipulated habitats, often feeding on the seeds of pioneer plants including *Crotalaria*, *Cassia*, *Sesbania* and *Indigofera* species, and weed plants such as *Hibiscus*, *Helianthus*, *Amaranthus*, *Bidens* and *Crotalaria* species. They will even take advantage of waste cereal grains such as oats, wheat, barley and sorghum.

Breeding

They are monogamous solitary nesters, breeding during the drier months from May to September, with a peak in June. The nest is a simple scrape, usually lightly lined with twigs and dry grass placed in a fairly well vegetated site, particularly where weedy fields are used. The 3 eggs are dusky-brown or tawny, with lines and blotches of umber occasionally forming a broad ring around the thickest part, and measure 45.8 x 33.9 mm. The female incubates by day and the male at night. The incubation period of 26–27 days is relatively long compared to that of smaller sandgrouse. When an incubating bird is approached, it first crouches on the nest and then walks off some distance before flushing.

Status and conservation

Their use of agricultural lands may expose them to the misuse of herbicides and to nest losses when these lands are ploughed during the late austral winter in preparation for planting. Nest predators include Banded Mongoose *Mungus mungo* and Pied Crow *Corvus albus*. Hunting may be detrimental where population levels may not be sufficient to allow for a sustainable off-take.

Crowned Sandgrouse
Ganga couronné

Pterocles coronatus

Pterocles coronatus (Lichtenstein, MHC, 1823), Nubia

Crowned Sandgrouse subspecies *P. c. coronatus* (photos by Tasso Leventis)

Classification

Crowned Sandgrouse are a sister species to Yellow-throated Sandgrouse *P. gutturalis* and Madagascan Sandgrouse *P. personatus*, all of which comprise the Short-tailed Group which have a morning drinking peak and also regularly drink in the late afternoon.

There are five subspecies recognised:

P. c. coronatus Lichtenstein, MHC, 1823 in the western and central Sahara to eastern Egypt and northern Sudan;

P. c. vastitas Meinertzhagen, R, 1928 in the Sinai Peninsula and north-eastern Egypt to Israel and Jordan;

P. c. saturates Kinnear, 1927 in northern Oman;

P. c. atratus Hartert, 1902 in the Arabian Peninsula to southern Afghanistan;

P. c. ladas Koelz, 1954 in Pakistan.

Description

- They are a relatively small (average mass 300 g) short-tailed sandgrouse.
- Males have a white forehead bordered by a black stripe from the base of the bill to the front of the crown.
- The sides of the face are white, the crown is pale rufous with a pale blue-grey stripe from above and behind the eye to the nape.
- The chin and upper throat are black with ochre-gold on the lower throat, cheeks and hindneck.
- The back is rufous sandy.
- Females are similar to the female Lichtenstein's Sandgrouse *P. lichtensteinii*, but have an unspotted yellow throat.
- Juveniles are similar to adult females but are more rufous-buff with coarser barring and a whitish throat.
- Downy chicks are rufous-buff above with a similar pattern to that of the downy chick of Namaqua Sandgrouse *P. namaqua*.

Distribution and habitat

- They are widespread across the Sahara from Morocco to the Nile River and on the Red Sea coast in Egypt and Sudan.
- They inhabit widespread hot, arid habitats from stony deserts to mountainsides.

Habits

They are not as gregarious as other sandgrouse. Flocks fly fast to water in the early morning, and not like many other sandgrouse will drink quite brackish water. The '*cla-cla-cla*' or '*cha-chagarra*' chattering call is high pitched and rises in pitch.

Food and feeding

Their diet consists almost exclusively of small hard seeds, particularly those of *Tephrosia apollinea* and *Asphodela tenuifolia*. They will also feed on spilled grains along roads.

Breeding

They are monogamous solitary nesters. Breeding is from May to July in Morocco and Algeria, and during March in Chad. The nest is an unlined scrape or natural hollow, sometimes with a ring of small stones round the rim. The clutch of 3 elliptical smooth eggs are cream to pale yellowish, evenly spotted and blotched with light brown and pale purplish grey. They measure 39.4 x 27.4 mm. Incubation is by the female during the day and by the male during the night. The incubation period is unrecorded.

Status and conservation

They are uncommon in Morocco, otherwise locally common and are the most common sandgrouse in the Ksours Mountains of Algeria.

Black-faced Sandgrouse
Ganga à face noire
Pterocles decoratus

Pterocles decoratus (Cabanis, 1868), Lake Jipe, Kenya

Pair of Black-faced Sandgrouse, male on the right (photo by Jacques Pitteloud)

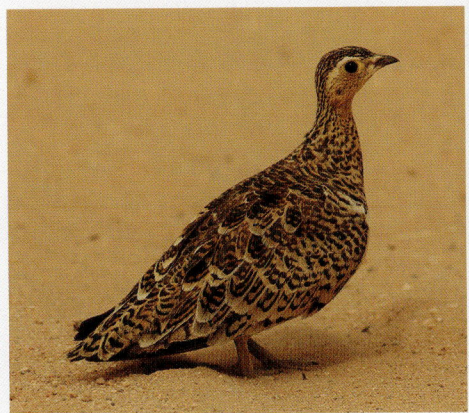

Female Black-faced Sandgrouse
(photo by Jacques Pitteloud)

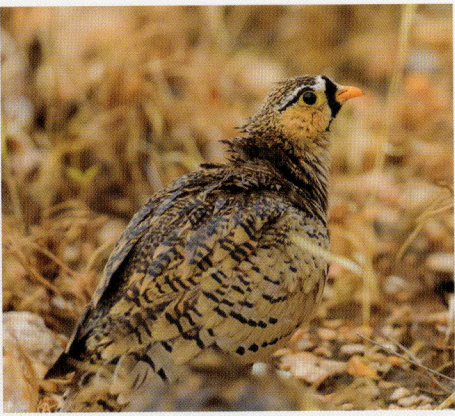

Male Black-faced Sandgrouse
(photo by Jacques Pitteloud)

Male Black-faced Sandgrouse calling (photo by Nik Borrow)

Pair of Black-faced Sandgrouse at a watering site in Ethiopia (photo by Peter W. Hills)

Classification

Black-faced Sandgrouse are sister species to Double-banded Sandgrouse *P. bicinctus*, Four-banded Sandgrouse *P. quadricintus* and Lichtenstein's Sandgrouse *P. lichtensteinii*, comprising the Nyctiperdix clade which drink only in the evening and *Dilophilus* has been suggested as the genus for this group.

There are three subspecies recognised:

P. d. ellenbecki Erlanger, 1905 in southern Ethiopia and southern Somalia to northern Kenya and north-eastern Uganda;

P. d. decoratus Cabanis, 1868 in south-eastern Kenya and eastern Tanzania;

P. d. loveridgei Friedmann, 1928 in south-western Kenya and central Tanzania.

Description

- They are a relatively small sandgrouse with a short tail and a black belly.
- Males have a black face patch from the fore crown down onto the throat and narrow black-and-white stripes curving backwards from above and behind the eyes.
- The narrow black breast band and broad white band across the upper belly distinguishes both sexes from all other sympatric sandgrouse.
- Lichtenstein's Sandgrouse *P. lichtensteinii* also have a black-and-white face pattern, but have no black on the throat and no pronounced supercilium.
- Juveniles are similar to adult females but have rusty upperparts with narrower, darker barring.
- Downy chicks are sandy to gold and grey above, with bold black mottling.

Distribution and habitat

- They are distributed across southern Ethiopia, southern Somalia, north-eastern Uganda, Kenya and in eastern and central Tanzania.
- They are found in dry open savanna, thorn bush, semi-desert scrub and coastal dunes, often seen in bare areas, road verges and in small open spaces in thick bush.

Habits

They are thought to be mostly sedentary. Mostly encountered singly or in pairs, they gather in flocks to drink. They usually drink 1–4 hours after sunrise, and sometimes at dusk. They frequently flock together with Chestnut-bellied Sandgrouse *P. exustus* in East Africa. Their flight-call is a repeated 3-note '*chuck-chuck-chuk*' or '*wop dela wiii*' whistle of two long syllables and one short syllable, and a wispy '*tseeoo whit-i-weeer whit-i-weeer*' flush call.

Food and feeding

Their diet consists mostly of seeds, mainly legumes, including *Trianthema salsoloides*, *Indigofera* species and *Heliotropium undulatifolium*.

Breeding

They are monogamous solitary nesters. They breed mostly from June to August. The nest is an unlined scrape on bare sandy or stony ground. The clutch of 3 long oval rounded greyish buff eggs, spotted or blotched with reddish brown and mauve-grey, measure 33.5 x 25.5 mm.

Status and conservation

They are not threatened globally and are locally common throughout their distribution.

Lichtenstein's Sandgrouse
Ganga de Lichtenstein
Pterocles lichtensteinii

Pterocles lichtensteinii (Temminck, 1825), Nubia

Male Lichtenstein's Sandgrouse (photo by Nik Borrow)

Female Lichtenstein's Sandgrouse (photo by Nik Borrow)

Classification

Lichtenstein's Sandgrouse are sister species to Double-banded Sandgrouse *P. bicinctus*, Four-banded Sandgrouse *P. quadricintus* and Black-faced Sandgrouse *P. decorates*, comprising the Nyctiperdix clade which drink only in the evening and *Dilophilus* has been suggested as the genus for this group.

There are five subspecies recognised:

P. l. targius Geyr von Schweppenburg, 1916 in Morocco and Mauritania east to Chad;

P. l. lichtensteinii Temminck, 1825 in north-eastern Chad, northern Sudan to Eritrea and northern Somalia, eastern and north-eastern Egypt to Jordan;

P. l. sukensis Neumann, 1909 in south-eastern Sudan, southern Ethiopia to central Kenya;

P. l. arabicus Neumann, 1909 in the southern Arabian Peninsula, through southern Iran and Afghanistan to Pakistan;

P. l. ingramsi Bates & Kinnear, 1937 in Hadhramaut, southern Yemen.

Description

- These small short-tailed sandgrouse appear dark because of their close barring.
- Males have a distinctive black-and-white marked crown and forehead, a white supercilium extending backwards, yellow breast with two black breast bands, an orange and a yellow breast band, and heavily barred neck and wing coverts.
- Females are uniformly barred, lacking any distinctive markings, similar to female Crowned Sandgrouse *P. coronatus*, but their face and throat are spotted, not plain yellow.
- Juveniles are similar to adult females, but are more closely barred above and below.
- Downy chicks are brown with light chocolate brown lores, supercilium, ear coverts and below the eyes, bordered below by a pale malar stripe and above by a pale lateral crown-stripe running from the bill to the nape.

Distribution and habitat

- They are distributed across northern and eastern Africa, southern Jordan, Arabia, Socotra, Iran and Pakistan.
- In Africa, they occur in southern Morocco, Mauritania, Senegambia, eastern Mali, adjacent Niger, southern Algeria, northern and eastern Chad, Sudan, south-eastern Egypt, Ethiopia, northern Somalia and Kenya.
- They inhabit rocky and bushy desert areas and arid bushveld with scattered shrubs, avoiding open desert.

Habits

They are less gregarious than other sandgrouse, and fly singly just above vegetation to drink after dark and before dawn. They are selective of drinking sites with low salinity water. They spend most of the day inactive in the shade of a rock or bush. Mostly silent in flight, but will utter a double liquid-whistle '*whittou-whittou*' call occasionally.

Food and feeding

Their diet consists largely of the seeds of *Vachellia* (*Acacia*) *seyal*, 'A'. *ehrenbergiana* as well as *Asphodelus*, *Cassia* and *Prospia* species. They will also eat the flowers and leaves of *Mesembryanthemum* species, and some insects (beetles, ants, ant-lions) and their larvae.

Breeding

They are monogamous solitary nesters, breeding mostly from May to July. The nest is an unlined scrape usually among scattered trees or rocks. The clutch of 2–3 elliptical olive, brownish-olive, pinkish or very pale buff eggs are blotched, spotted or sparsely marked with reddish brown and underlying purplish grey. They measure 42.0 x 26.3 mm. Their incubation biology is unknown.

Status and conservation

Their global population size is alleged to be stable in the absence of evidence for any declines or substantial threats, and they are generally locally common, although uncommon in West Africa, Sudan and Kenya.

Four-banded Sandgrouse
Ganga quadribande
Pterocles quadricinctus

Pterocles quadricinctus (Temminck, 1815), Senegal

ABOVE Female Four-banded Sandgrouse in Nigeria (photo by Tasso Leventis)

LEFT Male Four-banded Sandgrouse in Cameroon (photo by Tasso Leventis)

Classification

Four-banded Sandgrouse are sister species to Double-banded Sandgrouse *P. bicinctus*, Lichtenstein's Sandgrouse *P. lichtensteinii* and Black-faced Sandgrouse *P. decorates*, comprising the Nyctiperdix clade which drink only in the evening and *Dilophilus* has been suggested as the genus for this group.

This is a monotypic species with no subspecies recognised.

Description

- This is a smallish short-tailed sandgrouse.
- Males have a chestnut, white and black chest band, and a black-and-white forehead pattern similar to that of Double-banded Sandgrouse *P. bicinctus*, Black-faced Sandgrouse *P. decoratus* and Lichtenstein's Sandgrouse *P. lichtensteinii*, but are not sympatric with the former and lack the black throat of *P. decoratus* and barred throat and breast of *P. lichtensteinii*.
- They also have a plain buff-brown neck and upper breast.
- In flight, blackish flight feathers contrast with grey underwing coverts.
- Females have a plain buff breast and barred belly.
- Juveniles are more rufous than adults with finer black barring.
- Downy chicks have a dorsal pattern similar to most sandgrouse chicks, but with fewer white lines creating a single not double figure-eight pattern on the back.

Distribution and habitat

- They are distributed from Senegal and The Gambia across the Afrotropics in a narrow band to Eritrea, Ethiopia and western Kenya.
- They inhabit dry, open or partly wooded savannas, open and bushy grasslands, scrubby coastal dunes and cultivated pastures often on clay or stony soils.

Habits

They are usually seen in pairs or small flocks which are sedentary to partial migrant and mostly nocturnal, resting inactive during the day. When flushed, they have a zig-zag flight for a short distance before landing. They fly low to watering sites at sunset, thereafter scattering to feed until late at night. Their flight call is a piercing rhythmic whistled '*wur-wulli*' or '*pirrou-ee*', the last note tremulous.

Food and feeding

Like most sandgrouse, their diet consists mostly of small seeds.

Breeding

They are monogamous solitary nesters, breeding from November to June, but mostly from February to March. The nest is a bare scrape, or lightly lined with grass, on bare stony soil or shingle, or among scatter scrub such as *Bauhinia* trees. The clutch of 2–3 eggs equally rounded at each end are clay-pink or salmon-buff, spotted and flecked with orange-brown or pale brown and underlying mauve. They measure 39.6 x 27.6 mm. Their incubation biology is unknown.

Status and conservation

They are fairly common throughout most of their range, locally common in Senegambia, common in Mali, abundant in northern Ivory Coast during dry season, common in Nigeria and Chad south of 16°N, fairly common in Sudan and apparently uncommon in Kenya.

Double-banded Sandgrouse
Ganga bibande

Pterocles bicinctus

Pterocles bicinctus (Temminck, 1815), Great Fish River, south-eastern Namibia

Female Double-banded Sandgrouse (photo by Ian White)

Male Double-banded Sandgrouse (photo by Maans Booysen)

Male Double-banded Sandgrouse (photo by Ian White)

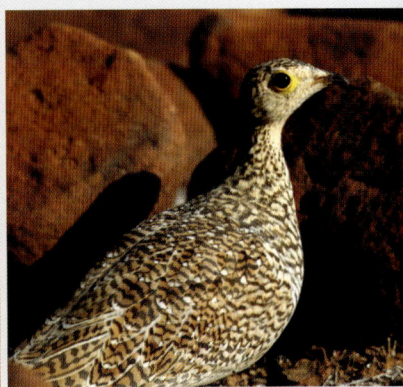

Female Double-banded Sandgrouse (photo by Tasso Leventis)

GAMEBIRDS

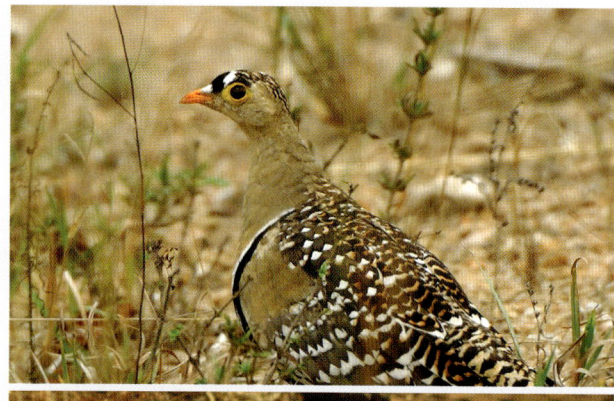

Male Double-banded Sandgrouse
(photo by Eric Stockenstroom)

Female Double-banded Sandgrouse
(photo by Maans Booysen)

Male Double-banded Sandgrouse (both photos by Ian White)

Classification

Double-banded Sandgrouse are sister species to Four-banded Sandgrouse *P. quadricinctus*, Lichtenstein's Sandgrouse *P. lichtensteinii* and Black-faced Sandgrouse *P. decorates*, comprising the Nyctiperdix clade which drink only in the evening and *Dilophilus* has been suggested as the genus for this group.

Four subspecies are recognised:

P. b. bicinctus Temminck, 1815 in north-western South Africa, Namibia, and Botswana;

P. b. multicolor Hartert, 1908 in north-eastern South Africa and eastern Botswana;

P. b. usheri Benson, 1947 in western Mozambique, Zambia and southern Malawi;

P. b. ansorgei Benson, 1947 in south-western Angola.

Description

- They are a medium-sized short-tailed sandgrouse.
- Males are the only sandgrouse in their range with a bold black-and-white band across the forehead, between the eyes and the beak, a lightly speckled crown and a yellow bill.
- Females are similar to female Namaqua Sandgrouse *P. namaqua*, but have a barred, not streaked upper breast and, as in the male, rounded tail feathers.
- Juveniles resemble adult females, but their back plumage is more pinkish-brown and has less barring.
- Their upperparts are speckled and finely mottled with black.
- The throat and upper breast are pinkish-buff, highlighted with light brown, with each feather having a brown bar.
- The crown of downy chicks has two dark brown patches, speckled and bordered with black and bisected and surrounded by white.
- The sides of the head are brown, and there is a white stripe above and two white stripes behind each eye.
- Their back has patches of rufous-brown edged with black and separated by white lines that form a double figure-eight pattern.

Distribution and habitat

- Widespread in southern African, they extend marginally into Angola, Zambia and Malawi.
- They are abundant in northern Botswana, northern Zimbabwe and along the Limpopo River system and are the only sandgrouse species in Mozambique.

- They are largely sedentary, although may move in search of water, especially in the dry season.
- They prefer wooded habitats, favouring *Brachystegia* and mopane woodlands and the savannas of the Okavango Delta region in Botswana, the Etosha Pan in Namibia, and the Limpopo River valley and Limpopo Province lowveld in South Africa.
- In the drier, western areas they prefer rocky hill slopes or gravel plains, often far less vegetated than in the eastern parts of their range.

Habits

They drink at last light, often after sunset. Birds weave through adjacent trees then flutter before dropping to the water's edge. Distances covered between feeding, roosting and watering sites are shorter than those travelled by open country sandgrouse species. They are largely inactive during the day, resting beneath scrubby vegetation. They are also less vocal in flight than other sandgrouse. Their flush call is a harsh '*chuck chuck*'. At the drinking site they give a musical rapid, 7–10 syllable '*pitee YOU'RE iti pur*'. When disturbed, they may give a growling '*churr*'.

Food and feeding

They forage during the cooler hours of the morning and evening, and late on moonlit nights. Their diet consists of the seeds of herbs and annual weeds, including *Requernia*, *Tephrosia*, *Cyperus*, *Bidens* and *Datura* species. When foraging, they search a restricted area particularly thoroughly for scattered seeds.

Breeding

They are monogamous solitary nesters breeding from May to October. The nest is a scrape, sparsely lined with dry vegetation, either well concealed in vegetation or more open. The clutch of 3 pinkish-buff eggs, spotted and streaked with reddish-brown and slate-grey, measure 37.1 x 26.6 mm. Unlike most other sandgrouse, the male incubates during various parts of the day and the female incubates at night. The incubation period is 23–24 days.

Status and conservation

An aspect of concern is where they are hunted as an added quarry during game hunts, since the peak game-hunting season during the austral winter straddles their breeding season. Also of concern is that they are shot when approaching their drinking site at dusk, resulting in birds being prevented from drinking at that site and them going through the night without drinking. This can be resolved by leaving nearby alternative watering sites undisturbed.

Burchell's Sandgrouse
Ganga de Burchell
Pterocles burchelli

Pterocles burchelli (Sclater, WL, 1922), near Griquatown, Northern Cape Province, South Africa

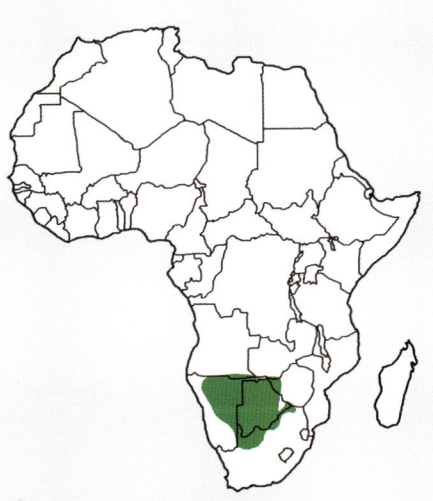

Male Burchell's Sandgrouse flushes from a drinking site (photo by Ian White)

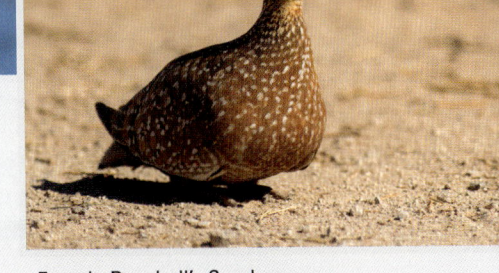

Female Burchell's Sandgrouse (photo by Dayne Braine)

GAMEBIRDS

Male Burchell's Sandgrouse (photo by Ian White)

Male Burchell's Sandgrouse approaching a watering site (photo by Ian White)

Two pairs of Burchell's Sandgrouse in their arid environment (photo by Andre Botha)

Classification

Burchell's Sandgrouse, which drink in the morning, are a weakly supported sister species to Pin-tailed Sandgrouse *P. alchata* at the base of the clade that comprises the Short-tailed and Long-tailed Sandgrouse.

They are monotypic with no subspecies recognised. In southern Africa, they are sometimes called Spotted Sandgrouse, but this creates confusion with the Spotted Sandgrouse *P. senegallus* of northern Africa.

Description

- They have a salmon-pink breast and belly feathers and brownish-yellow upperparts, with overall bold, white spotting.
- Males have a grey face and throat, and a prominent yellow eye patch, while females have a yellowish face with less prominent grey skin around the eye.
- They have a stocky build and relatively long legs.
- Juveniles resemble adult females, but the breast is buffy, with each feather having a pale tip above a light brown bar.
- The white spots on the wings are duller, and each feather is barred with buff.
- Downy chicks have a golden-buff forehead grading posteriorly to white and bordered with black.
- The crown is white in the centre, bordered with black and surrounded by light brown speckled with black.
- The face and sides of the head are buffy, with brown-and-white stripes, and there is a light brown ring around the eye.
- The back has a striking white double figure-eight marking, bordered with black.

Distribution and habitat

- They are a near-endemic in southern African, extending marginally into south-eastern Angola and south-western Zambia.
- Their distribution is centred on the sandy soils of the Kalahari basin, from western South Africa and extreme north-western Zimbabwe, across Botswana and the north-eastern half of Namibia, avoiding the driest southern and western regions of Namibia.
- They are mostly found on red Kalahari sands with dry savanna or scattered scrub, or shrub and grass tufts up to 50 cm tall, mostly in arid sweet bushveld and Kalahari thornveld.

Habits

Although largely sedentary, they may be nomadic in response to the availability of seeds. They arrive to drink 2–3 hours after sunrise, landing directly at the water's edge or even in the shallow water, drink rapidly and leave the watering site without delay. They avoid brackish, salty water. They are cryptic and secretive away from water holes, crouching before flushing at close distance when disturbed, or run with a hunched posture through the grass. They have a distinctive, mellow two-note '*chok-lit*' flight call.

Food and feeding

Their diet consists of small, dry seeds of legumes (Fabaceae), with a preference in the Kalahari for *Lophiocarpus burchelli*, *Requernia sphaerosperma* and *Tephrosia* species. They prefer to forage in grassy areas with well-drained, sandy substrata.

Breeding

They are monogamous solitary nesters and breed during the dry season from April to October. The nest is a scrape in the sand, usually placed next to a grass tuft or shrub. The clutch of 3 cream to tawny-olive eggs, with elongated smears of dark olive-brown and greyish-mauve measure 36.7 x 25.7 mm. The female incubates by day and the male at night. The incubation period is unknown.

Status and conservation

They have benefited from the provision of artificial watering sites, such as borehole livestock troughs, which have allowed them to forage further afield. The loss of breeding adults due to wing-shooting during their breeding season, added to big-game hunting and, coincidentally, during Namaqua Sandgrouse *P. namaqua* hunts can increase the mortality of eggs and flightless chicks. Fortunately, they favour habitats different from Namaqua Sandgrouse, and can therefore be excluded from sites where Namaqua Sandgrouse are regularly hunted by providing watering sites within their favoured habitats. Where they do drink at the same site, they also arrive for drinking later than Namaqua Sandgrouse, which can be recognised by their different call and shooting should then cease.

Madagascan Sandgrouse
Ganga masqué
Pterocles personatus

Pterocles personatus (Gould, 1843), Majambo Bay, Madagascar

Male Madagascan Sandgrouse (both photos by Dubi Shapiro)

A pair of Madagascan Sandgrouse in flight, female on the right (photo by Otto Schmidt)

Classification

Madagascan Sandgrouse are a sister species to Yellow-throated Sandgrouse *P. gutturalis* and thereafter to Crowned Sandgrouse *P. coronatus*, all of which comprise the Short-tailed Group which have a morning drinking peak, and also regularly drink in the late afternoon.

They are monotypic with no subspecies recognised.

Description

- They are short-tailed rufous-tan sandgrouse with black flight feathers.
- Males have a bold black face mask surrounding the bill, a yellow area of bare skin around the eye, a pinkish-buff breast, a light brown mottled back, brown wings and paler underparts barred with black.
- Females are generally duller with tan upperparts, finely speckled and barred with brown.
- Juveniles resemble females but have duller plumage.
- Downy chicks are warm buff above with a buffy-white median band and two transverse bands, and buffy white below, with buffy-white lines above and below the eye.

Distribution and habitat

- They are the only sandgrouse found on Madagascar.
- They are a common endemic to western and south-western Madagascar, commonly seen at the mouth of the Onilahy River near Augustin, at Lake Ranobe and Lake Amboromalandy.
- They inhabit open areas such as grasslands, savanna, open wooded plains and the surrounds of lakes and rivers at low altitudes down to sea level.
- They prefer level, sparsely vegetated ground, sometimes with rocks, including *Xerophyta* savannas, slightly degraded and open spiny forest.

Habits

They are usually found in small groups that fly fast and powerfully when flushed. They drink mainly in the early morning, but may appear at waterholes, including rivers, ponds and lakes, at any time of the day, typically in groups of 2–6, more exceptionally 20–40 individuals, with totals of 300–400 birds reported at favoured sites, particularly in the dry season. The flight-call is a distinctive, low pitched, nasal, repetitive '*katakataka*', '*ak-ak-ak-ak-ak-ak-ak-ak*', which may also be given on the ground.

Food and feeding

They forage in slightly degraded or open spiny forest or areas dominated by *Xerophyta* or introduced grasses. Their diet consists of seeds, and insects are also reported in their diet.

Breeding

They are monogamous solitary nesters, but sometimes nest in loose colonies. They breed through the late dry and early wet season (August–November) and again in the early dry season (April–June). The nest is a scrape in gravelly, sandy or hard ground, often lined with some plant fibres, usually on level or slightly sloping ground, occasionally at the foot of a shrub within relatively dense vegetation or under large *Tamarindus indica* plants, sometimes on lakeshores and even on coastal beaches. The clutch of 3 buff to greenish-brown eggs are finely marked with brown and grey, similar to those of Black-bellied Sandgrouse *P. orientalis*, and measure 45.0 × 32.6 mm. Incubation is by both sexes, but the period is unknown.

Status and conservation

They are not considered to currently have any specific conservation concern largely because they have a wide range within Madagascar and are common in the west and south of the country, although they are less common further north.

PART 6
Snipes, Greater Painted-Snipe & Eurasian Woodcock

SNIPES, GREATER PAINTED-SNIPE AND EURASIAN WOODCOCK

Classification

Snipes are wading birds of the Order Charadriiformes consisting of 25 species globally within three genera:

- *Coenocorypha* Gray, GR, 1855
- *Gallinago* Brisson, 1760
- *Lymnocrytes* Boie, F, 1826, in the family Scolopacidae

The three species of painted-snipes, including the Greater Painted-snipe *Rostratula benghalensis* of Africa, are not closely related to typical snipes, and are placed in their own family, the Rostratulidae.

The Eurasian Woodcock *Scolopax rusticola* is also a member of the family Scolopacidae.

Description

- Snipes are cryptic waders with relatively short legs, a characteristically disproportionate long and slender bill, and superbly camouflaged plumage.
- Unlike true snipes where the males and females appear very similar, painted-snipes have distinct sexual dimorphism, and even more unusual, the females are more striking than the males.

Natural history

Gallinago snipes have almost a worldwide distribution and include three of the African snipes, the genus *Lymnocryptes* includes Jack Snipe *L. minimus*, which occur in Asia and Europe, and are Palearctic migrants to central and West Africa, while *Coenocorypha* snipes are found only in the outlying islands of New Zealand. Pin-tailed Snipe *G. stenura*, which is a migrant between northern Russia and southern Asia, is only a rare vagrant to Socotra, Somalia and East Africa, and is not covered in this book.

Snipes favour various types of wet, marshy habitats including swamps, flooded grasslands, and along muddy rivers and estuaries with emergent vegetation. Snipes generally avoid areas with dense vegetation, preferring marshy areas with patchy mud openings to forage and avoid predators.

PREVIOUS PAGE A pair of Greater Painted-snipe with the female crouched on the right (photo by Andre Botha)

The Eurasian Woodcock is the only one of five woodcock species that visits northern Africa from the western Palearctic as a non-breeding migrant.

Evolutionary placement

- Snipes, painted-snipes and woodcocks are all waders, also known as shorebirds.
- The shorebirds are commonly split into two suborders or clades:
  - Scolopaci, which include snipes, painted-snipes, woodcocks, jacanas, sandpipers, curlews, godwits and dowitchers; and
  - Charadrii, which include plovers (lapwings), stilts, avocets, thick-knees and sheathbills.

Conservation

Their superb camouflage and tendency to stand motionless when approached make them elusive for the bird watcher and wing-shooter to detect, before their explosive flush. When flushed, snipes fly fast, some with a dodging flight path, which leaves the birder baffled and hunters with difficulty estimating a correct aiming lead for the bird's erratic flight pattern. It is suggested that the difficulties involved in hunting snipe gave rise to the term 'sniper'.

The two main threats to their population stability is netting in Africa, Europe and the Middle East, and the degradation and drainage of wetlands. Only two of the seven species covered in this section are threatened; both the Great Snipe *Gallinago media* and Madagascan Snipe *G. macrodactyla* are listed as Near Threatened (The IUCN Red List of Threatened Species v 2015-4).

Greater Painted-snipe
Rhynchée peinte
Rostratula benghalensis
Rallus benghalensis (Linnaeus, 1758), Bengal, Asia

Male Greater Painted-snipe (photo by Ian White)

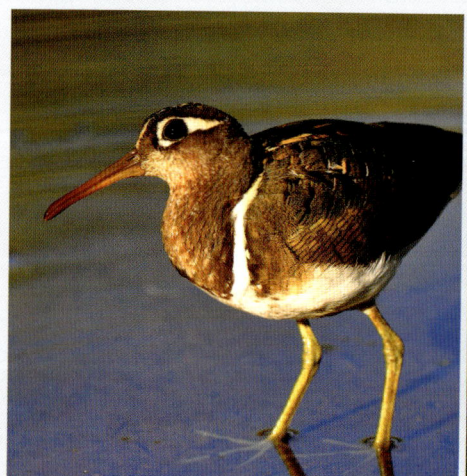

Female Greater Painted-snipe (photo by Ian White)

Female Greater Painted-snipe (photo by Andre Botha)

SNIPES, GREATER PAINTED-SNIPE & EURASIAN WOODCOCK

Two male Greater Painted-snipe (photo by Andre Botha)

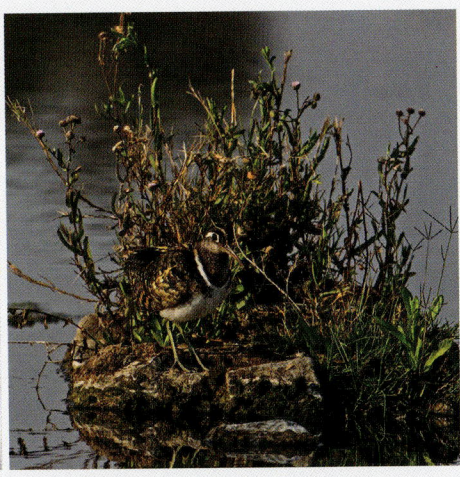

Male Greater Painted-snipe at the nest (photo by Andre Botha)

Female Greater Painted-snipe showing her attractive wing pattern (photo by Andre Botha)

Female Greater Painted-snipe landing (photo by Andre Botha)

Classification

They are monotypic with no subspecies recognised. A suggested separate race, *R. b. madagascariensis*, on Madagascar, based on being darker and greyer than mainland African birds is not yet recognised.

Description

- They differ from true snipes by having a white eye-ring which extends onto the ear coverts, a dark breast band and an obvious white breast which extends up onto the shoulders like white braces.
- They have rounded wings and a slow wingbeat.
- Their bill is pale, shorter than that of true snipes and is slightly decurved at the tip.
- The legs are longer than those of true snipes.
- Females are the dominant sex and are more strikingly marked, with a rich chestnut neck and breast, and uniform upperparts.
- Males and juveniles are more cryptic, with a grey neck, buff spotting on the upperparts and a conspicuous golden 'V' on the back.
- Juveniles are similar to the adult male in appearance, but are generally slightly greyer and the breast appears streaked rather than barred.
- Downy chicks are pale with a dark stripe on the crown and down the centre of the back, and another dark stripe across the side of the face and across the upper-wings on each side.

Distribution and habitat

- They have an extensive Old World range, from sub-Saharan Africa and Madagascar east to southern Asia and Japan.
- In Africa, they are patchily distributed from Senegambia across to Egypt and south to South Africa and Madagascar.
- They are absent from forested and desert areas.
- They are generally an uncommon resident and local nomad.
- Favoured habitats are marshes and flooded grasslands, particularly with good vegetation cover and receding water levels, and exposed mud flats between the vegetation.

Habits

They are usually solitary, in pairs, or occasionally in small groups. They are secretive, reluctant to flush, and can remain motionless for long periods. Flight is slow on large, broad wings, with legs often trailing, somewhat rallid-like. Silent when flushed. Females give a wheezy hiss and repeated '*wuk-oooooo*', repeated monotonously in display, often at night.

Food and feeding

Much like true snipes, they forage by probing mud with their bill, frequently bobbing their body. Their diet consists of worms, grasshoppers, crickets, crustaceans, snails and seeds.

Breeding

They are polyandrous, with a female mating with 2–4 males during each breeding season. The nest is a slight depression usually hidden in short sedges or grasses, with vegetation bent and trodden down to form the nest. The clutch of 2–5 eggs measure 35.5 x 25.0 mm, and are smooth creamy-beige with bold scrolls and blotches of dark brown and black. Incubation by the male only lasts for 17–19 days. Chicks are cared for by the male only and fledge at 30–35 days.

Status and conservation

Although there is no evidence of significant changes in distribution, local populations can be severely affected by rural development. Their favoured habitats can also be transformed by dam construction, wetland modification and the invasion of flood plains by tall vegetation, for example, Bulrushes *Typha capensis*, which interfere with streamflow and seasonal flooding cycles.

Jack Snipe
Bécassine sourde

Lymnocryptes minimus

Scolopax minima (Brünnich, 1764), Christiansø Islands, off Bornholm, Denmark

Jack Snipe (photo by Tasso Leventis)

Jack Snipe (photo by Markus Lagerqvist)

Classification

The Jack Snipe is monotypic with no subspecies recognised.

Description

- They are smaller and shorter-billed than the Common Snipe *G. gallinago*, with narrow wings and a buffy hind-neck.
- Unlike other African snipes, they have a distinctive head pattern where the crown lacks a pale central stripe, rather they have a double, pale buff supercilium which splits above the eye.
- They have two bold yellowish stripes on each side of the dark glossy upperparts and streaked breast and flanks.
- The upper tail also differs by being wedge-shaped and wholly dark.
- Juveniles are similar to adults but have white under-tail coverts with smaller and paler brown stripes.

Distribution and habitat

- They are an uncommon Palearctic migrant to the northern Afrotropics and Morocco, visiting the continent mostly from October to March.
- They are also a rare vagrant to Bird Island, Seychelles.
- They prefer brackish and freshwater habitats including moist and waterlogged areas with soft silty mud and short grass or sedges.

Habits

They are mostly crepuscular or nocturnal. They flush less readily than other snipes, preferring to freeze and rely on their camouflage. Their flight is also relatively slow and weak, less erratic, and they drop down into cover sooner. Generally silent in the non-breeding season, but when flushed, sometimes utter a faint '*gah*'.

Food and feeding

They usually feed singly or in small loose groups. When foraging they have a distinctive rhythmic bobbling motion while probing in soft mud or picking up food items from the surface. Their diet consists mostly of adult and larval insects, annelids, small freshwater and terrestrial gastropods and sometimes seeds or other plant material.

Breeding

They are a non-breeding migrant to Africa, breeding mostly in Scandinavia, Russia and Siberia in wet marshy bogs, tundra and meadows during the boreal summer.

Status and conservation

They are not globally threatened although populations have declined in some areas. The major threats are wetland degradation and drainage for agricultural intensification, afforestation and peat extraction. Hunting pressure is also a threat, where during the autumn migration, 5% of the European population is believed to be shot annually.

African Snipe
Bécassine africaine

Gallinago nigripennis

Gallinago nigripennis (Bonaparte, 1839), Cape of Good Hope, South Africa

African Snipe possibly subspecies *G. n. angolensis* at Lobatse, Botswana with sediment covered bill (photo by Ian White)

Camouflaged African Snipe (photo by Jacques Pitteloud)

African Snipe subspecies *G. n. nigripennis* at Marievale Bird Sanctuary, Gauteng, South Africa on frosty vegetation (photo by Andre Botha)

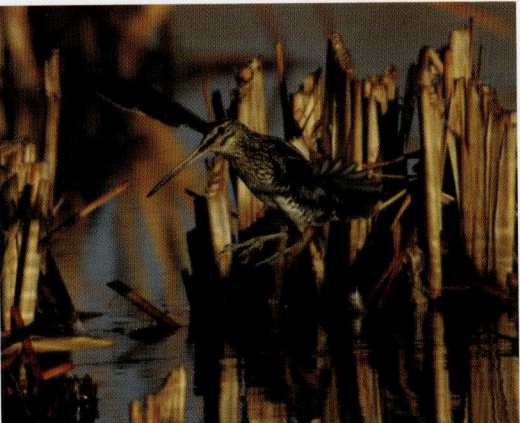

Landing African Snipe (photo by Andre Botha)

Classification

There are three subspecies recognised:

G. n. nigripennis Bonaparte, 1839 in southern Mozambique and South Africa;

G. n. aequatorialis Rüppell, 1845 in Ethiopia to eastern Democratic Republic of the Congo, eastern Zimbabwe and northern Mozambique;

G. n. angolensis Bocage, 1868 in Angola and northern Namibia across to western Zimbabwe and Zambia.

Description

- The African Snipe, also known as Ethiopian Snipe in some parts, is darker on top than the Common Snipe *G. gallinago*, and has heavily streaked neck and breast feathers, which contrast more with the white belly.
- In flight, they have short broad wings and also show more white in the outer-tail feathers, even though the five outer-tail feathers are barred black and white.
- The pale fringes to the greater coverts contrast more with the darker wings than for that of the Great Snipe *G. media*, the wings are shorter and broader and the bill is slightly longer.
- Juveniles are similar to adults, but are less strongly marked on the body and the wings are more mottled and barred.
- Downy chicks are rich tawny with a black spot above the base of the bill, a black streak through the lores and chin, and a band across the forehead.

Distribution and habitat

- African Snipe are common residents with varying local nomadism.
- They occur from central Ethiopia, down the Rift Valley, across to Angola and down to South Africa, with a separate population in western Kenya and northern Tanzania.
- Their favoured habitats include marshes and flooded grasslands, usually in muddy areas with short, patchy vegetation.

Habits

They usually occur as scattered individuals, but many can inhabit one wetland. If alarmed, they freeze, and their cryptic plumage provides effective camouflage when the bird stands motionless among wetland vegetation. When flushed they give a sucking '*scaap*' sound and their flight is more erratic than that of Great Snipe. Males make a whirring '*whu-whu-whu-whu-whu*' drumming sound with their stiffened outer-tail feathers during their stooping aerial display flights.

Food and feeding
They are mainly crepuscular or nocturnal foragers, probing soft mud for prey. Their diet consists of annelids, the larvae of beetles, dragonflies and flies, small molluscs and crustaceans.

Breeding
They are monogamous solitary nesters, breeding mostly after the rainy season. The nest is a small platform of grass within vegetation tussocks surrounded by wet or flooded ground. The clutch of 2–3 pale greenish or buffish eggs are strongly spotted and blotched blackish-brown, pale brown and slate grey mostly at the large end, and measure 41.2 x 29.6 mm. Incubation by the hen lasts for 19–21 days.

Status and conservation
They are threatened by habitat loss and degradation, such as decreases in the area of natural pastures and lake-edges and stream-edge marshes, agricultural expansion and increases in the area of lake mudflats due to increased siltation and reduced water supply because of bush encroachment, overgrazing, burning and the draining of wetlands.

Great Snipe
Bécassine double
Gallinago media

Scolopax media (Latham, 1787), England

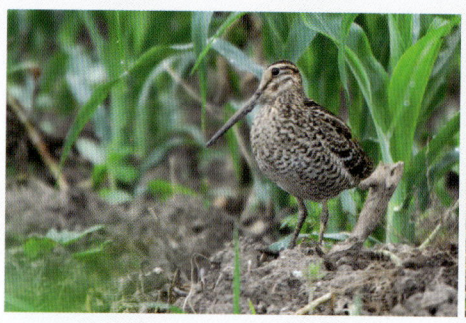

Great Snipe in a cropland in Lubumbashi, Kataga, Democratic Republic of the Congo (photo by Stéphane Doppagne)

Great Snipe (photo by Tasso Leventis)

Great Snipe flight patterns (photo by Bruno Portier)

Great Snipe (photo by Stéphane Doppagne)

Classification

The Great Snipe is monotypic with no subspecies recognised.

Description

- They are most easily distinguished from the other African snipes by their boldly barred flanks, belly and vent.
- Adults also have large, white tips to trailing upper-wing coverts forming prominent white wing bars and conspicuous white sides and tip of the outer-tail feathers.
- They differ from the Common Snipe *G. gallinago* by being slightly larger with a shorter bill, their underparts are more heavily marked, and they appear darker and heavier in flight, with a slower, more direct flight.

Distribution and habitat

- The Great Snipe is an uncommon Palearctic migrant to the flatter, open regions of West Africa, and from Sudan and Ethiopia in north-central Africa down to the northern parts of southern Africa, eastern South Africa and the Seychelles.
- They are most common in Africa from October to May.
- Similar to other snipes, their favoured habitats in Africa include marshes and flooded grasslands, but can also be found in short grass away from water.

Habits

They usually occur singly or in small loose groups. When flushed, they fly fast in a straight line, not dodging and jinking like the flight of African Snipe *G. nigripennis* and Common Snipe. Their flush flight is also usually fairly short. The bill is held more level in flight. They are generally silent, but occasionally utter one or two short croaks when flushed, deeper than that of the African Snipe.

Food and feeding

They are crepuscular or nocturnal foragers, feeding by probing in soft mud much like the other snipes. Their diet consists mainly of annelids, small molluscs, insects and some plant material.

Breeding

They are a non-breeding migrant to Africa, breeding mostly in Scandinavia and Russia in wet marshy bogs, tundra and meadows during the boreal summer.

Status and conservation

They are experiencing a population decline, owing primarily to habitat loss in their breeding range, including conversion of marshlands and floodplain meadows to intensive agriculture, wetland drainage and the submergence of river valleys during the creation of dams, as well as to hunting in eastern Europe and in their African wintering range. Their conservation status is therefore listed as Near Threatened (The IUCN Red List of Threatened Species v 2015-4).

Common Snipe
Bécassine des marais

Gallinago gallinago

Scolopax gallinago (Linnaeus, 1758), Sweden

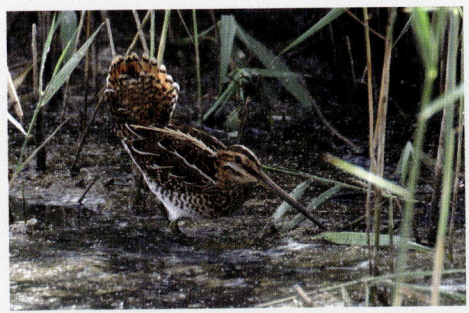

Common Snipe fan-tail display
(photo by Markus Lagerqvist)

Common Snipe showing the specialised tail feathers for the drumming display (photo by Tasso Leventis)

A moving flock of Common Snipe
(photo by Tasso Leventis)

Common Snipe (photo by Tasso Leventis)

> ## Classification
>
> There are two subspecies recognised:
>
> *G. g. faeroeensis* Brehm, CL, 1831 in Iceland, Faroe Islands, Orkney and Shetland Islands;
>
> *G. g. gallinago* Linnaeus, 1758 in Europe, Asia and Africa.

Description

- The Common Snipe is similar to the African Snipe *G. nigripennis*, but is slightly paler above and has much less white in the outer tail, with the white confined to the tail tips and outer margins of the outer tail feathers.
- Their bill is slightly shorter, and the wings are longer and more pointed.
- Another similar species is the Pin-tailed Snipe *G. stenura*, which is a rare vagrant to Socotra, Somalia and East Africa, not covered in this book. However, the Pin-tailed Snipe has a narrow pale grey trailing edge to the secondaries in flight, which is obvious and white in Common Snipe.
- Furthermore, the toes of the Pin-tailed Snipe project slightly beyond the tail tip in flight.
- The Pin-tailed Snipe is also slightly paler and has a broader pale eye-stripe from the base of the bill.

Distribution and habitat

- They are a common Palearctic migrant to Africa, presumably from Russia, during October to March and also a vagrant to the Seychelles.
- They are common across the northern Afrotropics down to the northern Democratic Republic of the Congo and northern Tanzania, less common in northern Zambia and Malawi.
- They prefer permanent and perennial swamps, marshy edges of lakes and dams, and seasonally flooded grasslands and rice fields.

Habits

Although largely solitary, they will form small groups. They are mainly crepuscular, resting in wetland vegetation during the day. They walk deliberately with the bill angled downwards. They squat when disturbed, but, if flushed, they have an explosive, zig-zag tilting flight, and utter a loud, harsh '*creech*', which is more rasping than that of the African Snipe. They will also perch on a low object while uttering an insistent '*chip-per, chip-per*'.

Food and feeding

They forage in shallow water sometimes up to their belly in the water, probing deeply and vigorously in soft mud, often immersing their bill up to eye level. Their diet consists of annelids, insects and their larvae, small molluscs and crustaceans, spiders, small frogs and some plant material.

Breeding

They are a non-breeding migrant to Africa, breeding mostly in the Azores, Iceland and widely through Europe, Russia and North America in wet marshy bogs, tundra and meadows during the boreal summer.

Status and conservation

They are generally common to abundant across the northern Afrotropics and are not globally threatened. The drainage or degradation of wetlands limits their foraging habitat. They are hunted fairly heavily in Europe.

Madagascan Snipe
Bécassine malgache

Gallinago macrodactyla

Gallinago macrodactyla (Bonaparte, 1839), Madagascar

Madagascan Snipe from Torotorofotsy Marsh, Madagascar (photo by Louise Jasper)

Madagascan Snipe from Vohiparara, Ranomafana, Madagascar (photo by Margaret Sloan)

Classification

Madagascan Snipe are monotypic with no subspecies recognised. They have previously been regarded as conspecific with Common Snipe *G. gallinago* and Noble Snipe *G. nobilis*, but they are resident in Madagascar.

Description

- Their relatively long straight bill and striped head are diagnostic.
- They are similar to African Snipe *G. nigripennis*, but with less contrast between the upperparts and the underparts, and their outer rectrices are greyer brown.
- They are also similar to Common Snipe and other close relatives, but they have a longer dark bill and their legs are dark yellow-olive. They have a narrow greyish trailing edge to secondaries, darker underwings and wing-coverts with warm olive-buff fringes.
- Females are very similar to males, but their average bill length is slightly longer.
- Juveniles are similar to adults but have narrower and paler warm olive-buff fringes to scapulars and mantle feathers.

Distribution and habitat

- They are the only snipe found on Madagascar.
- They are endemic to the eastern and central massif of Madagascar where they are common in the east and north-west.
- They are regularly seen at the Torotorofotsy marshes near Perinet-Analamazaotra and at the marshes and wetlands around Vohiparara in Ranomafana.
- They inhabit largely freshwater, grassy and sedge-covered marshes and swamps, flooded fields, muddy margins of water courses with dense vegetation and rice paddies, from sea level up to elevations of 2 700 m above sea level.

Habits

They are sedentary and secretive. Their flight is fast with a zig-zagging flight path. Their drumming in the courtship display is a noisy '*woo-woo-woo*' during the breeding season. When flushed, they give a harsh rapidly repeated '*eck-eck-eck-eck*' call.

Food and feeding

Outside the breeding season, they frequently forage in small groups of 4–8 birds, probing deep into mud on muddy flats or in shallow water. Their diet consists of insects and worms, seeds and other plant matter.

Breeding

They breed in wet marshy habitats mostly from July to January. The nest is a saucer-shaped depression scantily lined with dry grass, usually on a dry vegetation hammock covered with grass or sedges. The clutch consists of 2–4 eggs, but usually 3. No further information is available on their breeding biology.

Status and conservation

They are threatened by habitat transformation and drainage of natural wetlands, particularly with the spread of rice paddy fields, and hunting pressure may also be a threat. Their conservation status is therefore listed as Near Threatened (The IUCN Red List of Threatened Species v 2015-4).

Eurasian Woodcock
Bécasse des bois

Scolopax rusticola

Scolopax rusticola Linnaeus, 1758, Sweden

Flushing Eurasian Woodcock
(photo by Eduardo Gutierrez González)

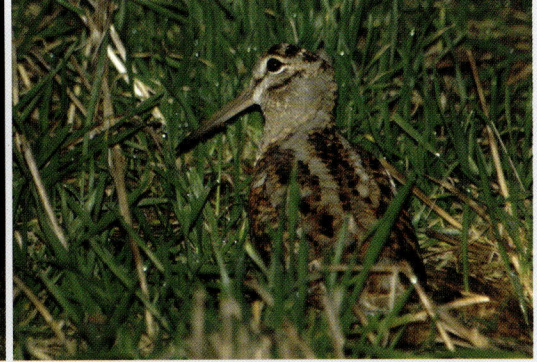

Eurasian Woodcock
(photo by Andrew Hoodless)

Two Eurasian Woodcocks
(photo by Andrew Hoodless)

Eurasian Woodcock in flight
(photo by Eduardo Gutierrez González)

> ## Classification
> The Eurasian Woodcock is a member of the family Scolopacidae, along with the snipes. They are monotypic with no subspecies recognised.

Description

- They are a bulky snipe-like bird with an average weight of 300 g.
- They have cryptic camouflage to suit their woodland habitats, with intricately patterned reddish-brown upperparts and buff underparts.
- Their head is barred with black, not striped like that of its close relatives – the snipes.
- They have large eyes located high on the sides of their head.
- The robust straight bill is flesh brown and darker at the tip.
- The sexes are similar and their heavy build, long broad rounded wings and slow wing-beat differentiate them from the snipes.

Distribution and habitat

- Their distribution is widespread across temperate and subarctic Eurasia, from western Europe to Russia and Siberia.
- They are a Palearctic wintering visitor to north-western Africa, arriving in October and departing in March.
- They inhabit damp open woodlands, coastal areas with thick cover and well vegetated gardens.

Habits

They are crepuscular and rarely active during the day. When flushed, they fly off with a whirring wing noise. They fly direct while migrating or crossing open country, but fly erratically with twisting and fluttering once in woodland. They are usually solitary and migrate singly, but may congregate where foraging conditions are optimal or to roost. When flushed they give a harsh snipe-like '*schaap*'.

Food and feeding

They forage by walking and probing deeply in soft marshy soil in thickets, usually well hidden from sight. They mainly eat earthworms, but also insects and their larvae, slugs, spiders, freshwater molluscs, some plant seeds and grass roots.

Breeding

They are a non-breeding migrant to Africa. In the breeding grounds, they nest on the ground in low cover in woodland or tall heather.

Status and conservation

In many countries, Eurasian Woodcock are hunted as game, and their size, speed and flight pattern make them a very challenging quarry. Recent research in the United Kingdom and France have disclosed results which call for caution in the harvesting of woodcock populations, particularly wintering in western France and Italy, and could be a forewarning of a decline. Other threats are degradation of habitats and harmful pesticides.

GLOSSARY

Antiphonal	Sung in alternation; calling involving two duetting birds, each giving components of what sounds like a single call.
Belly-wetting	During the breeding season, male sandgrouse soak up water in specially designed belly feathers to transport the water to flightless chicks in the desert.
Casque	Bony, horn-like growth covered with a sheath of keratin on the head (or upper mandible) of some birds.
Corm	A nutritious underground storage organ of certain geophyte plants.
Covey	A group of francolins or spurfowls, normally one or more family groups comprising a territorial adult male and female and their grown offspring from the previous breeding season.
Crepuscular	Mostly active at dawn and dusk.
Dust-bathe	Sitting and scratching in light, sandy soil which is worked into the feathers and expelled, presumably to remove parasites and debris in the feathers.
Egg-dumping	When one hen lays her eggs in another's nest.
Eye-stripe	Contrasting (dark or light) stripe on the side of the head running backwards above (supercilium) or at the same level as the eye.
Flight call	Call given as birds flush from cover.
Flush	Explosive flight from cover, normally employed only as a last resort when a bird is trying to evade danger.
Gregarious	Regularly associating in groups.
Incubation	Process whereby adult birds apply body heat to eggs, providing the appropriate temperature and humidity necessary for development of the embryo within.
Keets	Guineafowl chicks.
Migratory	Regular, predictable return movements over the landscape, usually on an annual basis, from a repeatedly used breeding ground to an area some distance away which may provide seasonally abundant food or some other key resource.

Miombo woodland	Mix of savanna and woodland dominated by trees such as *brachystegia*, *combretum*, *terminalia* and *burkea* species and grasses such as *aristida*, *digitaria* and *eragrostis* species.
Monogamous	Mating system in which one adult male mates with only one adult female. See polygynous.
Moustache patch	Strip of distinctively coloured feathers running from the base of the upper bill down the side of the head to below the eye.
Multiple-broods hypothesis	Suggestion that a breeding pair can lay and successfully rear chicks from more than one clutch of eggs in one breeding season.
Nomadic	Descriptive of irregular, unpredictable movements over the landscape, probably to exploit ephemerally abundant food resources.
Polygynous	Mating system where one adult male mates with more than one adult female.
Precocial	Descriptive of newly hatched young that are active and leave the nest immediately after hatching, and are therefore not fully dependent on their parents.
Resident	Descriptive of a bird that spends its entire life at or near the area in which it hatched or where it has established a territory, without seasonal movement.
Savanna	Vegetation with a mixture of grass and some bush and trees, often maintained by fire or feeding by elephants.
Sedentary	Tending to remain near a particular area (e.g. the site of hatching) for life, with minimal dispersal.
Sexual dimorphism	In which males and females of the same species differ markedly in their plumage and/or size.
Species	The fundamental products of evolution and units of conservation management; often identified by evidence of a lack of interbreeding with very similar birds occurring on the same ground.
Subspecies	Geographical races of a single species between which there are no intrinsic barriers to interbreeding.
Supercilium	A plumage stripe which runs from the base of a bird's beak above its eye, ending towards the rear of the bird's head.
Territorial	Process of defending a piece of ground from the intrusion of members of the same species; normally by males only.
Vermiculated	Refers to irregular, ill-defined, 'wormy' barring.

BIBLIOGRAPHY AND FURTHER READING

(References listed in Little and Crowe. 2011. *Gamebirds of Southern Africa*. (Struik Nature) have not been listed separately here.)

BirdLife International. 2016. *The IUCN Red List of Threatened Species* 2016: e.T22678901A92794026. https://dx.doi.org/10.2305/IUCN.UK.2016-3.RLTS.T22678901A92794026.en. Downloaded on 19 July 2020.

Borrow, N and Demey, R. 2004. *Birds of Western Africa*. London: Christopher Helm.

Borrow, N and Demey, R. 2011. *Birds of Senegal and The Gambia*. London: Christopher Helm.

Borrow, N, Demey, R, Owusu, EH and Ntiamoa-Baidu, Y. 2010. *Birds of Ghana*. London: Christopher Helm.

Bowie, RCK and Fjeldså, J. 2005. Genetic and morphological evidence for two species in the Udzungwa forest partridge. *Journal of East African Natural History* 94: 191–201.

Cohen, C. 2011. The phylogenetics, taxonomy and biogeography of African arid zone terrestrial birds: the bustards (Otididae), sandgrouse (Pteroclidae), coursers (Glareolidae) and Stone Partridge (*Ptilopachus*). Unpublished PhD thesis, University of Cape Town.

Crowe, T. 2016. African gamebirds are the key to understanding global avian evolution. *The Conversation* 24 February 2016. (retrieved from https://theconversation.com/african-gamebirds-are-the-key-to-understanding-global-avian-evolution-54970 on 11 March 2016).

Crowe, TM, Donsker, DB and Little, RM. 2020. Resolving nomenclatural 'confusion' vis- à -vis Latham's Francolin (*Francolinus/Peliperdix/Afrocolinus lathami*) and 'Red-tailed' francolins (*Francolinus/Ortygornis/Peliperdix* spp.). Addendum *Ostrich* 91(2): 134–136.

Crowe, TM, Little, RM and Turner, DA. 2019. Clarifying taxonomic, distributional and genetic information relating to subspecies of the Hildebrandt's Spurfowl *Pternistis hildebrandti* and the Yellow-necked Spurfowl *P. leucoscepus*. Addendum *Ostrich* 90(3): 279–280.

del Hoyo, J, Elliott, A and Sargatal, J (eds). 1994. *Handbook of the Birds of the World*. Vol. 2. Lynx Edicions, Barcelona.

del Hoyo, J, Elliott, A, Sargatal, J, Christie, DA and de Juana, E (eds). 2013. *Handbook of the Birds of the World Alive*. Lynx Edicions, Barcelona. (retrieved from http://www.hbw.com/node/54091 during July 2015 – March 2016 & March – April 2020).

Dinesen, L, Lehmberg, T, Vendsen, Jo, Hansen, LA and Fjeldså, J. 1994. A new genus and species of perdicine bird (Phasianidae, Perdicini) from Tanzania; a relict form with Indo-Malayan affinities. *Ibis* 136: 2–11.

Dowsett, RJ, Aspinwall, DR and Dowsett-Lemaire, F. 2008. The Birds of Zambia. Tauraco Press and Aves a.s.b.l., Belgium.

Gill, F and Donsker, D (eds). 2015. *IOC World Bird List* (v 5.3). doi: 10.14344/IOC.ML.5.3.

Hall, BP. 1963. 'The francolins, a study in speciation'. *Bulletin of the British Museum of Natural History (Zoology)* 10: 105–204.

Hockey, PAR, Dean, WRJ and Ryan, PG (eds). 2005. *Roberts – Birds of southern Africa*, VIIth ed. The Trustees of the John Voelcker Bird Book Fund, Cape Town.

Hunter, N, Mills, M and Cohen, C. 2019. Elgon Francolin *Scleroptila elgonensis* should be treated as a species distinct from Moorland Francolin *S. psilolaema*. *Bulletin African Bird Club* 26 (1): 92–100.

Little, RM and Crowe, TM. 2011. *Gamebirds of Southern Africa*. Struik Nature, Cape Town.

Mandiwana-Neudani, TG, Little, RM, Crowe, TM and Bowie, RCK. 2019. Taxonomy, phylogeny and biogeography of 'true' francolins: Galliformes, Phasianidae, Phasianinae, Gallini; *Francolinus, Ortygornis, Afrocolinus* gen. nov., *Peliperdix* and *Scleroptila* spp. *Ostrich* 90(3): 191–221.

Mandiwana-Neudani, TG, Little, RM, Crowe, TM and Bowie, RCK. 2019. Taxonomy, phylogeny and biogeography of African spurfowls Galliformes, Phasianidae, Phasianinae, Coturnicini: *Pternistis* spp. *Ostrich* 90(2): 145–172.

Morris, P and Hawkins, F. 1998. *Birds of Madagascar*. Pica Press, East Sussex, UK.

Redman, N, Stevenson, T, Fanshawe, J, Borrow, N and Small, BE. 2009. *Birds of the Horn of Africa: Ethiopia, Eritrea, Djibouti, Somalia and Socotra*. London: Christopher Helm.

Sinclair, I and Langrand, O. 2013. *Birds of the Indian Ocean Islands*. Struik Nature, Cape Town.

Sinclair, I and Ryan, P. 2010. *Birds of Africa south of the Sahara*. Random House Struik, Cape Town.

Stevenson, T and Fanshawe, J. 2002. *Field Guide to the Birds of East Africa*. T & AD Poyser, London.

Taku Awa II, Tamungang Simon A, Ashute Essebi Marcel and Djieto Lordon Champlain. 2015. Preliminaries on population status and distribution of the endangered Mount Cameroon Francolin, *Pterrnistis camerunensis*. *Newsletter of the IUCN-SSC Galliformes Specialist Group* 10: 13–17.

Töpfer, T, Podsiadlowski, L and Gedeon, K. 2014. Rediscovery of the Black-fronted Francolin *Pternistis (castaneicollis) atrifrons* (Conover, 1930) (Aves: Galliformes: Phasianidae) with notes on biology, taxonomy and conservation. *Vertebrate Zoology* 64: 261–271.

Urban, EK, Fry, CH and Keith, S (eds). 1986. *The Birds of Africa*. Vol II. Academic Press, London.

INDEX

ENGLISH COMMON NAMES

Francolin
- Archer's 105
- Bar-bellied 70
- Chestnut-breasted 79
- Coqui 54
- Crawshay's 111
- Crested 44
- Elgon 121
- Finsch's 114
- Forest (Latham's) 127
- Grant's 51
- Grey-winged 94
- Kirk's 47
- Kunene 102
- Moorland 117
- Orange River 98
- Pale-bellied 73
- Plain-bellied 63
- Red-winged 108
- Ring-necked 124
- Rufous-throated 88
- Schlegel's 82
- Shelley's 85
- Stuhlmann's 59
- Thika 66
- Ulu 91
- White-throated 76

Guineafowl
- Black 18
- Crested 29
- Helmeted 21
- Plumed 26
- Vulturine 32
- White-breasted 15

Painted-snipe
- Greater 312

Partridge
- Barbary 130
- Madagascan 142
- Nahan's 149
- Rubeho Forest 139
- Sand 133
- Stone 145
- Udzungwa Forest 136

Peafowl
- Congo 35

Quail
- Blue 257
- Common 250
- Harlequin 254

Sandgrouse
- Black-bellied 278
- Black-faced 287
- Burchell's 301
- Chestnut-bellied 271
- Crowned 284
- Double-banded 297
- Four-banded 294
- Lichtenstein's 291
- Madagascan 305
- Namaqua 268
- Pin-tailed 265
- Spotted 275
- Yellow-throated 281

Snipe
- African 319
- Common 325
- Great 322
- Jack 316
- Madagascan 328

Spurfowl
- Ahanta 202
- Black-fronted 187
- Cape 242
- Chestnut-naped 184
- Clapperton's 222
- Cranch's 163
- Djibouti 181
- Double-spurred 216
- Erckel's 178
- Grey-breasted 175
- Grey-striped 213
- Handsome 193
- Hartlaub's 232
- Harwood's 235
- Hildebrandt's 225
- Heuglin's 219
- Jackson's 190
- Mount Cameroon 196
- Natal 228
- Red-billed 238
- Red-necked 158
- Scaly 205
- Schuett's 208
- Swainson's 167
- Swierstra's 199
- Yellow-necked 171

Woodcock
- Eurasian 331

FRENCH COMMON NAMES

Bécasse
- des bois 331

Bécassine
- africaine 319
- des marais 325
- double 322
- malgache 328
- soured 316

Caille
- arlequine 254
- bleue 257
- de Madagascar 142
- des blés 250

INDEX

Francolin
- à ailes grises 94
- à collier 124
- à gorge blanche 76
- à gorge rousse 88
- à poitrine marron 79
- à ventre pale 73
- à ventre rayé 70
- à ventre uni 63
- coqui 54
- d'Ulu 91
- d'Archer 105
- de Crawshay 111
- de Finsch 114
- de Grant 51
- de Kirk 47
- de Kunene 102
- de Thika 66
- de Stuhlmann 59
- de Latham 127
- de Levaillant 108
- de L'Orange 98
- de Nahan 149
- de Shelley 85
- de Schlegel 82
- du Mont Elgon 121
- huppé 44
- montagnard 117

Ganga
- à face noire 287
- à gorge jaune 281
- à ventre brun 271
- bibande 297
- cata 265
- couronné 284
- de Burchell 301
- de Lichtenstein 291
- masque 305
- namaqua 268
- quadribande 294
- tacheté 275
- unibande 278

Paon
- du Congo 35

Perdrix
- de Hey 133
- gambra 130

Pintade
- à poitrine blanche 15
- de Purcheran 29
- noire 18
- plumifère 26
- sauvage 21
- vulturine 32

Poulette
- de rocher 145

Pseudofrancolin
- à bandes grises 213
- à bec jaune 219
- à bec rouge 238
- à cou jaune 171
- à cou roux 184
- à double éperon 216
- à front noir 187
- à gorge rouge 158
- à poitrine grise 175
- criard 242
- d'Ahanta 202
- d'Erckel 178
- de Clapperton 222
- de Hartlaub 232
- de Harwood 235
- de Hilderbrandt 225
- de Cranch 163
- de Jackson 190
- de Schuett 208
- de Swainson 167
- de Swierstra 199
- des Somalis 181
- du Mont Cameroun 196
- du Natal 228
- écaillé 205
- noble 193

Rhynchée
- peinte 312

Xénoperdrix
- des Rubeho 139
- de Tanzanie 136

SCIENTIFIC NAMES

Acryllium
- *vulturinum* 32

Afropavo
- *congensis* 35

Agelastes
- *meleagrides* 15
- *niger* 18

Alectoris
- *barbara* 130

Ammoperdix
- *heyi* 133

Campocolinus
- *albogularis* 76
- *coqui* 54
- *dewittei* 79
- *hubbardi* 63
- *maharao* 70
- *schlegelii* 82
- *spinetorum* 73
- *stuhlmanni* 59
- *thikae* 66

Coturnix
- *coturnix* 250
- *delegorguei* 254

Gallinago
- *gallinago* 325
- *macrodactyla* 328
- *media* 322
- *nigripennis* 319

Guttera
- *plumifera* 26
- *pucherani* 29

Lymnocryptes
- *minimus* 316

Margaroperdix
- *madagascariensis* 142

Numida
- *meleagris* 21

Ortygornis
   grantii 51
   rovuma 47
   sephaena 44
Peliperdix
   lathami 127
Pternistis
   adspersus 238
   afer 158
   ahantensis 202
   atrifrons 187
   bicalcaratus 216
   camerunensis 196
   capensis 242
   castaneilcollis 184
   clappertoni 222
   cranchii 163
   erckelii 178
   griseostriatus 213
   hartlaubi 232
   harwoodi 235
   hilderbrandti 225
   icterorhynchus 219
   jacksoni 190
   leucoscepus 171
   natalensis 228
   nobilis 193
   ochropectus 181
   rufopictus 175
   schuetti 208
   squamatus 205
   swainsonii 167
   sweirstrai 199
Pterocles
   alchata 265
   bicinctus 297
   burchelli 301
   coronatus 284
   decorates 287
   exustus 271
   gutturalis 281
   lichtensteinii 291
   namaqua 268
   orientalis 278
   personatus 305
   quadricinctus 294
   senegallus 275
Ptilopachus
   nahani 149
   petrosus 145
Rostratula
   benghalensis 312
Scleroptila
   afra 94
   crawshayi 111
   elgonensis 121
   finschi 114
   gutturalis 105
   jugularis 102
   levaillantii 108
   levalliantoides 98
   psilolaema 117
   shelleyi 85
   streptophora 124
   uluensis 91
   whytei 88
Scolopax
   rusticola 331
Synoicus (Excalfactoria)
   adansonii 257
Xenoperdix
   obscuratus 139
   udzungwensis 136

First published by Jacana Media (Pty) Ltd in 2016
Revised edition published by Jacana Media (Pty) Ltd in 2021

10 Orange Street
Sunnyside
Auckland Park 2092
South Africa
+27 11 628 3200
www.jacana.co.za

© Rob Little, 2016, 2021
© Distribution maps Bryan Little, 2016, 2021

All rights reserved.

ISBN 978-1-4314-3078-9

Cover design by Shawn Paikin
Set in Sabon 9.5/13pt
Printed by Tandym Print, Cape Town
Job no. 003753

See a complete list of Jacana titles at www.jacana.co.za

FRONT COVER A Grey-winged Francolin Scleroptila afra advertising his covey's territory in the landscape (photo by André Botha)

BACK COVER Pin-tailed Sandgrouse in flight (photo by Francois Mougeot)